LIBRARY OF LATIN AMERICAN
HISTORY AND CULTURE
GENERAL EDITOR:
DR. A. CURTIS WILGUS

EUROPE IN THE CARIBBEAN

THE POLICIES OF GREAT BRITAIN, FRANCE AND THE NETHERLANDS TOWARDS THEIR WEST INDIAN TERRITORIES

HAROLD MITCHELL
BERMUDES
M. A. (OXON)

NEW YORK
COOPER SQUARE PUBLISHERS, INC.
1973

TO MY FRIENDS IN THE CARIBBEAN

Originally Published 1963 by W. & R. Chambers Ltd.
Reprinted by Permission of W. & R. Chambers Ltd.
Published 1973 by Cooper Square Publishers, Inc.
59 Fourth Avenue, New York, New York 10003
International Standard Book Number 0-8154-0479-4
Library of Congress Catalog Card Number 73-75777

Printed in U.S.A. by
NOBLE OFFSET PRINTERS, INC.
New York, N.Y. 10003

220675

CONTENTS

MAPS

PREFACE

In our efforts to achieve world equilibrium we have to take account of the Caribbean as one of the unstable areas. To appraise the situation with its hopes and its potential dangers, an historical approach is essential, for only by some understanding of the past can the present be interpreted and assessed.

The Caribbean also provides a unique setting for a comparative study of the colonial problems of three colonial powers representing three distinct cultures and political traditions. Moreover, the policies of all three may be examined at work in a single and restricted theatre of operations. This is a matter of practical, as well as of academic, importance.

In making this study, I have concentrated on certain matters and have omitted others which would also be interesting. I have examined the policies of Great Britain, France and the Netherlands. The first five chapters of the book are introductory to the problems which have had to be faced since World War II and which are the theme of this book. The divergence in policy of these three experienced European nations is significant.

The position of Great Britain has been well stated by a distinguished Secretary of State for the Colonies who wrote: "The dominant theme of colonial policy had to be the careful and if possible gradual and orderly progress of the colonies towards self-government within the Commonwealth."[1] In application, this policy has met with difficulty and setbacks. The formation and collapse of the West Indies Federation has been studied in this book and an appreciation of the reasons for failure made. The political and racial problems of British Guiana which have caused in recent years great stresses in the territory have been examined, as has the special position of British Honduras. Situated in South and Central America respectively, they merit separate consideration even though historically Great Britain regarded them as part of its West Indian territories and hoped that they would join those territories in federation. The Bahamas have been excluded. Separated by Cuba from the Caribbean, more and more these islands have looked towards the United

[1] *The Memoirs of Lord Chandos* (London, 1962), p. 352.

vii

States and Canada rather than to the territories of the British Caribbean for the expansion of their economy.

France's policy of incorporating its ancient Caribbean territories as overseas departments stands out in contrast to the aims of Great Britain. I have undertaken to appraise the measure of success achieved by this endeavour to make Frenchmen out of the inhabitants of these countries.

With the loss of Indonesia in mind, and consequently with fewer colonial preoccupations to distract it than had either Great Britain or France, the Netherlands succeeded in negotiating a constitutional compromise which gave autonomy to Surinam and the Netherlands Antilles, yet did not confer independence. Here still another solution was evolved, which appears to have removed many of the objections associated with metropolitan control though involving a greater measure of integration than does membership of the Commonwealth.

If I have devoted more space to the British than to the French and Netherlands territories, my justification is that with a population more than double that of the combined French and Dutch territories, the British territories in recent years have been the scene of more numerous and varied experiments in political science.

No attempt has been made to assess and compare in the different territories the obviously great influence exerted by non-governmental bodies in the metropolitan countries. Churches of many denominations have had a profound effect upon the Caribbean from the campaign for the abolition of the slave trade to the present day. Their rôle in education has been especially significant. Cultural and charitable organizations have also played an important rôle. A comparative study would be of interest.

Spain has been excluded from this examination of policy, since its colonial interests ceased in the Caribbean after 1898, when it lost Cuba and Puerto Rico. An up-to-date study of the influence of the United States in the Caribbean would also be of value, including an assessment of its impact on the British, French and Dutch territories. The field, which requires separate study, would be rich and wide.

My link with the Caribbean is a long and close one. Since my first visit in 1936, I have been there every year, apart from the World War II period when I was in the army. In some years I have made more than one visit. For example, I made three in 1962 which took me to British Honduras, Jamaica, Curaçao, Surinam, British Guiana,

Trinidad, Martinique, Guadeloupe and Antigua. My association with agriculture in three territories, and with industry, commerce and the tourist industry, has given me insights into the Caribbean from different angles. Representing in the Caribbean the Headquarters of the Order of St. John of Jerusalem in London has brought me into close touch with other aspects of Caribbean problems, including the relief work arising from the aftermath of hurricanes and other disasters.

In order to have a proper understanding of the Caribbean, it is essential to have a knowledge not only of the territories which are under consideration but also of the surrounding countries, both island and mainland. Over several years I have also travelled extensively gathering material for lectures, delivered at Stanford University, which included the Latin American republics adjacent to the Caribbean, as well as Haiti, the Dominican Republic, and Cuba, which I visited both before and since the Castro revolution.

Education in the Commonwealth has interested me since, as a member of Parliament in 1933, I was invited to be a member of the Committee on Education and Training of Overseas Students. From this flowed a friendship with the late Sir James Irvine, Principal and Vice-Chancellor of St. Andrews University, who was also a member of the committee. Our friendship continued when he was actively associated with the establishment of the University College—now the University—of the West Indies. As chairman of the Princess Alice Appeal in Jamaica for the University College, I was able to see at first hand the fine work being done in the development of this important Caribbean centre of learning.

The greatest difficulty in studying the Caribbean is the dispersion of the source materials. No one library has more than a fraction of them. The proliferation of governments and administrations involves very considerable travelling within the area. Moves into independence or autonomy result in more documents being printed in local centres, and may involve delays in obtaining them. The metropolitan powers responsible for administration have also important sources. Geneva, with its excellent libraries and its convenient travel facilities, has proved a good base. My private collection of modern documents, books and pamphlets on the Caribbean has greatly facilitated my research.

In modern research involving politics, it is almost inevitable that many documents are not available. The correspondence of the West

Indies Federal Government with London on the one hand and with its constituent members, particularly Jamaica, on the other, would add to our knowledge of the reasons for the Federation's collapse. Of great interest too would be correspondence between Georgetown and London during the political crises in British Guiana in 1953 and 1962. It might also reveal whether or not Washington exerted influence on British policy. Examination of the main problem in the French territories is extremely difficult, since the whole official machine is inevitably dedicated to interpreting the experiment of integration as being a success. Nevertheless, there exists in the Caribbean a strong nationalist element which is opposed to the overseas departmental system.

Valuable studies of particular territories or groups of territories have been made. Many of these have been associated with the Universities of the West Indies and of Puerto Rico and are listed, where relevant, in the Bibliography of this work. In recent research the publications of the University of Florida at Gainesville have been of great use, particularly in regard to the French and Dutch territories where there is less information available than in the British territories. The University of Bordeaux, the Netherlands Universities Foundation for International Co-operation, and the University of Bristol which has continued to uphold the traditional association of the city with the West Indies, have all made significant contributions to scholarship in the area.

Newspapers have been of great value especially in studying the post-World War II Caribbean, the more so since freedom of the press at present exists in all the territories examined in this book. Articles by experienced journalists, whether resident in the area or making visits on behalf of foreign organs of the press, may be of major interest. The technique of interpretation and of comparison is, however, by no means easy. Here I have found four years' experience in writing for the *Hispanic American Report* of great help. The wealth of its archives in this field has been invaluable, including an excellent selection of cuttings from local newspapers in the area. The Press Library at the Royal Institute of International Affairs, Chatham House, London, has equally proved of assistance and has complemented that of the Hispanic American and Luso-Brazilian Institute at Stanford University.

Much of the justification for research covering recent events lies in the possibility of obtaining the views of individuals. Of major importance in this work have been conversations with men and women in all walks of life, including some who hold, or have held, the highest offices in these territories. In some cases these friendships commenced in the House of Commons. Of particular value have been the views of officials who by training take a dispassionate view. Yet with rising nationalism, the opinions of politicians are not less important. Businessmen and trade union leaders have provided other, often divergent, viewpoints. Finally, I have had the advantage, especially in Jamaica, the most populous territory, of very many friendships including those of workers in agriculture and industry which stretch back over a quarter of a century. Sometimes these have proved to be a key to the interpretation of public opinion which might otherwise be difficult to comprehend.

I am especially grateful to Professor Jacques Freymond, Director, and to Professor Louis J. Halle, of the Institut Universitaire de Hautes Études Internationales, Geneva, for their advice during the writing of this book. Their many suggestions have been invaluable. May I also thank Professor Ronald Hilton, Director of the Hispanic American and Luso-Brazilian Institute, Stanford University, who has read the manuscript and made many suggestions, and who has made available to me the files of the *Hispanic American Report* of which he is editor. I am deeply indebted to Dr. Hans G. Hermans, whose knowledge of the Netherlands Antilles and of Surinam is unrivalled. I had the benefit of his advice both at The Hague and in Curaçao, though he is in no way responsible for the views which I have expressed on these territories.

I wish to express my thanks to the staffs at the United Nations Library and Library of the Institut Universitaire de Hautes Études Internationales, Geneva, the Royal Institute of International Affairs, and the London Library, London, and the Hoover and Main Libraries at Stanford University, California.

I have had the benefit of the expert collaboration of John Bartholomew and Son Ltd. in preparing the maps, and I am equally grateful to Mr. Peter McIntyre for the index. My thanks are due to Mr. W. M. Todd of T. & A. Constable Ltd. for the personal interest which he has shown in the production and arrangement of this book. This continues an association commenced thirty-four years ago when his firm printed my first work.

My many friends in the Caribbean have by their knowledge guided me towards a more perceptive understanding of their area. The dedication of this book is the measure of my gratitude.

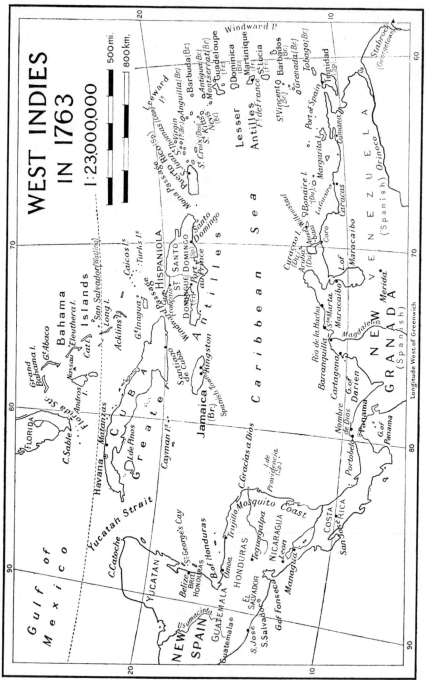

WEST INDIES
IN 1763
1:23,000,000

500 mi.

800 km.

Gulf of Mexico

FLORIDA

C. Sable

Florida Str.

Havana

Matanzas

C U B A

I. de Pinos

Cayman Is.

Great er

Santiago de Cuba

Spanish Town

Kingston

Jamaica (Br.)

Grand Bahama I.

Gt. Abaco

Bahama

Nassau

Eleuthera I.

Andros

Cat I.

Islands

San Salvador (Watling)

Long I.

Acklins

Gt. Inagua

Caicos Is.

Turks Is.

Windward Passage

Mole St. Nicholas

HISPANIOLA

Port au Prince (Fr.)

DOMINGUE

SANTO DOMINGO (Sp.)

Santo Domingo

Antilles

ST. SANTO

Mona Passage

PUERTO RICO (Sp.)

Leeward Is.

St. Thomas (Dan.) Virgin Is.

St. Juan

Anguilla (Br.)

St. Croix (Dan.)

St. Kitts (Br.)

Nevis (Br.)

Barbuda (Br.)

Antigua (Br.)

Montserrat (Br.)

Guadeloupe (Fr.)

Dominica

Martinique (Fr.)

Ft. de France

St. Lucia

St. Vincent (Br.)

Grenada (Br.)

Barbados (Br.)

Tobago (Br.)

Windward Is.

Lesser

Antilles

Caribbean Sea

Curaçao I. (Du.) Willemstad

Aruba I. (Du.)

Bonaire I. (Du.)

Amana (Du.)

Coro

Margarita

La Guayra

Caracas

Cumaná

Port of Spain

Trinidad (Sp.)

Orinoco

Stabroek (Georgetown)

Maracaibo

L. of Maracaibo

Rio de la Hacha

Sta. Marta

Magdalena

Barranquilla

Cartagena

G. of Darien

Merida

V E N E Z U E L A

(Spanish)

N E W   G R A N A D A

(Span. ish)

Longitude West of Greenwich

Nombre de Dios

Panama

G. of Panama

Portobelo

I. de Providencia (Sp.)

C. Gracias a Dios

Trujillo

Tegucigalpa

Mosquito Coast

NICARAGUA

Leon

Managua

COSTA RICA

San José

Omoa

B. of Honduras

HONDURAS

Belize

St. George's Cay

BRIT. HONDURAS

C. Catoche

YUCATAN

Yucatan Strait

N E W

S P A I N

Usumacinta

GUATEMALA

Guatemala

EL SALVADOR

S. Salvador

S. José

G. of Fonseca

© — John Bartholomew & Son. Ltd.

CHAPTER I

THE BEGINNINGS OF COLONIALISM

With a lead of more than a century in the Caribbean, Spain had ample time to consolidate its rule. Geographical insight, combined with excellent strategic judgment, enabled it to select the most fertile lands as well as the points of most effective control. As the world's most powerful nation and fortified both by papal sanction and by treaty, Spain, guided by its imaginative leaders, selected footholds in the Antilles which held firm over the centuries until the mighty El Morro fortresses at Havana, Santiago de Cuba and San Juan surrendered to the modern armament of the United States fleet.

The enemies of Spain, who were to challenge its monopoly in the Antilles, began their assaults early, though at first these were of a guerilla character. The Elizabethan seamen of England were partly concerned with harassing the Spanish navy, until the defeat of the Armada had diminished that navy as a threat; and partly with securing booty. Queen Elizabeth I herself was essentially a woman whose policy is difficult to unravel and whose motives were often mixed or even opportunistic.

Often allied with the English, the Dutch were at first motivated by an even more fanatical hatred of Spain. Alba's terror in the Spanish Netherlands was equalled by the barbarities of the Sea Beggars: the execution of the Dutch garrison at Haarlem[1] matched that of the Spanish garrison at Flushing.[2] Religious intolerance had created conditions of hatred and barbarity which were soon to be reflected in the New World.

The first attempts at colonization in the Caribbean by Spain's competitors took place in the seventeenth century. New Spain and later Peru had lured the more adventurous spirits from the Greater Antilles, all of which Spain held. More and more the islands came to be regarded as garrison outposts guarding the Spanish route to Mexico and the Isthmian mule-track to the Pacific.

[1] All the 1600 survivors (except the Germans) of the garrison of 4000 men who had defended Haarlem were killed in cold blood after the city surrendered.

[2] In 1572.

The Lesser Antilles, inhabited by Caribs, far more difficult to subdue than the Arawaks of the islands which Spain had occupied, provided opportunities for Spain's rivals. The early British colonization in St. Kitts[1] and in Barbados[2] was essentially European. In the same way France, in addition to sharing St. Kitts, developed Martinique and Guadeloupe[3] with its own emigrants. This was the period of grants to influential subjects or to companies. A colony was looked upon by the mother country as being a source of profit to its owners and to the sovereign making the grant. Though Columbus had performed a superb task in his four voyages of exploration to the Caribbean,[4] little was known of the interior of these islands, often densely covered with trees and bushes, which masked the rocky ground underneath.

The developing demand for tropical products provided a challenge to the enterprising merchants of London, Bristol, Amsterdam and Bordeaux, whence distribution to other centres took place. England, France and Holland were seeking to take advantage of the increasing weakness of Spain, its communications overstretched both in Europe and still more in America. With its administrative skill, as it were, offset by commercial incompetence, Spain brought textiles from the Spanish Netherlands for use in far off Salta, Lima and Buenos Aires. Meanwhile commerce in the homeland shrivelled and the economy was kept alive by shipments of precious metals from the Americas. Spain proved an ineffective commercial competitor because its leading citizens, unlike those of Britain, France or Holland, disdained commerce. Its rivals also had been interested in the search for precious metals, as exemplified by the voyages of Sir Walter Raleigh in search of El Dorado. Yet the great mines of the New World, the output of which was large enough to affect the price structure of Europe, were found within the vast territories of Spanish America.

As Spain declined in military power after the middle of the seventeenth century, it became more and more vulnerable along its lines of

[1] In 1624 Thomas Warner established the first English settlement in St. Kitts.

[2] By 1640, Barbados had over 30,000 British colonists, about 200 to the square mile. J. H. Parry and P. M. Sherlock, *A Short History of the West Indies* (London, 1960), p. 56.

[3] Colonized in 1635.

[4] Samuel E. Morison, *Admiral of the Ocean Sea* (Boston, 1942), pp. 669-71. Cf. Salvador de Madariaga, *Cristóbal Colón* (Buenos Aires, 1940), pp. 561-3.

communications, though so strongly was it entrenched that its hold on its American mainland territories, though weakened by raids, remained unshaken for more than a century longer. The treasure fleet that brought home the precious metals became an early essay in the convoy system, though sometimes the attacks of its enemies were successful. Military considerations caused the Dutch to seize Curaçao in 1634 for use as a base to harry the shipping of their enemy. They had appreciated the strategic advantages of Annabay, which they proceeded to fortify. Commercial development followed but was not the original motive.

The capture of Jamaica by Cromwell's fleet[1] further dented the Spanish defence system, even though the island had been ill-garrisoned and unfortified. In the long run it was to prove a useful consolation prize for the inglorious British failure before Santo Domingo of those quarrelsome leaders, General Robert Venables and Admiral William Penn. At the end of the century, the western portion of Hispaniola, which became known as St. Domingue, was ceded by Spain to France.[2] Once again the Spanish position in the Greater Antilles had been breached.

A perceptible change in the balance of power was taking place which had become clear in the Peace of Westphalia. With Spain weakened, Britain, France and the Netherlands were able to devote more time to the development of their commerce, even if they were still overshadowed in the New World by their mighty rival.

[1] In 1655.
[2] By the Treaty of Ryswick, 1697.

CHAPTER II

THE EIGHTEENTH-CENTURY POWER STRUGGLE IN THE CARIBBEAN

The planting of sugar cane, largely to the exclusion of other crops, drastically changed the outlook in the Caribbean. This was accelerated by the expulsion of the Dutch from Brazil, then the greatest producer of sugar. Together with some of the Portuguese Jewish exiles who had accompanied them from Amsterdam to Pernambuco, they began to concentrate in the Caribbean. Europeans proved unsuited to the heavy work in the canefields. African slaves, formerly imported in small numbers[1] for the use of the Spaniards who often employed them for domestic work, were now in even greater demand. Thus the notorious slave trade grew up, in which Great Britain, France, the Netherlands and other countries participated. Excluded from Africa by the Treaty of Tordesillas with Portugal, Spain relied on the ships of these countries for its supplies of imported labour, though French and British planters provided the principal market. Brazil, the largest importer of slaves, drew its supply mainly from the Portuguese African territories, especially Angola.

Though the new economic ideas were early being propounded by writers like the Abbé Raynal in France and Professor Adam Smith in Scotland, the mercantilist theory of trade continued to dominate the attitude of metropolitan powers towards their colonies. It had been inherent in the vigorous reforms of Jean Baptiste Colbert, which had produced such radical changes in the commerce of France and which had been extended to the French overseas possessions. The former policy of detachment of Baron de Pointis and of the French West India Company was replaced by centralization. When the eighteenth-century sugar boom carried St. Domingue into first position in the Caribbean, the colonial theory of the mercantilists appeared to have been justified.

The eighteenth-century power struggle in Europe was projected

---

[1] Sir John Hawkins (1532-1597) was a pioneer in the slave trade between the Guinea coast of Africa and the Spanish possessions in the New World.

into the Caribbean as it was into North America and the East. In the race for empire in the Caribbean, the Netherlands was the first to be forced out by its more powerful rivals. The failure to hold Antwerp in the sixteenth century[1] resulted in the compression of the Netherlands into a small area. Holland was compelled to look out to sea. Yet though its merchants had been as efficient as any in the world, by the mid-eighteenth century "Dutch commerce had long since passed its highest point".[2] The wealthy merchants had lost the zeal and drive of former days. Assisted by naval strength,[3] the overseas trade of Britain increasingly challenged that of its old rival. At the same time British yards were turning out fast ships which were manned by excellent crews, a matter of importance not only in speed of peacetime communications and transport but also for meeting conditions of war which prevailed when privateering was rife and every merchantman armed. Many were furnished in wartime with *letters of marque*.[4]

[1] There was a saying among the Prince of Parma's troops: "If we get Antwerp you shall all go to Mass with us; if you save Antwerp, we will all go to Conventicle with you." John L. Motley, *History of the United Netherlands* (London, 1875), Vol. I, p. 132.

[2] Petrus Johannes Blok, *History of the People of the Netherlands* (New York, 1912), Vol. V, p. 67.

[3] Of great significance was the introduction by Sir Charles Douglas (Rodney's fleet captain) of gunnery innovations which greatly increased the rapidity of fire. This made a major contribution to the British victory at the Battle of the Saints in 1782. E. B. Potter and Chester W. Nimitz, *Sea Power* (Englewood Cliffs, New Jersey, 1960), p. 100.

[4] Miss E. Arnot Robertson in *The Spanish Town Papers* (London, 1959), p. 9, describes the widespread issue of *letters of marque* by "the angry King George III".
This state of turmoil is also brought out in a letter, one of a collection in the possession of the author, from Aretas Akers, a prominent St. Kitts planter, written from Antigua, to which island he had just voyaged, and dated March 30, 1777. During the short voyage between these neighbouring islands, he describes how H.M.S. *Hynd* on which he was travelling was approached by four vessels, believed to be American privateers. The *Hynd* was cleared for action, but the vessels turned out to be British ships from Bristol. However, another British vessel, which had set out with them from St. Kitts and had straggled, was in the writer's words "chased by a privateer, after we parted from her, but on his altering his course bearing down on her and giving her a gun or two she sheered off". The policies of the European powers certainly made the Caribbean an exciting and dangerous place, as Akers found when the French captured the island of St. Kitts five years later and he wrote home "with a heart full of grief, with empty pockets and an almost empty belly . . .".

5

Typical of the decline in the commerce of the Netherlands was the weakening position of the Dutch West India Company, whose dividends decreased during the first half of the eighteenth century with a consequent fall in the value of its shares.[1] However, the policy of remaining out of the Seven Years' War provided a welcome opportunity for the Dutch West India merchants to make large profits, even if the Netherlands may have violated its neutrality in its lust for gain.[2]

The Seven Years' War was a turning-point. Thenceforth the French dream of Caribbean power linked to a Louisiana-Canadian Empire was shattered. If victory in the American Revolutionary War rested with the North American colonists, defeat came not alone to Great Britain but in reality to America's French, Dutch and Spanish allies as well. The British surrender at Yorktown had been matched by the burning of Dutch St. Eustatius and the destruction of the French fleet at the Battle of the Saints. The Netherlands in particular, squeezed between the greater power of Britain and France, had paid a heavy price when it entered the American War of Independence, probably more in the hopes of material gain than out of sympathy with the colonists.[3] Still later, not even Napoleon could save St. Domingue for France. The final restoration of the French and most of the Dutch colonies at the end of the Napoleonic wars was of small political significance.[4]

The commercial policy of the European colonial powers was closely related to the sugar industry. British and Dutch merchants exerted considerable political influence. In England the seaport

[1] Blok, *op. cit.*, p. 73.

[2] E. S. de Klerck, *History of the Netherlands East Indies* (Rotterdam, 1938), Vol. I, p. 57.

[3] Bernard H. M. Vlekke, *Evolution of the Dutch Nation* (New York, 1945), pp. 267, 269, suggests that the conservative Dutch political leaders and merchants were not attracted by revolution in the American colonies. John Adams, when he visited the Netherlands, interpreted this correctly. The motives for entering the war were the chance of breaking the British trading monopoly with the colonies and the hope of profitable smuggling. However, W. J. M. van Eysinga, *Lectures on Holland for American Students* (Leiden, 1924), p. 19, considers that the spectacle of the American colonies fighting for their independence against Great Britain evoked in the Netherlands "very great semi-official sympathies".

[4] Demerara, Essequibo and Berbice were ceded by the Netherlands to Great Britain in 1815.

6

towns were heavily over-represented in Parliament.[1] Elections were usually more corrupt in the boroughs where electorates were smaller and therefore more open to bribery. The wealthy West Indies planters were well represented in the House of Lords and the House of Commons. Their power was soon to be demonstrated in the struggle over the abolition of slavery. In the Netherlands, the state of Zeeland and the city of Amsterdam had large overseas holdings, but powerful families like the van Aerssen exerted great influence. Absentee owners were numerous, though France, unlike England, disapproved of them. Faced with a long and uncertain voyage in a small sailing-ship, the proprietor made but infrequent visits. He controlled his land and slaves through an "attorney",[2] himself often resident in the island capital perhaps a day's journey or more from the property which was looked after by a resident overseer. The owner, when visiting, resided at the Great House. His stay might well be for several months and his influence was often stronger than might appear at first sight, even if sometimes after a prolonged absence, such as that of "Monk" Lewis,[3] conditions on his return might shock him. The wealthy merchants in cities such as London, Bristol and Amsterdam who financed the sugar crop exerted both commercial and political influence on the colonies.

In *Tom Cringle's Log*,[4] colonial Jamaica, even if caricatured, at times comes to life, as it does in Lady Nugent's[5] description of her ride with her husband, the Governor, through the northern parishes of the island. Perhaps the fine eighteenth-century colour prints, usually inscribed to some prominent landowner whose property is

[1] Almost one-third of the parliamentary boroughs were seaports. "This again was a heritage from the early times when even inland trade, carried on mainly by river and coastwise, centred in towns on the seaboard. But soon the tendency to concentration set in in the sea-borne trade, and London, together with a dozen 'out-ports', swallowed up the trade of the smaller harbours. However much decayed, these still retained their parliamentary representation, henceforth their most lucrative branch of business." L. B. Namier, *The Structure of Politics at the Accession of George III* (London, 1929), Vol. I, p. 80.

[2] He held a power of attorney for the absentee owner and was not necessarily a lawyer. This use of the word still survives in the British Caribbean.

[3] Matthew G. Lewis, *Journal of a West India Proprietor* (London, 1834), pp. 116-18.

[4] Michael Scott, *Tom Cringle's Log* (London, 1894), *passim*.

[5] *Lady Nugent's Journal*, ed. F. Cundall (London, 1907), pp. 103-20.

depicted, can best conjure up the period. From them one would deduce that the metropolitan power regarded its territory as a sugar-bowl. The owner or attorney rides top-hatted in a tight-fitting coat and cravat, on a small short-tailed thoroughbred horse, usually escorted by a slave, to inspect the property and sugar-works, or to watch the barrels of sugar being rolled on to small boats for transport to the sailing-vessel lying at anchor. To protect this commerce was part of the justification for the costly naval estimates of the day. The army too played its part, for the coasts of the coveted islands had to be defended. Isolated from the remainder of the British territories, and less than a hundred miles from Cuba and little more from St. Domingue, the north coast of Jamaica was especially vulnerable. Fortified posts with batteries of guns were established at different coastal points.[1] The picture of a red-coated sentry on the heights above English Harbour, the British naval base of the period at Antigua, typifies the never-ending watch which Britain's policy towards its Caribbean territories made necessary. The price that Britain paid is also manifested in the numerous memorial tablets to men who died on service (usually from yellow fever) at Port Royal and other stations.

The political systems, the culture and the languages of the different territories in the Caribbean were settled by force of arms in the eighteenth and nineteenth centuries. The violent changes which characterized the French Revolution produced strong reactions in the Caribbean. The influence of French philosophy was most marked in St. Domingue, a clear indication of the rise of power in one monarchy and its decline in the other. By the end of the eighteenth century, French commercial ability had transformed the agriculture of St. Domingue.[2]

The cultivation of the plantations, some of which were irrigated,

[1] The author dug out one of these guns embedded in the sand at Frankfort Bay, on the north coast of Jamaica, which C. S. Forester, when visiting Frankfort, dated as a late eighteenth-century naval gun.

[2] At the outbreak of the French Revolution, the colony's combined annual exports and imports exceeded $140 million. Nearly two-thirds of the foreign commercial interests of France centred in this territory. The trade in sugar, coffee, indigo and cotton in a good year employed 700 ocean-going vessels and 80,000 seamen. J. G. Leyburn, *The Haitian People* (Yale University Press, 1941), p. 15, quoting Pamphile de Lacroix, *Mémoires*, II, p. 277. Cf. H. Herring, *A History of Latin America* (London, 1954), p. 249.

required large numbers of labourers.[1] In consequence, the racial composition of the territory changed radically. By 1790 this formerly poor and empty territory, inherited from the buccaneers, had a population of more than 450,000 slaves, 40,000 whites and 28,000 free persons of colour.[2] Many of the free coloured group had acquired wealth. They probably owned at this period about a fifth of the land and the slaves, and their affluence was increasing rapidly. With the prosperity of the rising group fanning the jealousy of the whites, colour prejudice mounted. Each free section sought to turn the doctrines of the French Revolution to its own end and to further its own bid for power. While the two factions quarrelled, the slaves in 1791 revolted. The pent-up anger of years of ill-treatment exploded. White men, women and children were slaughtered: the plantations of the fertile Plaine du Nord were largely laid waste. In the words of Professor Hubert Herring, "the French set off the explosion by outlawing slavery".[3] But the influence of France went back much earlier. The wealth of the country had facilitated frequent visits of the planters to Paris, and of the merchants to Bordeaux. There was no barrier of language, such as handicapped the introduction of French literature into the Spanish colonies, nor, as in the latter case, any strict censorship of French books.

Order was gradually restored by Toussaint l'Ouverture, a former slave, who proved a remarkable national leader and an effective military commander. So strong, however, were the forces of revolution that not even Napoleon at the height of his power could stem the tide. His troops, commanded by General Charles Leclerc, his brother-in-law, gained a temporary success. Toussaint l'Ouverture, "the gilded African", was deported to a Jura fortress, where he died. But as a result of yellow fever, which killed Leclerc and played havoc with his army, the French finally withdrew and Haiti achieved its independence in 1803. France had lost St. Domingue, its richest colony, by a policy of confusion, both at home where there was no agreement on what course to pursue and in the colony where white and mulatto planters had been at loggerheads. Martinique and

---

[1] St. Domingue competed strongly with the British colonies for the African slave cargoes.

[2] The free coloured group originated in the Code Noir of Louis XIV, which permitted a slave liberty in return for a cash payment or by an act of manumission.

[3] Herring, *op. cit.*, p. 249.

9

Guadeloupe were also affected, but their white population, proportionately larger than in St. Domingue, did not lose complete control, though civil conflict broke out in Martinique. In 1794 both islands were occupied by the British, whose help had been requested by the large planters fearful of a repetition of the massacres of St. Domingue.

The Convention and Directory had devoted only intermittent attention to the colonies, and had no clear-cut policy. Napoleon, to whom dreams of empire overseas made a strong appeal, had failed to reconquer Haiti just as he failed in his colonization scheme in French Guiana. Though France had regained its captured territories[1] at the Peace of Amiens in 1802, it lost them again in 1809 after the resumption of hostilities with Britain, only to recover them once more in the final settlement at Vienna.

When territorial settlement was achieved in 1815, Great Britain gave back to France and the Netherlands what it did not require for strategic or commercial purposes.[2] St. Domingue was lost to France for ever. St. Eustatius, the Netherlands' richest post, remained a heap of ruins. The struggle had been won by Great Britain even if it proved an arid victory. The settlement was to affect profoundly the attitude of all three colonial powers in the Caribbean. The prosperity of the islands, which had been considered for more than a century and a half to be among the richest agricultural lands in the world, was drawing to a close.

An epoch had come to an end for all the colonial powers. The sugar monopoly was drawing to a close as was the slave trade and the slavery on which it had been built. Great Britain had won its victories on the sea. Its navy would ensure a period of tranquillity in the islands for most of the nineteenth century. Of more importance, British command of the Caribbean, in silent agreement with the United States, whose influence was rising, would facilitate the revolutions against colonial Spain which were soon to refashion the Spanish Main. In retrospect, the eighteenth-century wars seem sterile and unproductive. Yet the very sterility of the policy which

[1] Martinique and Guadeloupe.

[2] D. W. Brogan writes of the 1815 settlement as regards France: "A few West Indian islands like Martinique, Réunion in the Indian Ocean, Saint-Pierre and Miquelon in the St. Lawrence, Cayenne in South America, a few decaying trading posts in India, a few more on the African coast—these were scattered fragments of what had once been a great colonial system." *The Development of Modern France (1870-1939)* (London, 1940), p. 217.

initiated them may have encouraged the liberal break-through which characterized the years that followed. The message of Philadelphia, reiterated in Paris, was soon to reverberate in Port-au-Prince and Caracas, even if a century or more would elapse before colonialism faded in Havana.

CHAPTER III

THE CARIBBEAN POLICY OF
GREAT BRITAIN FROM 1815 to 1939

The immense efforts which Great Britain had put forth to defeat and finally ruin Napoleon resulted in British dominance in the Caribbean. Yet the very efficacy of the British blockade had led to the active development of the continental sugar-beet industry. The result from this increasing competition was a gradual deterioration in the economy of the West Indies. From being possessions which had seemed to justify to Parliament the massive base at English Harbour and the costly garrison in Jamaica, they were eventually to become territories dependent either directly on grants from the British Treasury to enable them to survive or upon sheltered markets for their products which could not meet open competition. As it turned out, the fruits of victory at Waterloo and at Vienna, so far as the British West Indies were concerned, were destined to wither.

England in the seventeenth and eighteenth centuries was in many ways in advance of other colonial powers in the administration of its colonies. Basically the system consisted of a Governor appointed by the Crown; an Upper House nominated by the Crown through the medium of the Governor; and a Lower House elected on a property franchise by the freeholders, and modelled on that of Great Britain.[1] A basic principle was that the Crown could not legislate in Council.

Colonial Assemblies had developed considerable independence, even prior to the events leading to the independence of the American colonies.[2] For example, in 1678 Jamaica refused to allow London to interfere by sending draft Bills to the island.[3] In the next century, a

---

[1] This system exists practically unaltered today in Bermuda. Universal franchise is, however, expected to be introduced before the next General Election.

[2] Parry and Sherlock, *op. cit.*, pp. 209-11.

[3] Sir Alan Burns, *History of the British West Indies* (London, 1954), pp. 330-2.

decision of Lord Mansfield regarding pressure being exerted on Grenada to levy an export duty still further enhanced the status of these Assemblies, by making it clear that they could be coerced only by Act of Parliament.[1] Thus the basic principle that the Crown could not legislate for them in Council was upheld. Probably because of the constitutional difficulties which it had encountered in dealing with its colonies, the British attitude changed in the nineteenth century. The former progressive approach was slowed down. Demerara, Berbice, Trinidad and St. Lucia were not given representative government.

The freeing in 1834 of three-quarters of a million slaves, who formed the bulk of the British West Indies population, would at any time have created formidable social, political and economic problems. Since it occurred at a time of depression in the major industry of the area, it is remarkable that the adjustment was not even more difficult than it proved to be.

The Colonial Office, which had experience of Crown Colony government in the newer West Indies colonies, preferred this system to the wrangles with elected colonial legislatures. The utterly unrepresentative character of the Houses of Assembly, usually chosen by a small number of landowners and merchants, was enhanced after emancipation. In 1839, despite protests from Jamaica, a Bill was introduced into the House of Commons to vest powers of legislation in the Governor and his Council to the exclusion of the Jamaica Assembly.[2] Opposed by Sir Robert Peel and the Tory Party, the Bill passed on its second reading by a majority so narrow that the Whig Government resigned. Eventually a compromise, aided by a change in the governorship in Jamaica, was achieved with the Jamaica House of Assembly. This resulted in the continuance

---

[1] Alexander Campbell, a British subject, was charged duty on sugar which he had exported from Grenada. Lord Mansfield held that while the King originally had the power to tax the people in this conquered colony, he had abandoned this power when he granted a constitution and authorized elected Assemblies. Cowper's King's Bench Reports (Great Britain), 1774-1778.

[2] A quarrel had arisen between the Colonial Office and the Jamaica Assembly over "An act for the better government of prisons in the West Indies" which was passed by the British Government in 1838. Though there was much to be said for the measure, tradition, always powerful in British political life, had been broken. Burns, op. cit., p. 641. Cf. F. R. Augier et al., The Making of the West Indies (London, 1960), p. 22.

of the Colonial Parliament. Curiously, the British House of Commons, which had so recently begun the long process of reforming itself, did not advocate a gradual widening of the franchise in the colonies.[1]

With an improving Civil Service, Colonial Office officials were convinced that they could do a better job than the elective Assemblies in the colonies,[2] overlooking the fact that the apprenticeship for legislators, as for civil servants, is a long one. Unfortunately, the office of Secretary of State for the Colonies was still of secondary importance and was often filled by mediocre ministers. According to Sir Alan Burns, himself a distinguished former Colonial Governor, "It was now more than ever obvious that the irresponsible and unrepresentative Assemblies could no longer be allowed to hamper the progress of the colonies by their captious and selfish approach to all problems."[3] When the dislocation brought about by the abolition of slavery, combined with the price collapse of sugar and accentuated by an Act of Parliament which repealed in instalments the preferences enjoyed by the British colonies in the British market, finally caused severe rioting in Jamaica with some deaths and executions, the Jamaica House of Assembly solved the problem for the Colonial Office by abolishing itself.[4]

Crown Colony government was set up with effective power exercised by the Colonial Office through the medium of the Governor. Most of the other enfranchised Caribbean colonies also gave up the representative system,[5] which in the Caribbean was retained only in Barbados and the Bahamas. In the words of Burns, "The Houses of Assembly in most of the colonies were at this time very reactionary and difficult to handle, and of all of them that of Jamaica was easily

[1] In 1863, Jamaica with a population of about 450,000 had only 1799 registered voters, of whom 1482 recorded votes. In the other islands, the vote was equally restricted. In St. Kitts, in the 1855 census, out of 20,741 persons, only 166 had the franchise. Of their number, 81 electors made use of their franchise to elect 24 members at the 1856 General Election. Burns, op. cit., p. 653.

[2] Augier et al., op. cit., pp. 221-2. They also comment on the success of Crown Colony administration, p. 218.

[3] Burns, op. cit., p. 652.

[4] In 1865. The immediate cause of the riots was the mishandling of the situation by Governor E. J. Eyre.

[5] Changes in the composition of the colonial Assemblies giving complete or increased control by means of nominated members took place in St. Kitts, Nevis and Antigua (1866); in St. Vincent (1867); and in Grenada (1875). Burns, op. cit., p. 655.

the worst."[1] The Colonial Office had won this important round in its efforts to control what one of its Governors was later to call "the blessed island".[2] Yet in the long run, the wisdom of replacing elected members by a Government and Council entirely composed of civil servants and members nominated by the Governor may well be questioned.

To Whitehall, the new system was much more convenient. In the short run it resulted in more efficient government. But it could not possibly be termed democracy or even adequate preparation for democracy.[3] The gradual widening of the franchise, from the era of the "rotten boroughs" of the eighteenth and early nineteenth centuries through the Reform Bill of 1832 to virtual adult suffrage in 1918, undoubtedly contributed to the maturity of the British electorate and the training of successive generations of political leaders. With more zeal for immediate results and less vision of the future, notwithstanding the lesson of the American colonies, the British Parliament was party to the destruction of the two-centuries-old Jamaica House of Assembly. Yet a quarter of a century before, Great Britain had implemented the Durham Report by passing the Act of Union which reunited Upper and Lower Canada largely to allay racial discord in Canada. Power in that case had been transferred to an Assembly which, though universal franchise had not then been introduced into Great Britain, was none the less relatively representative. Two years after the Jamaica House of Assembly had abolished itself, the British North America Act received royal assent. Far-seeing statesmanship which laid the foundations of the future Commonwealth was matched by a myopic and unprogressive approach contributing to the constitutional problems in the British Caribbean territories at a later date.

A major change in British colonial policy stemmed from the great influence exerted by Joseph Chamberlain whom the Conservative Party, skilled in drawing strength from its opponents, had attracted

---

[1] Burns, *op. cit.*, p. 642.

[2] Lord Olivier, *Jamaica, the Blessed Island* (London, 1936).

[3] Though sharply critical of the incompetence of the West Indies elected Assemblies, Augier *et al.* write: "It is doubtful, however, whether the Colonial Office view, that dispensing with the assembly was the only way of securing the interests of the unrepresented masses, was in the long run justified." F. R. Augier *et al.*, *op. cit.*, p. 218.

to its ranks. With Chamberlain as Secretary of State, the Colonial Office for the first time became a post of major importance. Though many of his aims were to be fulfilled only after his death, more than any man he reshaped Britain's attitude towards its overseas territories. His period of office was overshadowed by events in South Africa, yet he was deeply interested in the West Indies, where his son Neville had been a planter for several years on Andros in the Bahamas; although destined to be Prime Minister, the young Chamberlain had failed to make sisal growing profitable on that barren island.[1] The Colonial Secretary had to grapple with the serious problem of the West Indies sugar industry which continued to struggle for its very life against subsidized continental sugar-beet.[2] He was the main-spring of the long struggle between protective tariffs and free trade which was the centrepiece of British politics from 1904 to 1931. His influence on the attitude of Great Britain to its colonies was profound.

Again and again Great Britain had shown itself sensitive to boundary disputes and had always acted tenaciously over its Carib-bean interests, as may be seen in its negotiations over British Honduras[3] with Spain in the seventeenth and eighteenth centuries and with Guatemala in the eighteenth century. To Joseph Chamber-lain as Colonial Secretary fell the task of finding a diplomatic path through the tangle of problems occasioned by the long-drawn-out dispute between Great Britain and Venezuela over the British Guiana boundary. In 1895 President Grover Cleveland announced that an American commission would be appointed to settle the boundaries of Venezuela which of course equally involved British Guiana, a British colony.[4] Though Chamberlain was faced at that time with increasing difficulties in South Africa and with a hostile Germany, he tenaciously

---

[1] Iain MacLeod, *Neville Chamberlain* (London, 1961), pp. 24-36 *passim*.

[2] Charles W. Boyd writes in reference to Joseph Chamberlain: "In the West Indies he had found the sugar industry suffering from the invasion of continental beet importers propped up by the bonuses of their several governments. He was prompt in applying remedies good and good enough; but these were accounted less than the warmth with which Mr. Chamberlain pressed on home audiences the responsibilities of the mother country." *Mr. Chamberlain's Speeches*, ed. Charles W. Boyd (London, 1914), p. 316.

[3] William J. Bianchi, *Belize* (New York, 1959), pp. 1-9, 59-91.

[4] J. L. Garvin described it as "a violent ultimatum in effect". *The Life of Joseph Chamberlain* (London, 1932), Vol. III, p. 67.

resisted the American demand, negotiating patiently first in London[1] and then travelling to the United States to discuss the problem with Secretary of State Richard Olney. Finally the dispute was resolved by international arbitration.[2] In retrospect it seems amazing that a man whose responsibilities covered some 10 million square miles and 50 million people should have found time to conduct personally this struggle over a piece of territory that had proved to be no more an El Dorado than had Andros Island.

Though Chamberlain's policy which sought to cement imperialism with Empire Preference was rejected by the British electorate in 1906 and 1910, it had nevertheless taken root in the country. If his ideas appear today at times jingoistic, as do the writings of Rudyard Kipling, it may be that time will redress the balance by taking into account the period. After World War I, the orthodox Liberal Free Traders found their party squeezed between a strong Conservative revival on the one hand and an equally strong advance of socialist philosophy expressed in the rise of the Labour Party. Inevitably these happenings affected the attitude of Great Britain towards its colonies, including those in the Caribbean.

World War I, which had devastated great areas in France and Belgium, brought in its wake prosperity to the Caribbean. The cane-sugar industry boomed, assisted by the destruction of many sugar-beet factories in Europe. Unfortunately this temporary improvement was short-lived for there was a disastrous sugar crash in 1920, largely due to the policies of the United States and Cuba which dominated the market.[3]

The interesting two-day debate on imperial preferences which took place in 1924 revealed the incipient interest of the first Labour Government in Empire Preference. Though he opposed the Conservative motion, J. H. Thomas,[4] Colonial Secretary, showed that he had

---

[1] With Thomas F. Bayard, American Ambassador.

[2] The Treaty of Washington of 1897 provided for a tribunal of five jurists, two from Britain and two from the United States with the distinguished Russian Frederick F. Martens as a neutral president. The Schomburgk boundary was confirmed, apart from minor adjustments, by the award made in 1899.

[3] Parry and Sherlock, *op. cit.*, pp. 255-6.

[4] Hansard 174, col. 1989. The influential Clydeside Independent Labour Party member and publicist Thomas Johnston voiced his criticisms of colonial sweated labour. He was also critical of Free Trade. Hansard 174, cols. 2040-2047 *passim*.

an open mind on the question in contrast with the Liberal leaders, including Herbert Asquith and Sir John Simon.

The Conservative Party, mindful of its recent defeat,[1] had been careful to play down the tariff issue during the General Election which it won later in the year, but its leaders still favoured a major fiscal change to combine the sheltering of British industries from foreign competition with a policy designed to extend Empire trade. Thus it was that when the financial crisis of 1931 brought down the second Labour Government, the commercial policy of Great Britain was drastically changed by the coalition government of Ramsay Macdonald and Stanley Baldwin, which included leading Liberals like Sir John Simon. The change to protection presented no difficulty to J. H. Thomas. At the Ottawa Conference the following year the West Indies colonies were included in the framework of the agreement.

In the 1930s Britain was beginning to be increasingly conscious of the need to advance independence for its overseas territories. The Balfour Declaration and the Statute of Westminster had demonstrated the intentions of Parliament, even if the National Government did not hesitate to revoke the constitution of Newfoundland when it got into financial difficulties. Yet the application of self-government to the Caribbean territories was a leisurely study. Attention was, however, concentrated on them when strikes and rioting occurred in several of the islands.[2] The House of Commons debate on the Trinidad riots in 1938 laid bare some of the problems that faced the Colonial Office. W. G. Ormsby-Gore, Colonial Secretary, pointed out how his powers differed from colony to colony, recalling that while in Trinidad he had an official majority and could therefore have his measures enacted; in Barbados, which had self-government, he had no power to initiate any vote of money or any legislation nor to alter the franchise or the Constitution except by the introduction in the British House of Commons of a Bill to take away self-government. All parties in the House of Commons were in fact committed to self-government. Much of the Labour criticism was directed at the large corporations which were appearing in some of the Caribbean colonies and which the Opposition feared would lead to exploitation of the labourers. However, large-scale agricultural and industrial

---

[1] In the General Election of 1923.

[2] In St. Kitts and St. Vincent (1935); in Trinidad, British Guiana and Jamaica (1938).

development was generally welcomed by the Government supporters.[1] The outcome of the riots was the setting up of the carefully
chosen Moyne Commission.[2]

In art and architecture, the influence of the colonial powers may
readily be seen.[3] The solid yet well-proportioned Georgian architecture of eighteenth-century Jamaica is seen to advantage in the
square at Spanish Town, laid out when it was the capital of the island.
While many buildings have been destroyed, there are examples
throughout the islands, including some of the small Great Houses,
often in ruins, in Nevis, or the more celebrated Rose Hall in Jamaica.
Curaçao at once recalls the Netherlands with its ornate gables and
impressive curved steps. Even in the occasional canal, the Dutch
influence has been displayed, just as France stamped its artistic
pattern on Martinique and Guadeloupe. Paramaribo and Georgetown, outside the hurricane belt, have each a number of distinctive
and delightful eighteenth-century buildings.

Furniture resistant to insects is found throughout the Caribbean.
In Jamaica, it resembles that of the same period in Britain, though it
is heavier in design. One may note the same tendency in the collection at the Curaçao museum, influenced by the Netherlands work of

[1] This division of opinion was clearly illustrated in the debate on the
Trinidad riots of 1938. Labour members including Arthur Creech Jones
(afterwards Secretary of State for the Colonies, 1946-1950), Aneurin Bevan,
James Maxton and Ben Riley regarded the new large-scale oil and sugar
enterprises with suspicion, fearing that the workers, with weak trade unions,
would not get a square deal, particularly since the franchise in the West
Indian colonies was very restricted. Conservative speakers such as W. G.
Ormsby-Gore (Secretary of State for the Colonies), Captain Victor Cazalet,
and Harold Mitchell welcomed the new industries, believing that they would
result in higher wages and more employment. Hansard 332, cols. 766-858
passim.

[2] The West India Royal Commission of 1938-1939, under the chairmanship of Lord Moyne (Walter E. Guinness, Minister of Agriculture and
Fisheries, 1925-1929).

[3] Angus W. Acworth considers that the best buildings had been constructed from the mid-eighteenth to the mid-nineteenth century during the
period of prosperity. He remarks: "Jamaican architecture is particularly
interesting since from the Georgian beginnings it developed on distinct lines
of its own, so that by 1846 there was to all intents and purposes a Jamaican
style, a 'vernacular', which though largely forgotten in the past hundred
years, is still recognizable in contemporary buildings of which the designers
have looked at home rather than abroad for inspiration." *Colonial Research
Studies No. 2* (HMSO, London, 1951), p. 5.

19

the period. If craftsmen came out to the colonies, they were unlikely to be the most expert. The African slaves, natural workers in wood, had not the skill of the best European workmen of the period, even if Alejandinho proved the exception in Brazil.

Imperialism reached its zenith towards the end of World War I, after the Imperial War Cabinet had been constituted in London. Speaking to the Empire Parliamentary Association,[1] Sir Robert Borden, Prime Minister of Canada, saw in it the "birth of a new and greater Imperial Commonwealth", while General J. C. Smuts, Minister of Defence of the Union of South Africa, envisaged the solution of its problems through political thought turned into new channels.[2]

Yet critics had also appeared who were opposed to the whole concept that colonies were a source of profit or of strength. Norman Angell attacked colonialism as unsound, arguing that military and political power did not bring commercial advantages to a nation, and that colonies were costly to defend[3], an argument which E. M. W. Tillyard considered valid, applying it to that period in Athenian history when "a nation of craftsmen was becoming a nation of fighters".[4]

[1] House of Commons, April 2, 1917.
[2] *The Voice of the Dominions* (London, 1917), pp. 20-1.
[3] Norman Angell, *The Great Illusion* (London, 1909), pp. 29-30.
[4] E. M. W. Tillyard, *The Athenian Empire and the Great Illusion* (Cambridge, 1914), p. 20.

CHAPTER IV

THE CARIBBEAN POLICY OF
FRANCE FROM 1815 to 1939

With disaster engulfing France's colonial policy, a change of policy was clearly needed. Louis XVI had sensed this when in 1787 he extended his new system of local *parlements* from France to the colonies. However, it was too late, for revolution overtook France two years later. The remaining years of the eighteenth century were associated in the French Caribbean territories with slave revolts, intrigues with the enemy and the occupation of French territory by Great Britain and Portugal.

Surprisingly enough, Napoleon I succeeded in re-establishing slavery, which had been abolished during the Revolution.[1] The planters in Martinique, Guadeloupe and French Guiana were embittered and discouraged. Owing to the excess of the death-rate over the birth-rate, partly due to the preponderance of male over female slaves, and partly due to poor living conditions, the supply of slaves had to be constantly replenished. The economy depended upon slavery, which in turn depended upon the slave trade, now outlawed by the Treaty of Vienna. For several years after the Restoration, France's efforts to enforce abolition were ineffective,[2] but the threat to the planters' interests remained, for many of the planters' own slaves had for a time been freed. Moreover, the revolt of Spain's mainland colonies which half encircled the Caribbean contributed to the general feeling of uneasiness.[3] Slaves brought to France became automatically free in 1836, more than half a century

[1] By the Convention in 1794. Slavery was reintroduced by Napoleon Bonaparte when First Consul in 1802.
[2] Herbert I. Priestley, *France Overseas* (New York, 1938), pp. 65-7.
[3] Simón Bolívar had moved through the Caribbean mobilizing opinion against colonialism and slavery. President Alexandre Pétion of Haiti promised him aid, stipulating only that he should free the slaves in Venezuela after he had won victory, a promise Bolívar fulfilled. His famous letters of September 6, 1815, and September 28, 1815, to *The Royal Gazette*, Kingston, Jamaica, set forth his feelings of revolt, e.g. "And our enemies are intent on reducing us once more to slavery".

after a similar ruling had been made in England. Twelve years more elapsed before Victor Schoelcher could force through emancipation in the colonies.

The "Utopian" administration of 1848 was replaced by the authoritarian Second Empire. Each major change in France was immediately reflected in the Caribbean territories until they were permanently incorporated in 1875 as French Departments.[1] The colonies were shuttled between the Minister for the Navy and the Minister for Commerce, until a decree of 1894 established a Minister for the Colonies.[2] Gradually they became more and more assimilated as French Departments. The commercial policy of France had veered from the protective system of *l'exclusif*[3] to an approach to free trade in 1861, when the colonies were permitted to export and import freely in the liberal system of the period. A decade later the pendulum in France began to swing back to tariffs.

After 1870[4] France adopted the policy of assimilation for its West Indies colonies. Steadily they were incorporated as part of France,[5] with the laws of France applying basically to the Caribbean territories. Adult franchise was introduced by France far in advance of Great Britain in their respective colonies. Education was modelled on that of France.

Though the demand for sugar expanded during the eighteenth century, the traditional export monopoly into France began to be challenged by the cheaper products of Cuba and the British islands. A tax on foreign sugar had been imposed in 1832, but competition om home-produced beet sugar increased.[6] An important producer

[1] This had been envisaged in Article 109 of the Constitution of 1848. Universal suffrage obtained in 1848 had been lost.

[2] Alpheus H. Snow, *The Administration of Dependencies* (New York, 1902), pp. 479-80.

[3] The principle of *l'exclusif* prohibited the colonies from trading other than with the mother country, and from shipping goods in other than French bottoms.

[4] Universal suffrage was granted in Martinique in 1870; and in 1875 its representation in the French Parliament was fixed according to the decree of 1871, at two deputies and one senator.

[5] In 1938, Mr. Arthur Creech Jones said in the House of Commons, "In the French West Indies, there is adult suffrage and this ought to be extended to the British West Indies." Hansard 332, col. 797. In that year Jamaica with a population of about 1,100,000 had only 66,000 persons entitled to exercise the franchise, while in Trinidad only one person in fifteen could vote.

[6] Priestley, *op. cit.*, p. 47.

of this commodity at home, France found itself in a more difficult position to help its colonies than did Great Britain, which did not then produce sugar.[1] In the case of Martinique, the position was alleviated by the reputation which the island had built up for its rum, until the eruption of Mont Pelée in 1902 destroyed an important rum-producing area around the volcano, halving production.[2]

France's efforts to colonize French Guiana, though determined, were both costly and profitless, notwithstanding exploration work which had been carried out by La Condamine, and by the botanists Pierre Barrère and Christian Aublet.[3] Though the emigration scheme of the Duc de Choiseul, who had obtained a vast concession[4] from Louis XV in French Guiana, had attracted 13,000 to 14,000 persons, this considerable attempt at colonization by France failed through poor management. Many of the colonists died of typhus on board ship and others soon after landing.[5]

The confusion of French policy was broadly illustrated in French Guiana, which had been denuded of labour because a large number of the liberated slaves moved into the hinterland, refusing to work on the hated plantations. The Directory sent out from France a shipload of exiles—its political opponents. This policy inevitably ended in disaster since, quite unsuited to manual work, many of these men soon died. After the Peace of Amiens, Napoleon I had proposed a development scheme which he wished General Charles Pichegru, one of the Directory's prisoners, to put into effect. Not surprisingly, Pichegru refused.

Finally, in 1854, French Guiana received a heavy influx of unsolicited immigrants. The gold which had eluded Raleigh and his fellow-explorers had at last been discovered, but the boom proved

[1] Marcel Guieysse, "La Martinique", Les colonies françaises d'Amérique (Paris, 1923), p. 79.

[2] Ibid., pp. 82-3. Martinique permanently lost some of its market to Guadeloupe and to the British territories. Finally, France adopted a policy of a rum quota for Martinique and Guadeloupe to replace unrestricted importation.

[3] Others included François-Simon Mentelle, engineer, geographer and explorer (1731-1799), who went out with the colonists sent by Turgot to study the coast of French Guiana, and Samuel Guisan, born in the canton of Vaud, Switzerland, who was in charge of drainage.

[4] Between the Kourou and the Maroni River. Léon Jacob, "La Guyane", Les colonies françaises d'Amérique (Paris, n.d.), p. 98.

[5] 10,000 emigrants died in five months.

short-lived. Indeed, it damaged France's policy of agricultural development, since many left the land for the goldfields of Le Haut-Approuague, never to return to farm labour.

Volatility characterized the policy of France towards its Caribbean territories in the nineteenth century. Political changes in the metropolis resulted in fluctuating attitudes towards the West Indies. The survival of French control is little short of amazing when we consider the stunning impact of the reimposition of slavery, nourished by active, if illegal, slave trading. At times France's interest appeared to falter and wane. Yet centralization, aided by geography, had proved such an important factor in the development of a powerful France from the days of Richelieu to the twentieth century that it finally overcame the indecisiveness of lesser men. Government reached out once more from the metropolis to the ancient colonies which it had nurtured. Their economic weakness made the prospect of closer union attractive. Unlike Great Britain, France offered equality of citizenship with direct political representation. Moreover, France stressed its education and culture.[1] Assimilation, which Portugal also attempted with much less success in its overseas possessions, was the cornerstone of France's policy in the West Indies. From it derived economic integration, and with it the concept of the unrestricted entry of colonial products into France with French goods supplying the Antillean departments. Thus Colbert's policy of integrating the Caribbean colonies with the economy of France was fulfilled; but the profit expected from this policy failed to materialize. Losses resulted which involved France in a policy of subsidizing its colonies.

The divergence between French and British colonial policy as exemplified in the Caribbean had become clarified. France increasingly felt that its mission was to create Frenchmen out of its Antillean subjects.[2] Emphasis was placed on education, which probably surpassed that provided in the British West Indies during the eighteenth and the first half of the nineteenth centuries. The fumbling French policy over emancipation and the inconsistencies

[1] Ernest-Théophile Boulanger, the first Minister for the Colonies, emphasized the importance of its being "known to all the world that France, however far distant, proposes to exercise upon its Colonies its moral and civilizing influence". Report by Boulanger to the President of the Republic, May 5, 1894.

[2] G. H. Bousquet, *La politique musulmane et coloniale des Pays-Bas* (Paris, 1938), pp. 158-9.

24

over colonial trade, which make France's nineteenth-century attitude seem hesitant, gradually crystallized into a firmer mould. Yet France was not altogether satisfied with its colonial achievements. Inevitably, perceptive people in every European nation which administered colonies were beginning to make comparisons with the achievements of other colonial powers. Writing at the end of World War I, Camille Fidel admires the fine buildings, colonial agencies and exhibitions which he saw in London, contrasting the enthusiasm of the British with what he regarded as the apathy of the French towards their respective colonies in the Caribbean.[1] Yet he might equally have compared the well-developed roads in some French or Dutch colonial territories of the period with an often much less adequate road system in British colonial territories. France appreciated the "imperial perception"of Great Britain, while it felt its own mission was to pursue unceasingly its civilizing rôle in the world.[2]

[1] Camille Fidel, *La paix coloniale française* (Paris, 1918), p. 6.
[2] *Ibid.*, p. 234.

CHAPTER V

THE CARIBBEAN POLICY OF THE NETHERLANDS FROM 1815 to 1939

In the Netherlands major changes marked the close of the Napoleonic Wars. A kingdom was established, unnaturally linked with Catholic Belgium, until this union was dissolved in 1830. William I ruled both countries autocratically. He was head of the army and navy and had also exclusive direction of both foreign and colonial policy.[1] Reaction to revolutionary France, which had swept over most of Europe and was manifested in the Holy Alliance with all that that implied to the New World, also gripped the Netherlands. The Dutch constitution of 1814, though promising civil liberties and personal security to its citizens, was essentially an autocratic document, as was the 1815 constitution which soon replaced it. Though William I, the "Merchant King", used his power to restore the fortunes of his country which had suffered under the French occupation, he was quite unable to revive the lost prosperity of the Netherlands West Indies. Yet with the termination of the Dutch West India Company, administrative responsibility rested with the Crown. The West Indies colonies were the concern of the King and not of the people of the Netherlands.

In the eighteenth century Surinam had possessed some degree of self-government since the colonists elected, on a restricted franchise, a representative council. Since Amsterdam bankers and merchants owned most of the plantations, the council was in reality controlled by absentee owners. In 1816 this body was transformed from being elective to co-optative, modelled on Dutch oligarchic lines. In 1828 a governor was appointed by the King to administer the territory: Curaçao and the other Netherlands West Indies were similarly treated.[2] The system had some similarity to the Spanish practice of personal rule in the colonies instituted by Ferdinand and Isabella.

---

[1] "The Power exercised by the Prince with the Council of State, as adviser, was almost supreme." *Nederlandse Regeringsvoorlichtingsdienst* (The Hague, 1948), No. 4, p. 2.

[2] Vlekke, *Evolution of the Dutch Nation, op. cit.*, p. 299.

With the growing importance of European sugar-beet production which had been stimulated during the Napoleonic Wars when the British blockade had cut off overseas supplies, the Netherlands West Indies fell on hard times.[1] Moreover, the slave economy on which the cane-sugar industry depended was threatened by the measures adopted against the slave trade at the Congress of Vienna, even though these measures were ineffectively applied.

Not surprisingly, the enterprising merchants of Amsterdam who were already familiar with the Eastern trade began to concentrate increasingly on the extensive East Indies possessions of the Netherlands, which comprised 735,000 square miles, as compared with the 55,000 square miles of the West Indies. As the nineteenth century progressed, the introduction of steamships and the opening of the Suez Canal each in its own way shortened the voyage from Europe to the East Indies and stimulated the change in trade. This interest, stimulated by the establishment of rubber plantations following the successful smuggling of hevea seeds from the Amazon, steadily increased until the dream of a Dutch-Indonesian partnership finally vanished after World War II.

In the revolutionary year 1848, William II, who had succeeded his father,[2] made a necessary *volte-face*, in his own words changing from "very conservative to very liberal within 24 hours".[3] With constitutional power passing from the king to the people, or at least to that still small part of it which had been enfranchised, more attention began to be paid to the colonies and to the native populations. Gradually the sense of obligation towards them grew in the Netherlands.

While the hardships of the period were mitigated by the business ability of the Portuguese Jewish merchants and by the trading opportunities of the revolutionary wars in Venezuela and of the American Civil War, the increasing interest of the United States in the Caribbean, following the Spanish-American War and the opening of the Panama Canal, revived interest in the Dutch West Indies.

---

[1] To make matters worse, Paramaribo, the Surinam capital, suffered disastrous fires in 1821 and 1832. *The Netherlands*, ed. Bartholomew Landheer (Berkeley, 1943), p. 400.

[2] William I, disappointed over the loss of Belgium and mortified by criticism of his administration, abdicated in favour of his son in 1840.

[3] *Nederlandse Regeringsvoorlichtingsdienst, op. cit.*, p. 5.

Stimulated by the attitude of the United States, the Netherlands quickly appreciated the changed commercial climate.[1]

Wars often generate change, even for neutrals. In 1920 the Commission on Revision which the Netherlands Government had appointed to advise on constitutional amendments, brought out its report. In it was the Dutch concept that the Dutch East and West Indies should each enjoy a substantial measure of self-government but should remain part of the Kingdom of the Netherlands.[2]

Prior to this, both Curaçao and Surinam[3] had suffered from adverse balances of payments. Inevitably the control of the home government was tighter both in legislation and administration over these territories than in the wealthy and prosperous East Indies. Since 1865 the Colonial Council of Curaçao, wholly appointed by the Crown, and the elected Colonial States in Surinam, had taken part in legislative matters. The governor of the colony was required to execute exactly the commands of the king. The colonial budgets expressed the hopes of each territory; what it received, however, depended on the legislative body of the Netherlands, who were the paymasters.[4] In the years following World War I, the revenues of Curaçao and Surinam were not sufficient to defray their expenses. The attitude of the Netherlands Government, like that of the British Government towards its grant-aided colonies, was firm. Ministers had to defend their requests for money, and were subject to criticism from the representatives of the Dutch taxpayers.

As in the case of Great Britain and France, the Netherlands imported labourers from British India in 1863 to make good the shortage of workers which arose after emancipation. On completion of their indentures, these immigrants were given the choice of repatriation to India or of settlement on small-holdings in Surinam. Many elected to stay and were established around Paramaribo and Nickerie. Some

[1] Cf. Hans G. Hermans, *The Caribbean* (University of Florida Press, 1958), pp. 53-72.

[2] *The Netherlands and the World War* (Studies in the War History of a Neutral) (Yale University Press, 1928), Vol. III, J. H. Carpentier Alting and W. de Cook Buning, "The Effects of the War upon the Colonies", p. 144. Cf. *ibid.*, Vol. IV, p. 189; *Nederlandse Regeringsvoorlichtingsdienst, op. cit.*, fourth document, p. 10.

[3] *The Netherlands and the World War, op. cit.*, Vol. IV, G. Vissering and J. Westerman Holstijn, "War Finances in the Netherlands", p. 196.

[4] *Ibid.*, Vol. III, J. H. Carpentier Alting and W. de Cook Buning, *op. cit.*, pp. 9-10.

Indians became large farmers and owners of rice-mills. The indenture system was terminated by British India in 1916, but since the beginning of the twentieth century it had begun to be superseded by the use of Javanese labour which it was natural for the Netherlands to encourage. Gradually the policy of the indenture system had been replaced by that of free immigration with settlers receiving allotments and financial assistance for settlement. Though descendants of old families, long ago established in the colony, had adapted themselves and were taking a significant part in the business of the country, the climate was unfavourable to white settlement. The encouragement of immigration from the East Indies indicates the Dutch policy in this matter, though the shortage of farmland in the Netherlands led to some immigration into Surinam after World War II, not always with success.[1]

The end of World War I was marked by the establishment on Curaçao by the Royal Dutch Shell Company of an important refinery to process its newly exploited oilfield on Lake Maracaibo. The company, heavily financed as it was with Dutch money and operated from the Netherlands, preferred to place its large installations, soon to become one of the largest petroleum plants in the world, on Dutch rather than Venezuelan soil. Memories of the international difficulties of President Cipriano Castro may have been in the minds of directors of the company. President Juan Vicente Gómez was accommodating, but his dictatorship would one day end. In addition, the sand bar across the mouth of Lake Maracaibo, which at that time had not been dredged, prevented the entry of large ocean-going tankers. The fine harbour at Willemstad, Curaçao, on the other hand, was ideal as a trans-shipment point for oil.

The Royal Dutch Shell Company re-created Dutch interest in Curaçao. The company pursued a policy of extending its refining processes. Labour which came in from Surinam, the Dutch Windward Islands, as well as from the British West Indies, rapidly augmented the population.

The increasingly successful development of the Maracaibo basin led to the establishment by the Standard Oil interests of a refinery on the island of Aruba, influenced no doubt by the example of Royal Dutch Shell and by the policy which the Netherlands had consistently

[1] This viewpoint was expressed to the author by Dr. Hogenboom, manager of the Dutch land settlement at Holambra in the state of São Paulo, Brazil.

followed of admitting foreign capital on the same footing as that of Netherlands subjects.[1]

The Netherlands intensified its interest in its colonial problems as the potentialities of the Dutch East Indies became clearer. From the middle of the nineteenth century the training of administrative officials had been undertaken by the Royal Academy at Delft. Since 1874 lectures were given at Leiden University in the languages, law and ethnology of the East Indies. After 1906 it became the main centre for the training of administrative officials, while Utrecht University started an Indological course.[2] Inevitably the emphasis was heavily on training for the East Indies. The Caribbean territories were far too small to have attracted the same attention, but they undoubtedly benefited from the increasing Dutch colonial interest. Writing of the Dutch administration in the East Indies, W. Preger noted that young men arrived at their posts well equipped with the book knowledge available, and inspired by their reading and by their own national traditions. They were selected not only for intellectual qualities but also for qualities of character and personality.[3] This might be compared to the British system, where character and personality were always taken into consideration in addition to academic qualifications.[4] The Dutch approach to their overseas territories was efficient and just, even if paternalistic and perhaps a little uncompromising.

In the conclusion to his important treatise on Dutch colonial policy[5] published in 1931, Dr. de Kat Angelino made a powerful appeal for more understanding of colonial problems by the people of the Netherlands. Though he came out strongly on the side of the

[1] J. H. Carpentier Alting and W. de Cook Buning, *op. cit.*, p. 37. With the sand bar across the entrance to Lake Maracaibo cut through in 1956, the production of the Venezuelan oilfields, which has so far increased, has made possible the erection of refineries on the mainland without interfering with refining offshore. Yet it is possible that this situation may change. Gilbert J. Butland, *Latin America* (London, 1960), p. 126. Cf. Preston E. James, *Latin America*, 3rd ed. (New York, 1959), pp. 84-5.

[2] W. Preger, *Dutch Administration in the Netherlands Indies* (Melbourne, 1944), p. 16.

[3] *Ibid.*, pp. 17-18.

[4] The author, when a Member of Parliament, served in 1934-1935 on the Consular Selection Board which interviewed candidates for the Consular Service.

[5] A. D. A. de Kat Angelino, *Colonial Policy* (The Hague, 1931), Vol. II, p. 648.

Dutch administration and was inevitably devoting most of his attention to the Netherlands East Indies, a spirit of uneasiness may be detected in his work. He felt that within the framework of the League of Nations "one would like to detect an effort more consciously directed towards this special sphere entrusted by world history to Dutch leadership. Holland must bring to the world more than the contribution of its eleven provinces."[1] He adds, "We must begin to train for membership of the organic Greater Netherlands. A good basis has been laid since 1900 by the work of many interested people, of associations, universities, reviews, exhibitions, and journals."[2] The general policy of the Netherlands towards its East and West Indies at this period was similar both in its ideals and its philosophy. To de Kat Angelino, Dutch colonial policy was uniform. The Netherlands was convinced of the importance of its colonial mission.

In the concluding chapter of his book,[3] Professor G. H. Bousquet, himself a faculty member of a French overseas university,[4] contrasts Dutch colonial philosophy with that of France. He finds it hard to define exactly the Dutch colonial spirit. Referring to de Kat Angelino, Bousquet writes, "On a le sentiment que la Hollande aimerait bien être considérée comme mandatée par l'univers pour administrer son domaine colonial." Queen Isabella of Spain would have understood.

[1] *Ibid.*, p. 648.
[2] *Ibid.*, p. 653.
[3] G. H. Bousquet, *op. cit.*, p. 149.
[4] The University of Algiers.

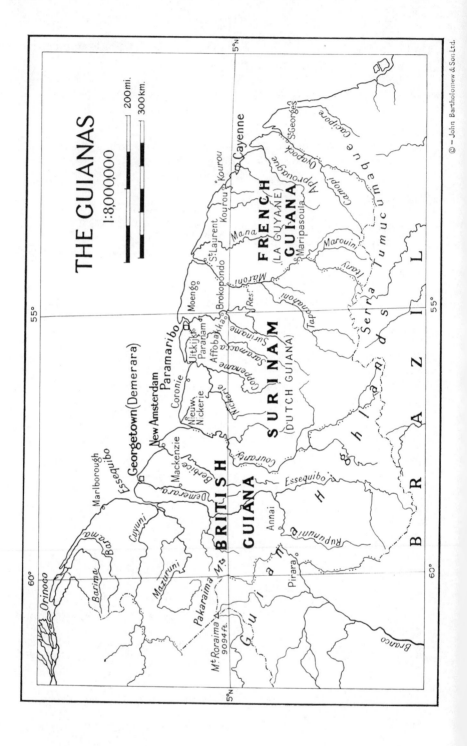

THE GUIANAS

1:8,000,000

200 mi.

300 km.

© – John Bartholomew & Son Ltd.

CHAPTER VI

THE COLONIES IN TRANSITION

In retrospect, the rise of nationalism seems slight during the years preceding World War II. Undoubtedly the concept was advancing of a British Empire composed of self-governing units, held together by tradition, sentiment and the Ottawa agreements. It was assumed in Great Britain that the progress towards self-government would be very gradual and that this would be in harmony with the wishes of the colonial peoples, still backward and with many illiterates in most of the territories. More and more, however, the traditional policy of control from London was being questioned, even if less brusquely than it had been in eighteenth-century North America. The two most difficult issues involved Eire,[1] which gradually moved to complete independence, and India, whose problems caused a temporary crack in the solid ranks of the supporters of the National Government: in both cases the solutions adopted were examples of Great Britain's extraordinary capacity for illogical compromise. Nationalism in the West Indies, as in other colonial territories, was not yet easy to discern.

The new colonial empire which France had carved out during the nineteenth and twentieth centuries differed sharply in character from the wrecked empire it replaced. France was fortunate in its leaders, including General Joseph Simon Gallieni and Marshal Louis Lyautey. Together they illustrated the indirect approach to colonial problems by working through local rulers in the territories, as opposed to the system of integration with France which had been designed by Colbert and had continued in the older colonies, aided by a substantial white plantocracy in a slave economy. As a young man Gallieni had served in Martinique, though it was in Tonking and Madagascar where his colonial reputation was established. Lyautey,

---

[1] The tradition of free movement of citizens between Great Britain and the Republic of Eire has been continued to the present day, despite the restrictions imposed by the Commonwealth Immigrants Act. This not unnaturally caused heart-burning in the British Caribbean territories which found it difficult to understand Great Britain's claim that it could not control a frontier of 200 miles.

who had served under Gallieni in Tonking and Madagascar, brilliantly exemplified the same methods of working through local rulers, a system also adopted by Lord Lugard in Nigeria. This concept of colonial rule was in complete contrast to that in the older French colonies which included the Caribbean departments. The hope of any closer integration with France for these more recent colonies was rudely shattered by World War II. "Un grand vent d'émancipation a soufflé sur les populations d'Afrique et d'Asie."[1] Despite the attempt to administer through local rulers, Paul Alduy considered that French administration had pulverized the framework of local institutions which had resulted in a policy of racial segregation. Only in the Antilles and in Senegal, where several centuries of coexistence had succeeded in breaking down racial barriers, had this been avoided.[2] He also declared that the change from a feudal to a modern economy, based upon immigrants from France and Spain living side by side with the Moslem population of North Africa, had caused a major revision in capital values. The hostility to colonialism of former colonies in North and South America added to the difficulties which France faced in its efforts to assimilate its overseas citizens.

The careful, logical and legalistic Netherlands approach to its colonies, strictly and capably administered, envisaged a gradual move towards closer partnership with the metropolitan power. To many students of colonial affairs it was the Netherlands East Indies which appeared to exhibit colonial administration at its most efficient.[3] Unlike Great Britain and France, the Netherlands had only two important territories to administer, Java and Sumatra, on which they were able to concentrate. Interest in the Netherlands West Indies was slight.

[1] E. Revert, "La politique coloniale de la France: étude retrospective", *Principles and Methods of Colonial Administration*, Colston Research Society and University of Bristol (London, 1950), p. 31.

[2] Paul Alduy, *"La naissance du nationalisme outre-mer"*, *ibid.*, p. 127.

[3] The author, when studying coal-mining, visited in 1925 the Oembilin coal-mines, a Dutch Government enterprise at Sawah Loento in the interior of Sumatra. The underground operation which involved hydraulic stowage of the waste was modern and efficient. About 7000 Javanese were employed, some of them convicts. The coal was shipped from Emmahaven, the port of Padang. Most of it was supplied to Dutch steamship lines and the Java State Railways. This remote company town provided an excellent glimpse of Dutch enterprise and policy in the East Indies. Cf. Sir Harold P. Mitchell, *In My Stride* (London, 1951), pp. 39-40.

Like a tidal wave, World War II swept over the world affecting each one of the colonial powers. Great Britain was largely cut off from its overseas territories. Its shipping had to run the gauntlet of an enemy submarine network. Yet after the invasion of France, Belgium and Holland in 1940, Britain depended on the Commonwealth more than ever before both for troops and supplies.[1] The well-protected strong-points in so many parts of the world proved of the greatest assistance to the Commonwealth and its allies, as they had in previous wars. In establishing the convoy system, the harbours in the Western Atlantic and the Caribbean provided bases of immense value to the allied navies. Halifax and Bermuda matched Kingston and Port-of-Spain. Food became increasingly scarce, with ration cards entitling the people to less and less. Great Britain's desperate situation was reflected in an increasing demand for sugar from the Caribbean territories, and contracts were later made for the supply of concentrated orange juice for children.[2] The export of bananas from Jamaica to Great Britain was discontinued, the crop being purchased by Great Britain and sold back at a low price for local consumption. The refrigerated ships previously employed in this trade were needed for other purposes.[3]

Perhaps the most striking example of the British Government's awareness of its colonial problems and of its desire to solve them arose out of the Moyne Report, which was in the hands of the Government in the early days of the war even though it was not issued in full until 1945. The report called attention to the deplorable housing and health conditions existing in the Caribbean. It was generally believed in the House of Commons that the withholding of publication was due to the Government's anxiety lest the information it contained should cause trouble in the colonies. Notwithstanding the strain of war which had compelled Great Britain to impose even heavier taxation on its citizens and to mobilize for sale its foreign securites to provide exchange, the British Government obtained Parliamentary approval for the setting up of the Colonial Welfare and Development Fund. To vote £1 million per annum for twenty

[1] After the withdrawal of France, the Polish armed forces, which at that time were mainly based in Great Britain, were the largest allied force apart from British imperial forces.

[2] Supplied from Jamaica, British Honduras and Trinidad.

[3] E.g. for carrying meat. Losses were heavy since these ships were often too fast for convoys and voyaged unescorted.

years at a time when the standard of living at home was being steadily reduced showed the appreciation by all political parties of the urgency of the problems in the colonial empire and not least in the West Indies.

In the grim days of the early summer of 1940, General Charles de Gaulle appealed in the name of France for continued resistance. "A l'heure qu'il est, je parle pour l'Afrique du Nord française, pour l'Afrique du Nord intacte. . . . Il ne serait pas tolérable que la panique de Bordeaux ait pu traverser la mer."[1] Marshal Pétain, however, had sufficient influence to keep General Nogues in North Africa with him. Even if de Gaulle's words at first fell mainly on deaf ears in Africa, he was able to announce two months later that Tchad and Cameroun had rallied on August 27, 1940, to the Free French Forces, followed the next day by Brazzaville, the capital of French Equatorial Africa.

With their leaders divided, the choice was not an easy one for Frenchmen. A patriotic soldier like General de Lattre de Tassigny, who had served the Vichy Government, and whom Lord Norwich (Alfred Duff Cooper) described as "the last of the Beaux Sabreurs", underwent trial and imprisonment rather than carry out orders with which he disagreed, before finally escaping to serve Free France in Africa and in North-West Europe, and afterwards in Indo-China.[2] The line of defiance taken by de Gaulle was magnificent, but it had many critics. Commenting on de Gaulle's memoirs,[3] General Maxime Weygand considered that the armistice with the Germans which was the alternative to unconditional surrender had obligated France to follow the path of Pétain, and that it had been acceptable to the vast majority of the French people.[4]

Perhaps the confusion of the period is best summed up by de Gaulle himself when describing the unsuccessful British action against Dakar, which he had discussed on the spot with Admiral Sir Andrew Cunningham. He writes, "Les Britanniques, gens pratiques, ne parvenaient pas à comprendre comment et pourquoi, à Dakar, les autorités, la marine, les troupes, déployaient cette énergie pour se battre contre leurs compatriotes et contre leurs alliés, tandis que la

[1] London, June 19, 1940. Charles de Gaulle, *Discours de guerre* (Fribourg, 1944).
[2] Sir Guy Salisbury-Jones, *So Full a Glory* (London, 1954), pp. 114-21.
[3] Charles de Gaulle, *Mémoires de guerre* (Paris, 1954).
[4] Maxime Weygand, *En lisant mémoires du général de Gaulle* (Paris, 1955).

France gisait sous la botte de l'envahisseur. Quant à moi, j'avais, désormais, renoncé à rien étonner."[1]

Martinique had proved equally confusing. When France was collapsing in June 1940, the Banque de France sent a large shipment of gold to Brest, where it was placed on board the fast cruiser *Emile Bertin*. The warship proceeded to Halifax and then to Fort-de-France, Martinique, where the gold was stored. In view of the large quantity involved, a rigid blockade of Martinique was imposed by British warships after France's surrender. With shortages of goods occurring and prices rising, eventually Great Britain agreed to the United States' replacing its patrols around the island. In December 1940, when President Roosevelt toured the bases acquired on lease from Great Britain at the Bermuda Conference, France agreed to the United States' patrolling its Antillean waters. However, Admiral Georges Robert, who had been appointed High Commissioner for the French Antilles by the Vichy Government, remained in control.

At a press conference in London on May 27, 1942, de Gaulle was questioned on the march of events in Martinique and their relation to the internal situation in France. He replied that Martinique was at the bottom of nearly all current world discussions on the subject of France and naturally of Fighting France. It was necessary to know if the general interests of France were or were not represented among the democracies.[2] De Gaulle's remarks were often cryptic. In 1942, he said, "En outre, il s'est créé dans la nation et dans le monde une sorte de mystique de la libération française qui est un élément capital, pour le présent et pour l'avenir, de l'unité et de la grandeur du pays"[3]; and he ended this speech, "Les Français n'ont qu'une seule patrie. Il s'agit de faire en sorte qu'ils ne livrent qu'un seul combat. La France est et restera une et indivisible." A country partly occupied by the enemy with the remainder of its territories split between two governments, one of which was at war and the other neutral, was in no condition to plan the future of its vast overseas territories.

[1] De Gaulle, *op. cit., L'appel 1940-1942*, p. 107.

[2] "Quand il se produit un fait comme celui de la Martinique, je vous prends à témoin que, ou bien la question est tranchée unilatéralement par une puissance étrangère et alliée, ou bien elle est tranchée par un accord entre cette puissance alliée et M. Laval, c'est-à-dire en dernier ressort, M. Hitler. Ni l'une ni l'autre de ces solutions ne sont désirables. Elles ne font pas entrer en ligne de compte la représentation des intérêts généraux de la France parmi les Alliés." [3] London, December 28, 1942.

In quick succession the war submerged first the Netherlands[1] and less than two years later the Netherlands East Indies.[2] The Netherlands Government in exile in London perceived that action was required in the field of colonial reform. A committee[3] was set up to investigate the opinions and aspirations of the different racial and social groups in the East Indies. Though its work was completed prior to the Japanese invasion in 1942, no action could be taken, but the added emphasis on speedy colonial reform and self-government began to be expressed by the Dutch Government, increasingly influenced as the war continued by the outspoken views of President Franklin D. Roosevelt.

The speeches of Queen Wilhelmina of the Netherlands, one of the most experienced constitutional sovereigns in modern times, who had already reigned for forty-four years when invasion forced her with her Government into exile in London, were at first an affirmation, in which her Prime Minister, P. S. Gerbrandy, joined, of the determination of her people to resist. She emphasized that from Curaçao to New Guinea the Empire stood fast; she also stressed the material and moral aid being provided by the Netherlands East and West Indies in the crisis.

During the course of the war Queen Wilhelmina faithfully expressed the increasingly progressive ideas of her ministers and advisers towards the Netherlands overseas territories, including those in the Caribbean, which alone had escaped invasion. In a radio address over Radioorange, the Netherlands station in London, on December 7, 1942, she amplified the views of her Government on post-war reforms. Declaring her conviction that, after the war, it would be possible to reconstruct the Kingdom of the Netherlands "on the solid foundation of complete partnership", she added that this political unity would express the ideals for which the United Nations were fighting and which were set out in the Atlantic Charter. There would be no room for discrimination according to race or nationality; only the ability of individual citizens and the needs of the various

[1] Germany invaded the Netherlands on May 10, 1940.
[2] Japan invaded the Netherlands East Indies on March 8, 1942.
[3] Dr. Franz H. Visman, a member of the Council of the Indies, was appointed on September 14, 1940, by the Governor-General of the Netherlands Indies as chairman of a committee to investigate "what wishes, trends of thought, and opinions concerning the political developments of the country, nationally and locally, exist among the different racial and social groups of the community of the Netherlands Indies", and report its findings.

38

groups of the population would determine the policy of the Government. The Queen envisaged a commonwealth in which the Netherlands, Indonesia, Surinam and Curaçao would participate, with complete self-reliance and freedom of conduct for each regarding its internal affairs, but with the readiness to render mutual assistance.

In the autumn of 1941, with the approval and collaboration of the Netherlands Government in London, American troops were stationed in the Netherlands West Indies[1] in order to strengthen these vital points. Queen Wilhelmina referred to the importance of Surinam bauxite and Curaçao oil products to the Free World when she addressed the United States Congress the following year.[2] Naturally the policy of the Dutch Government in exile towards strengthening its Caribbean territories was violently assailed by the Nazi-controlled radio in Holland, which described the transaction as the sale of the colonies "for a few silverlings despite the work of generations of Netherlanders".[3]

The German occupation had stifled the press of the Netherlands, but underground publications had begun to appear. That the Queen in her broadcast had used "Indonesia" instead of the "Netherlands East Indies" was considered as symbolic of a forward policy on the part of the Netherlands Government, since the name had been created by native nationalists.[4] On July 30, 1943, the Dutch underground newspaper *Vrij Nederland* commented, "Our Queen and various Government spokesmen have already clearly indicated that independence in some form or other must be granted to the overseas territories." It added that enemy occupation had given the people of the Netherlands a greater appreciation of their urge for freedom. Another underground paper, *Vrij Katheder*, devoted a special number to the Indonesian problem, claiming that the Netherlands Government would have to be adapted to "existing modern democratic institutions".[5] Inevitably the emphasis was on the relationship

[1] L. de Jong and Joseph W. Stoppelman, *The Lion Rampant* (New York, 1943), pp. 157-8.   [2] August 6, 1942.
[3] De Jong and Stoppelman, *op. cit.*, p. 158.
[4] The Dutch underground press, July 8, 1943.
[5] *Vrij Katheder*, September 13, 1943, quoted by *The Netherlands Commonwealth and the Future* (The Netherlands Information Bureau, New York, 1945). This publication notes that the various underground papers, including *Je Maintiendrai*, *Vrij Nederland*, *Het Parool*, and *Vrij Katheder*, had all supported the proposition that the mutual relationship between the homeland and the Indies must be based on co-ordination and not subordination.

of the Netherlands to Indonesia, further dramatized by invasion, but the acceptance of the Caribbean territories into the partnership was implicit throughout.

The Dutch policy statements were favourably received abroad. The *Washington Post* considered the proposal of Queen Wilhelmina for the "future governance of the far-flung Netherlands Empire" as a great contribution to constructive statesmanship. It added with a measure of prescience that no good end would be served if by the drastic implementation of the Atlantic Charter the world was balkanized so that an effective international society became impossible.[1] The *Christian Science Monitor* also commended the Queen's speech as showing how the principles of the Atlantic Charter could be applied to the Pacific. "British opinion", it added, "has long recognized such a return to the *status quo ante* to be impossible. Its pledge of freedom for India and its surrender of extra-territorial rights in China are proof of this. Queen Wilhelmina's statement shows that what is happening in the British Empire is part of a world trend. It helps to assure all peoples that the trend will be well established before the war is over."[2]

In a thoughtful analysis the *Washington Star* considered that the plan was novel and differed from the British Commonwealth and the United States' system for the Philippines. Both the Commonwealth and the Philippines concepts involved greater separation of the territories from the mother country. Under the Dutch system, the overseas partners would be brought closer to the mother country while the plan would extend independence and educate them politically.[3]

In the House of Representatives, Clare Booth Luce commended the progressive attitude of the Dutch towards their colonial responsibilities. She referred to the recent decentralization of the six islands of the Netherlands West Indies group, in order that each island should have its own lieutenant-governor and administration operating on a democratic basis. She visualized in the future a commonwealth of the Netherlands, Indonesia, Surinam and Curaçao, with complete internal freedom for each part and readiness to co-operate for mutual assistance.[4]

[1] *Washington Post*, December 2, 1942.
[2] *Christian Science Monitor*, December 9, 1942.
[3] *Washington Star*, December 8, 1942.
[4] *Congressional Record*, May 15, 1944.

Though based in London where it might have been expected to be influenced by the British approach to overseas problems, the Dutch Government does not appear to have been attracted to the concept of independent "dominions". The elastic British system, which was later to include independent republics within the framework of the Commonwealth "Club", made little appeal to the legalistic and logical Dutch mind, which was steeped in constitutional precedents.

The Atlantic Charter, which set forth the views of President Roosevelt and Prime Minister Winston Churchill and was proclaimed at their 1941 meeting off Newfoundland, stressed the aim of freedom. Though Churchill may have had reservations which he characteristically expressed at the Lord Mayor's Banquet in London in 1942[1] and which were shared by many British people, as the war proceeded the views of the American President seemed more and more to be in tune with events. Though the Charter of the United Nations placed power in the hands of the Security Council, the principle of one vote to each member large or small in the General Assembly was of major importance to the new countries which were soon to become independent. Perhaps the West, including the colonial powers, was over-optimistic that the emerging African and Asian peoples would continue to accept its guidance.

Major problems faced each one of the colonial powers. For Great Britain, the quest for a solution in India overshadowed all other overseas problems. But attention was also paid to a small territory like Jamaica, which in 1944 received a new constitution.

When World War II was at its height in 1942, the Anglo-American Caribbean Commission was set up to promote scientific, technological and economic development in the Caribbean area; its first West Indies Conference was held in 1944. Both major powers had recognized the need for action to relieve the poverty of the islands, a poverty aggravated by wartime shortages. The Commission was later joined by France and Holland in 1945, and renamed the Caribbean Commission.[2] Though at first its impact on the West Indies was not

[1] *The Times*, London, November 11, 1942.
[2] The first meeting of the expanded Commission took place in St. Thomas, U.S. Virgin Islands, in February 1946. At a meeting in Washington in July 1946, representatives of member governments established the Caribbean Commission with headquarters at Port-of-Spain, Trinidad. Two of the four members of the British section were non-officials, Norman Manley from Jamaica and Garnet Gordon from St. Lucia. Thus the people of the Caribbean territories participated in the Commission's work. Cf. Hansard 427,

very considerable, it served to draw the islands together and to make them aware of one another's problems.[1] A parallel may be seen in the inauguration by Australia and New Zealand of the South Pacific Commission in 1947.

World War II caused profound changes even if they were not always perceived at the time; such changes were much more marked than in World War I, which had also affected colonial territories, particularly in Africa, where a long campaign had been waged over the German colonies and in which African troops had been involved. The effect of the war on each of the colonial powers varied. Despite the immense cost of the war to Britain and the Commonwealth, which had to be borne at first with little outside aid, despite the heavy damage from air attack to its cities and factories, Parliament was increasingly conscious of its colonial responsibilities. The shock of the rapid collapse of Malaya when invaded by Japan in 1942, followed by the surrender of the great base at Singapore upon which so much money had been lavished, stunned the country. Thoughtful people began to wonder what it signified.

The French position was more confused, with part of the overseas territories in association with Vichy and part garrisoned by foreign troops, as in the case of certain areas of French North Africa, while other colonial territories declared with fervour for Free France.[2] It was still too soon for France, torn asunder by invasion, to formulate the future of its colonial empire.

---

col. 313. In October 1946, Arthur Creech Jones, Secretary of State for the Colonies, described the Commission as follows: "The Caribbean Commission is an advisory international body of the four metropolitan countries, France, the Netherlands, the United Kingdom and the United States, which have territories in the Caribbean. Its purpose is the encouragement and strength-ening of co-operation amongst the member governments and their territories, with a view to improving the economic and social well-being of the peoples of those territories." Hansard 427, cols. 311-312.

[1] In 1959 the Caribbean Commission was reconstructed as the Caribbean Organization, with headquarters at San Juan, Puerto Rico, the Caribbean territories now being directly represented. Of the colonial powers, only France was represented by reason of the status of its territories as French Departments. The Commission has never included the Caribbean republics.

[2] The author, when on a mission to Africa in 1942 for General Wladyslaw Sikorski, commander in chief of the Polish army, has a vivid recollection of the general emotion which he shared as he stood beside the French naval commander at Douala, French Cameroun, at the sounding of a bugle for the lowering of the Tricolour at dusk.

Of the three countries, the Netherlands had been the most completely overwhelmed, with all of the homeland and most of its colonial empire in enemy hands. Nevertheless, the very isolation of its Government which had remained united in exile behind Queen Wilhelmina gave time for reflection. The invasion of the East Indies hastened the realization that a radical change of policy was required.

The three most experienced colonial powers had all reached a climax in their history of administering overseas territories. Faced with increasingly difficult problems, each was to attempt a different solution.

CHAPTER VII

PROBLEMS OF CLOSER UNION
IN THE BRITISH CARIBBEAN

The end of World War II involved the colonial powers in many new appraisals of policy, which extended beyond the bounds of the belligerents. Victory for Great Britain had indeed solved some of its problems; it had also created others. If the British Empire and Commonwealth had responded magnificently to the Nazi-Fascist challenge, the vicissitudes of war, involving the moving of hundreds of thousands of troops and the occupation by the enemy of large areas of territory such as Malaya and Burma, had caused enduring changes. Great Britain had accepted the fact that the old concept of empire must radically alter.

Yet Britain's problems were both widespread and scattered. The grim middle years of the war had emphasized the tenuous nature of Empire and Commonwealth communications.[1] Australian and New Zealand troops had fought valiantly in North Africa, in Malaya and in New Guinea, while the Japanese invasion of their home territories had appeared to them imminent. Australia and New Zealand had a definite and expressed interest in South-East Asia. British bases, and the treaties which in some cases gave Great Britain special rights, contributed to the complexity of what still appeared to be a life line facilitating the movement of ships and of airplanes between Commonwealth countries.

Great Britain's desire to fulfil its promises of independence to those countries which appeared ready for it had necessarily to be adjusted to Britain's obligations to its Commonwealth partners and its allies. In addition, it had to consider the vital supply of oil from the Middle East. The strain on the British coal industry, increased by the exigencies of war, was making the oil ever more important. Though

---

[1] Lord Chandos well describes the complications which had to be tackled in the Middle East at this time in *The Memoirs of Lord Chandos* (London, 1962), pp. 215-79, as does his successor as Minister of State in the Middle East, Lord Casey, in *Personal Experience* (London, 1962), pp. 93-166. Cf. Mitchell, *op. cit.*, pp. 200-8.

44

Middle East problems were interrelated, in that most of them involved strategic as well as economic considerations, no general plan could be adopted. What more diverse group of territories could be found than Cyprus, Egypt, Aden, Palestine and Iraq linking Great Britain via Gibraltar and Malta with India, Burma, Malaya and Australia? Affecting all was the Suez Canal. In some cases, peace was even to heighten tensions. Solutions were to be reached only after agonizing decisions.

In the ancient West Indies colonies, the position was very different. Strategic considerations no longer existed. British bases had been gradually given up. Bermuda[1] in the North Atlantic was already dominated by two great American bases on these islands, and the British base there would soon be closed. The United States' preponderance of power was equally marked in the Caribbean. In the final analysis, the proximity of the Panama Canal and the vital Venezuelan oilfields made American strategic control inevitable. There were no British minorities to be evacuated if sovereignty changed. Intermarriage had largely softened asperities between Europeans and the remainder of the population.

With all political parties committed to an advance towards self-government throughout the colonial territories, Great Britain was enabled to give free play to its liberal instincts which favoured independence. Moreover, some of the West Indies colonies had had the added advantage of a long experience of partial self-government. The greatest problem was the smallness of the islands and the distances which separated them, while the larger but impoverished mainland territories faced other difficulties. To the British Colonial Office, the continuance of a proliferation of small and costly governments appeared illogical. Closer union seemed essential. Thus Great Britain was to present to West Indian statesmanship the challenge of independence within a federation.

A modest measure of federation had already been attempted in the nineteenth century to reduce the cost and complications of administering a large number of tiny islands with an ailing economy. In 1871 the Leeward Islands reluctantly became a federal colony by Act of Parliament.[2] However, when Great Britain attempted in 1876 to

[1] Though outside the Caribbean, Bermuda had been closely linked with the Caribbean colonies. After World War II the British naval dockyard was closed in April 1957 and finally the British garrison withdrew on March 31, 1958.   [2] 34 & 35 Victoria, cap. 107.

45

federate Barbados with the Windward Islands, the Barbadians rioted, and the proposals were abandoned.[1] The clumsy, if well-meant, British attempt to bring about needed reforms had ended in violent opposition from the Barbados assembly and in loss of life. Governor John Hennessy was recalled, and even federation among the Windward Islands without Barbados was postponed. It was a clear indication of the rugged individualism of West Indian leaders. The Royal Commission of 1882-1883, under the chairmanship of Colonel William Crossman, M.P., recommended setting up a separate federation of the Windward Islands, and this was carried out.[2]

Despite the continuing belief of the Colonial Office in the principle of union of the smaller colonies, West Indies public opinion remained opposed to it, fortified by the ancient constitution which Barbados had retained intact. Even in 1921 Major Edward F. Wood (afterwards the Earl of Halifax), as Under-Secretary of State for the Colonies, considered that the unpopularity of proposals for federation made them impracticable. The opinion of this astute statesman was re-echoed in 1936 by Lord Olivier, who believed that Jamaicans would never consent to having the domicile of their government outside the island and in so essentially different a political and social atmosphere as that of Barbados or Trinidad.[3]

The year 1945 not only marked the end of World War II with the total defeat of first Germany and then Japan. It also produced a crushing reverse for the Conservative Party and its allies at the

[1] John Pope Hennessy, who had previously governed the Bahamas and who had thus had experience of a similar constitution of the old colonial pattern, which involved a scattered group of islands, was appointed Governor of Barbados in 1875 to promote federation with the Windward Islands. In fact, this "old and proud colony" strongly objected to giving up its long-established assembly for Crown Colony government. Though labourers on the estates favoured the progressive policy of Hennessy, who had tried to introduce prison and hospital reforms, and who thought that federation might bring about higher wages, the Barbadian planters were strongly opposed to the suggested reforms. They formed for this purpose a Barbados Defence League. To suppress Negro riots, troops had to be sent to Barbados from Jamaica and British Guiana. Augier et al., op. cit., pp. 235-7; cf. Burns, op. cit., p. 658; Parry and Sherlock, op. cit., p. 286.
[2] Report of the Royal Commission appointed to inquire into the public revenues, expenditures, debts, and liabilities of the Islands of Jamaica, Grenada, St. Vincent, Tobago and St. Lucia, and of the Leeward Islands (1884).
[3] Lord Olivier, op. cit., p. 431.

General Election which took place in Great Britain shortly after the German surrender. With an overwhelming majority behind him, Clement Attlee succeeded Winston Churchill as Prime Minister. For the first time Labour was in power without dependence on Liberal votes.

In the new approach to the colonies, the Labour Government made use of two main instruments to further its colonial policy: the Colonial Development Fund established in 1929, and the Colonial Development Corporation which the Attlee Government set up. In 1945, Parliament voted £120 million to be spent in the colonies over a ten-year period under the Colonial Development and Welfare Act.

With a lively recollection of the help given by the colonial empire during World War II, in which half a million men from the colonies had served in the Armed Forces, much attention was devoted to the Commonwealth and particularly colonial territories. The Prime Minister emphasized this point of view when he welcomed nearly a hundred delegates from the Dominions and colonies to the sixth Imperial Press Conference in London.[1] A month later, George Hall, Secretary of State for the Colonies, making what he termed the first peacetime statement on colonial policy since the 1945 General Election, said in his opening remarks, "I can say without hesitation that it is our policy to develop the colonies and all their resources so as to enable their peoples speedily and substantially to improve their economic and social conditions and, as soon as may be practicable, to attain responsible self-government." He added that the Labour Government regarded the colonies as a great trust: the colonies would progress towards self-government as quickly as they showed themselves capable.[2] An interesting feature of this important debate was the tribute which the Secretary of State paid to his Conservative predecessor, Oliver Stanley, for laying the foundations for much of the work which had been carried out in the colonies during the preceding year. Stanley, who spoke next, commented on the similarity of the Labour Secretary of State's policy to his own, though

[1] In the course of his address, Mr. Attlee said, "In the presence of the delegation from the West Indies, I must mention too, the debt we owe to the sons and daughters of the Caribbean, who from the very outset of the war flocked to the colours, and who won honour in every service and in every theatre of the world-wide war."

[2] Hansard 425, col. 238.

47

he added that constitutional changes had been dramatic in Jamaica, Ceylon and Nigeria.[1]

The post-war years were a period of remarkable political evolution in the Commonwealth. India, Ceylon and Ghana advanced rapidly to independence, with almost every British-administered territory in Asia and Africa pressing forward to the same goal. The slower progress of the Caribbean territories may seem strange. A tradition of independence, with the larger units having their own governors, and a belief that each territory was selling its exports in competition with the others, discouraged integration. This feeling of isolation had been fostered by poor inter-island communications. Events, however, were speeded up by the development of air travel, aided by the fine chain of airports which the United States had constructed on leased bases during World War II and which civil aviation was afterwards able to use. Thus the way was prepared for a new approach to the political organization of the British Caribbean.

In 1947 a conference of the West Indies colonies held at Montego Bay, Jamaica, approved the principle of a federation on the Australian model, laying heavy stress on the rights of the individual territorial governments while severely limiting the central government. With Jamaica, the largest island, more than a thousand miles distant from Trinidad, not even speedier communications had overcome the traditional reluctance towards any form of union. There was general agreement that only by closer association could economic problems be solved, including the centralization of technical help and the provision of services beyond the reach of individual small units. It was also

[1] Hansard 425, col. 264. The continuity of thought between the two main British political parties may also be seen in a speech of the author, speaking at Cardiff on May 13, 1944, when Vice-Chairman of the Conservative Party Organization of Great Britain: "There are now over forty different colonies which are administered by governors and officials who are directly responsible to the Colonial Office. This system sometimes makes administration costly. My view is that, where possible, colonies should be grouped on a regional basis. . . . You might combine some of the colonies in the Caribbean area—Jamaica, British Honduras, the Bahamas, Barbados, Trinidad and, probably, British Guiana. The problems of all of them are somewhat similar. There are many which they cannot tackle adequately working alone. As a unit their problems might be successfully overcome. These colonies grow a variety of products, in the cultivation of which they encounter similar obstacles. For example, over here each has its own marketing machinery. Why should not that be pooled for efficiency?" Harold P. Mitchell, *Into Peace* (London, 1945).

48

recognized that other countries preferred to make trade agreements with a single large unit. Yet controversy and disagreement between the units, which was to mar the short career of the Federation, were early exhibited.

Following the report of the British Caribbean Standing Closer Association Committee, which had been set up by the Montego Bay Conference under the chairmanship of Sir Hubert Rance, a conference was called in London in 1953. This, on the whole, weakened still further the concept of central government. The raising of loans, which had been a federal matter, was now put on the concurrent list, which included those spheres of activity open to both the federal and unit governments. So also was income tax, with the additional proviso that during the first five years the power to impose an income tax was to be withheld from the Federal Government. It was becoming more and more clear that all parties to this proposed "marriage" were showing increasing reluctance, despite the encouragement of Great Britain's veiled promises of a suitable "dowry".

A further London conference was held in 1956. By this time difficulties which had arisen over the free movement of the population between the islands appeared to have been overcome. Trinidad's concern over unwanted immigrants was partly allayed by the grant of authority to decide this matter for five years by local legislation. But, no solution to the knotty problem of a customs union had been found. Since agreement over the location of the capital could not be reached, an impartial Site Commission from outside the West Indies was set up to furnish a report, with the ultimate decision in the hands of the Standing Federation Committee, which remained in being until the creation of the new Federal Government after the first federal elections.

In January 1957 the Standing Federation Committee met in Jamaica primarily to settle the issue of the site of the new capital. The order of choice of the Site Commission, which had been (1) Barbados, (2) Jamaica and (3) Trinidad, was reversed, Trinidad being selected. Whether the decision was a wise one may well be questioned. Trinidad had perhaps the most humid climate in the proposed Federation, a matter affecting the capacity to work of persons whether of African, Indian or European origin. Brazil, in changing its capital from Rio de Janeiro to Brasília, was considerably influenced by this consideration, as well as by the desire to secure a

49

more central location, something which Trinidad did not have in relation to the Federation. The discovery that the American base at Chaguaramas was the only suitable site in Trinidad caused a further deadlock. The United States, having established this base at great cost, was disinclined to give it up, especially at a time of international tension. Consequently, the Federal Government had to be squeezed into an already overcrowded Port-of-Spain.[1]

With the complications which had already occurred in the setting up of the West Indies Federation, the selection of the first Governor-General of the West Indies was of great importance. The appointment of Lord Hailes was unexpected, since many had believed that one of the former Governors of some Caribbean territory would be chosen. It reflected the view of the British Government that someone with a wide knowledge of the workings of Parliament should hold the post. Clearly, complex constitutional problems were likely to arise within a federation which was politically so loosely bound together and geographically so scattered. Though the post of Chief Whip, which Lord Hailes held for seven years, is one of the most important parliamentary appointments, it is also one which receives little publicity. Yet on his ability in the division lobbies may sometimes hang the fate of a government. If Lord Hailes had required all his qualities of tact and persuasion in Parliament when Government and Opposition were evenly matched, he would need them at least as much in the complex politics of the West Indies. He also benefited from having no former association with any territory in the West Indies which, island jealousies being what they are, might have added to his task.

At the beginning of 1958 a Federal General Election was held to elect the first members of the House of Representatives. The Federal Labour Party was formed with Norman Manley as leader, assisted by Sir Grantley Adams as deputy leader. It had the support of the People's National Party in Jamaica, the People's National Movement in Trinidad, which Dr. Eric Williams had led to victory two years before, and the Barbados Labour Party. Since all these

[1] After prolonged negotiations a solution was reached in 1961 whereby the United States relinquished 21,000 acres of its lease in Trinidad, including unused portions of the naval base. The lease had been acquired under the bases-for-destroyers agreement signed in 1941 with the United Kingdom Government. Thus the way was opened for the establishment of the Federal capital at Chaguaramas. *Hispanic American Report* (Stanford University, California), Vol. XIII, p. 885.

island parties were entrenched in office, the new Federal Labour Party had powerful backing and was expected to win an easy victory. In opposition to it, however, the Democratic Labour Party led by Sir Alexander Bustamante, supported by his Jamaica Labour Party and the opposition Democratic Labour Party in Trinidad, secured a majority of seats both in Jamaica and in Trinidad. The Federal Labour Party was only able to obtain a slender overall majority from its successes in the small islands. Observers noted that, in Jamaica, the Democratic Labour candidates who, following Bustamante's example, made a critical approach to federation, were the more successful.[1] The Jamaica electorate seemed lukewarm to federation, the full implications of which Jamaicans hardly as yet appreciated.

Since neither Manley nor Williams, occupied with the problems of their respective governments, had felt able to forsake island for federal politics, Sir Grantley Adams was the obvious choice for Federal Prime Minister, and he was selected. Though shrewd and experienced, his orientation was towards the smaller islands from which he derived his support. In fact, he set up a government dominated by the small islands. This was forced on him partly by the paucity of experienced Federal Labour Party members elected in Jamaica and Trinidad. The effect of this was to exaggerate the importance of the small islands and to cause increasing anxiety in the two larger islands which had to bear the burden of financing the Federation. In all this, Great Britain, committed to a policy of handing over power as quickly as possible, was perforce a spectator. Such influence as remained in London could only be expressed through governors whose powers all over the British Caribbean were steadily being reduced.

On April 22, 1958, Princess Margaret, on behalf of Queen Elizabeth II, inaugurated the newly elected federal legislature. The House of Representatives, or Lower House, was established with 45 members, of which 17 were from Jamaica, 10 from Trinidad, 5 from Barbados,

---

[1] Charles H. Archibald suggested that the supporters of the People's National Party in Jamaica and of the People's National Movement in Trinidad resented the intrusion of the Federation in their domestic politics. An assessment of the result of the Federal General Election could only lead them to the conclusion that, for party purposes, federal sentiments should be played down. Although neither Manley nor Williams had contested seats, Archibald felt that the messianic aura surrounding them had been disturbed by the setback. "The Failure of the West Indies Federation", *The World Today* (London, June 1962).

2 each from Antigua, St. Kitts-Nevis, St. Lucia, Grenada, St. Vincent and Dominica, and 1 from Montserrat, all elected by adult suffrage. The Senate of 19 members—2 from each territory, except Montserrat, which was represented by 1—was appointed by the Governor-General in consultation with the Prime Minister. No member of either Federal House was permitted to serve on the legislative or executive council of any territory. It was expected that this would be advantageous in the long view, since it would result in more persons gaining experience of politics than if island leaders had been permitted to add to their duties by serving also in the Federal House. Except in the case of Trinidad, distance had also to be taken into account, together with poor telephone and postal services in most of the islands. On the other hand, Manley and Williams might have entered federal politics had they been able also to continue to head their island's government. Manley favoured the right of members to sit in both Houses. Bustamante opposed it strongly. The executive was vested in a Council of State of 14 members, normally presided over by the Governor-General and composed of the Prime Minister and 10 Ministers. Three other persons holding office in the public service of the Federation were nominated by the Governor-General. The Federal Supreme Court had jurisdiction in proceedings concerning the Federation as a whole or involving more than one territory.

The financing of the Federal Government was to derive mainly from a levy on unit governments, Jamaica paying 43 per cent., Trinidad 39 per cent. and Barbados 9 per cent. The Federal Government was not permitted to levy more than BWI$9,129,000 in any one year. Thus the immediate financial resources available were very small, the more so as a federal income tax had been ruled out for the first five years.

The path of the new Federation proved stony. In January 1959 a conflict of ideas occurred between Adams and Manley, with the former threatening to impose retroactive taxation.[1] Spurred on by the attacks of Bustamante, who was becoming increasingly critical of federation, Manley reacted sharply to Adams' threat, sensing that the issue might become a serious one in Jamaica, where the public had already shown its lukewarmness to federation by electing a majority of Democratic Labour Party candidates who were allied to Bustamante. The taxation controversy was the first serious breach

[1] *Hispanic American Report, op. cit.*, Vol. XII, p. 33.

between the Federal Government and Jamaica. Since Adams could not have imposed the taxation before 1963 when a new General Election was due which there was no certainty that his party would win, he appeared to have stirred up unnecessary trouble. This sterile argument began to blight the relations between the Federation and Jamaica. The Jamaica Labour Party continued to warn Jamaica of the drawbacks and dangers of federation to Jamaica, of the inequity of Jamaica's proportional representation, and of its heavy financial implications. Manley's People's National Party was placed in an awkward position.[1] It could hardly claim that it was in agreement with Jamaica's having only 17 members in the Legislative Assembly of 45, when its population entitled it to 22 or even 23 members.[2]

With a federal conference to consider constitutional revision scheduled to be held in June 1959, controversy raged in Jamaica over terms that would be acceptable to the island. Talk of secession became increasingly audible, though the fact was overlooked that there was no constitutional provision for a unit to leave the Federation. The approach of a General Election made the issue a difficult one, particularly for Manley.

Adams made the situation more difficult by announcing that the federal conference on constitutional revision would be postponed. He also said that it was his profound conviction that there was no danger whatever to the success of federation.[3] The conference postponement produced a storm. Manley claimed that the conference was essential and must be held in 1959. Bustamante suggested that Adams' reason for postponing the conference was his fear that it

[1] Opinion within the People's National Party was not unanimous over the advantages of federation. Wills Isaacs, Minister of Trade and Industry and, as First Vice-President, the leading member of his party after Manley, whom he was expected to succeed should Manley enter federal politics, had grave doubts over the advantages to Jamaica of its entry into federation. Though Isaacs supported his party over federation on terms acceptable to Jamaica, he had a keen appreciation of the problems which federation would present to Jamaica's economic policy of attracting new industries, aided by tax relief and tariffs, which he was energetically implementing.

[2] The West Indies population was estimated at 3,115,113 as at April 7, 1960, of whom 51·6 per cent. lived in Jamaica, 26·5 per cent. in Trinidad and Tobago, and 7·5 per cent. in Barbados. *Daily Gleaner* (Kingston, Jamaica), August 26, 1960.

[3] At a meeting of the British Caribbean association in London, April 21, 1959.

might prejudice Manley's electoral prospects.[1] Williams commented that many West Indians did not want constitutional reform at any level.[2] Sensing the danger into which the Federation was moving, *The Times* devoted two editorials[3] to the subject, expressing its apprehension over secession by Jamaica. Without an integrated trading policy within the Federation it felt that Jamaica, which favoured high tariffs to protect its nascent industries, could not for long remain within the Federation. The *New Statesman* considered that although the Federal Government was concerned over the weakness of its powers, the real problem was over its relationship with Jamaica.[4] *Time and Tide* suggested that the establishment of a national newspaper in the West Indies would assist the integration of federal units.[5] Opinion in Jamaica was expressed by the influential *Daily Gleaner*, which put forward the not unreasonable argument that Jamaica could not be expected to agree to issues on customs union until it was fairly represented with its rightful number of seats in the Federal House.[6]

Though the press both in Great Britain and in the West Indies was clearly aware of the danger that was looming for the future of federation, the British Government remained optimistic. After a Caribbean tour, Julian Amery, Parliamentary Under-Secretary of State for the Colonies, gave his assurance at a press conference in Port-of-Spain that he had not met anyone in Jamaica or in any other Caribbean island he had visited who was against federation.[7] A visiting Minister naturally follows a carefully arranged programme and meets selected people, but it seems almost incredible that Amery's itinerary allowed him to form an opinion so wide of the mark. However, the confidence of the British Government was reflected in the announcement in the Queen's Speech[8] of the grant to Jamaica of self-government within the West Indies Federation.

A crucial by-election in Kingston, Jamaica,[9] which both the

[1] *Hispanic American Report, op. cit.*, Vol. XII, p. 211.
[2] *Ibid.*, Vol. XII, p. 271. [3] May 11 and May 30, 1959.
[4] London, April 25, 1959. [5] *Ibid.* [6] May 29, 1959.
[7] *Sunday Gleaner* (Kingston, Jamaica), May 31, 1959.
[8] On Prorogation of Parliament, September 18, 1959. Hansard 610, col. 796.
[9] The by-election had been caused by the death of Noel Nethersole, Jamaica's Finance Minister, who had recently negotiated a $12·5 million bond issue in New York for the Government of Jamaica. This was the first occasion on which a British colony with political autonomy had floated an

People's National Party and the Jamaica Labour Party had regarded as a rehearsal of the General Election expected later in the year, resulted in a Government victory. Correctly assessing this expression of public opinion, Manley quickly announced a General Election for July 1959.

The People's National Party won a decisive victory, securing 30 out of 45 seats, the balance being won by the Jamaica Labour Party. With both parties agreed that the federal constitution had to be radically amended if Jamaica were to stay in, the election was in the end fought largely on local issues. Speakers of both parties attacked the shortcomings of the federal constitution. A critical attitude was expressed by the Government party, and a hostile one by the Opposition. This may well have had its influence on the referendum vote later on, since for the first time the public had been made aware of the difficulties of federation. The country districts where the Jamaica Labour Party was strong were particularly affected.

Following the Jamaica General Election, which was quickly interpreted as favourable to the future of the West Indies Federation, attention was concentrated upon the postponed conference on revision of the constitution which became an issue of increasing importance. There were several reasons for this. Manley had obtained his electoral victory with the promise to obtain radical alteration of the federal constitution. These were matters which concerned Great Britain, whose approval was necessary for any alteration, though clearly it would give its blessing to any changes that could be agreed upon by the quarrelling units of the Federation. Jamaica's representation in the Federal House of Assembly remained the major issue, while Trinidad had not failed to notice that its representation was less than a proportional distribution would have granted. Not less difficult were the problems of a customs union and the free movement of citizens within the Federation. Convinced that industrialization was a solution to many of Jamaica's problems, the Manley Government was fearful of the effect of a lower tariff on its

issue payable in U.S. currency. Both parties nominated prominent candidates. Vernon Arnett, who had been Secretary of his party since 1939, was the People's National Party candidate. David Clement Tavares, solicitor and Honorary Secretary of the Jamaica Labour Party since 1953, represented the opposition. Immediately after the by-election, Arnett was appointed Finance Minister. Tavares became Minister of Housing in the Jamaica Labour Party government in April 1962.

new industries. Trinidad's apprehensions were different from those of Jamaica. With the strongest economy in the Federation and with some of the neediest islands near by in the Eastern Caribbean, it feared lest its economy be swamped by an influx of immigrants from the small islands. Moreover, both Jamaica and Trinidad felt instinctively that the Federal Government might be more sympathetic to the point of view of the small islands than to themselves. To be fair to the two larger islands, though their economies were more prosperous than the other's, there was poverty enough in both. In 1959 only Jamaica, Trinidad, Barbados and St. Kitts were not in receipt of grants from Great Britain. As the *West Indian Economist* pointed out,[1] the Federal Government had the choice of developing the smaller islands until they could pay their way, or of accelerating the development of the two larger islands so that some of their increased revenue could be diverted to aid the distressed governments of the smaller islands. The probability of extra taxation on the larger islands loomed as a cloud on the horizon, even if the British Treasury may have viewed it with some relief. *The Times* suggested that the reconciliation of the views of Jamaica with those of the Federal Government would be a test of Manley's statesmanship.[2]

Under pressure from Jamaica and Trinidad, whose differing problems required urgent solution, the postponed Inter-Governmental Conference on Federal Constitution Revision was opened in Trinidad on September 28, 1959. It was attended by Adams and by delegations which included the principal Ministers from all the units in the Federation. The *Daily Gleaner* felt that there was no reason for optimism over its outcome.[3] In a forthright speech, Governor-General Lord Hailes declared that the goal of Dominion status could only be attained if the West Indies became self-financing and could undertake its own defence responsibilities and its representation abroad.[4] This represented the standpoint of Great Britain in regard to any territory seeking to enter the Commonwealth.

Despite the recent hotly contested election in Jamaica, the island's delegation led by Manley included Donald Sangster, deputy leader of the Jamaica Labour Party, together with senior civil servants. Electoral hatchets were temporarily buried in order to present a common front to the rest of the Federation. Manley at once took a

1 *West Indian Economist*, Vol. II, No. 2, p. 8.
2 London, August 4, 1959.   3 Jamaica, October 13, 1959.
4 *Hispanic American Report, op. cit.*, vol. XII, p. 492.

56

strong line, refusing to discuss any other matter on the agenda until the controversial issue of the representation of each territory in the Federal House of Assembly had been settled. Winning this point of procedure, he suggested that a new constitution should provide for representation on the basis of population in an enlarged House of 65 seats. Thus Jamaica would have received the right to elect half of the members. After a week of argument, Manley offered to compromise by accepting 31 seats out of the total proposed. When this offer was declined, he led the Jamaican delegation home.

Jamaica had now made clear its determination to obtain a major change in the constitution. Opinion in Great Britain was pessimistic. *The Times* declared editorially that Jamaica was in a position to drive a hard bargain. It speculated whether the island was preparing to leave the Federation.[1] The *Daily Telegraph* criticized Williams for pressing forward the independence issue and for attempting with some of the smaller islands to coerce Jamaica.[2] On his return home, however, Manley, at heart a Federalist, still appeared to consider that Jamaica would not secede.[3] He even agreed that he and Arnett, his new Finance Minister, should represent Jamaica on two committees, set up by the ill-fated conference, to examine the constitutional, financial and economic problems of the ailing Federation. Among his advisers would be Sangster.

The quarrel with Jamaica was temporarily obscured by a different imbroglio. Williams had embarked on direct negotiations with the Venezuelan Government over customs problems.[4] Technically this was a breach of sovereign rights, since Great Britain represented in the person of its ambassador to Caracas both the West Indies Federation and its component parts, of which Trinidad was one. The British Government, presumably wishing to avoid difficulty, agreed to delegate to the West Indies Federal Government the responsibility of negotiating and signing agreements with Venezuela in this matter. The Trinidad Government announced that its discussions with Venezuela were in a state of indefinite suspension. Great

[1] London, October 9, 1959.   [2] *Ibid.*
[3] At the annual conference of the People's National Party on October 25, 1959, at Kingston.
[4] With only 15 miles separating Trinidad from Venezuela across the Dragon's Mouth of the Gulf of Paria, smuggling had for long been prevalent. In October 1959 Venezuela had sent a mission headed by Pedro Archambaud, its director of customs, to Port-of-Spain, Trinidad, to negotiate a settlement of these difficulties.

57

Britain had by its timely concession shown that it fully supported the Federal Government. Williams had been sharply rebuffed.

Although the major points of disagreement within the West Indies Federation remained unsettled, Adams hinted that Dominion status might be attained even before April 22, 1960, which was the date that had been proposed by Williams. In December 1959 the House of Assembly unanimously endorsed a Government motion to request the British Government to amend the West Indies Constitution to provide for a complete cabinet system and to grant Dominion status as early as possible in 1960.[1] This optimism proved unjustified. In its 1960 New Year review of the Commonwealth, *The Times* commented that this sovereign status could be achieved in 1960, but only if agreement could be reached over the constitutional weight of Jamaica in the Federation. Declaring that the Federal Government and the House of Assembly had overridden the position taken by Jamaica at the Inter-Governmental Conference in September 1959, Manley hurried to London, accompanied by Arnett. It was understood that he discussed with the British Government its future attitude in the event of Jamaica's withdrawing from the Federation. On his return to Jamaica he declared that if Jamaica could not obtain satisfactory agreement over its requests for constitutional change, it would leave the Federation and seek independence on its own. Manley added that he was very satisfied with his visit to London. Iain Macleod, who had succeeded Alan Lennox-Boyd as Secretary of State for the Colonies in October 1959, announced shortly after Manley's visit that he could not agree to any date for independence for the West Indies until the Inter-Governmental Conference on Federal Constitution Revision had reached agreement. He said that he would invite representatives of the territorial governments to London for a constitutional conference to determine the final shape of the constitution after independence. Manley had found Macleod very accommodating. The visit to London was to have far-reaching effects on the future course of federation.

Strengthened in his views by his reception in London by Macleod, Manley announced in the Jamaica House of Representatives in February 1960 his terms for remaining in the Federation. They included Jamaica's proposal for limiting the powers of the West Indies Constitution. The amended Constitution would provide for a Council of Ministers from the units, while the Federal Government would

[1] *Hispanic American Report, op. cit.,* Vol. XII, p. 670.

58

have the right to raise loans for itself. This right would also be enjoyed by the units, co-ordination being achieved through a Loan Advisory Council. He added that if the reasonable demands of Jamaica were not met, it might leave the Federation. From this it was clear that his attitude had stiffened following his London visit. The *Trinidad Guardian* warned editorially that there had been too much glib talk of early Dominion status. More sober thinking, it declared, was required.[1]

As had happened before, a diversion from the main constitutional issues in dispute was provided by Trinidad, whose police were rounding up and deporting immigrants from the small islands at the rate of twenty-five per week. This led to an angry exchange of views at a meeting of the Regional Council of Ministers at Port-of-Spain, Trinidad, when Chief Minister Ebenezer Joshua, leader of the St. Vincent delegation, complained to Patrick Solomon, the Trinidad Minister for Home Affairs. Joshua was reported to have been supported by Adams and several politicians from the small islands who criticized the deportations. Solomon retorted that there were 13,000 illegal immigrants in the island. The Trinidad police attributed the high incidence of crime in the island to these immigrants.[2] The publicity surrounding this controversy was unfortunate, since voices were beginning to be raised in Great Britain against immigration from the West Indies.[3]

The quarrel over the right of free government was soon overshadowed by one which received international publicity, and which involved not only the Federal and Trinidad Governments but Great Britain and the United States as well. The Chaguaramas base, which was generally regarded as the best site for a federal capital, remained in the possession of the United States. Williams, who had for some time been pressing for its return, had been encouraged by the U.S. decision to release to the St. Lucia Government the naval air station at Gros Islet.[4] He attacked Adams, declaring that the Federal Government was the stooge of the British Colonial Office. Adams repudiated this sharply.

[1] February 8, 1960.
[2] *Hispanic American Report, op. cit.*, Vol. XIII, p. 109.
[3] *The West Indian Comes to England*, ed. S. K. Ruck (London, 1960), pp. 115-16; cf. *The Times*, May 25, 1959, report of demonstrators in Trafalgar Square proclaiming their intention to "keep Britain white" which coincided with the arrival in London of Carl D. La Corbiniere, deputy Prime Minister of the West Indies Federation. [4] In March 1959.

The shooting of Africans at Sharpeville, South Africa, aroused strong resentment throughout the West Indies. It had the momentary effect of uniting all territories and all political parties in the Federation in protest against the South African Government. Trinidad at once placed a ban on the import of South African goods, which Jamaica had already put into force.[1] The People's Progressive Party in British Guiana denounced the South African Government at its annual conference in April 1960. The *West Indian Economist* called for a complete trade boycott of South Africa, which it considered the most effective way to destroy the racial tyranny there.[2]

The chances of survival of the Federation remained in the balance. There were indications that the studies in committee of the Inter-Governmental Conference on Federal Constitutional Revision were producing proposals nearer to Jamaica's point of view, with the agreement of the representatives of the smaller islands. It appeared that a full customs union might cost Jamaica £4 million per year in revenue. To alleviate this, a transitional period of seven years was suggested. Returning to Jamaica from a visit to Trinidad in May 1960, Manley expressed optimism in regard to the Federation since the value of the Jamaican proposals was now appreciated by other territories. Williams' opinion was different. In an interview given to the *New York Times*, he speculated that the West Indies Federation might not last.[3]

The announcement was made in June that Bustamante had resigned as leader of the federal Democratic Labour Party, and that the opposition Jamaica Labour Party, the leadership of which he retained, would not contest a federal by-election in St. Thomas, Jamaica. In each case the reason given was that the Jamaica Labour Party had decided to advocate the secession of Jamaica from the West

[1] In July 1959. Lennox-Boyd, when Secretary of State for the Colonies, had deprecated this action as a discriminatory measure against another Commonwealth member on an issue of domestic politics.

[2] Its editorial stated: "We are convinced that when a later generation of free South Africans writes the history of this tragic period, they will accord a special place of honour to the small island of Jamaica for having led the way in showing how the white South African tyranny can be brought to its knees. Unhappily the government of Britain, for all the fine sentiments of its Government Ministers, is still unwilling to act, still takes refuge in 'non-interference in the internal affairs of others'. But in the face of a great evil we are all, nations as well as individuals, our brothers' keepers." *West Indian Economist*, Vol. II, No. 10.

[3] May 6, 1960.

Indies Federation.[1] Shortly afterwards, Morris Cargill, deputy opposition leader in the Federal House of Representatives, in which he represented St. Mary, Jamaica, resigned his seat, declaring that he could no longer accept the taxpayers' money for something which he was convinced was harmful to Jamaica.[2]

Sensing that the opposition to federation was substantial, Manley announced in the House of Representatives that a referendum would be held in 1961 to decide whether or not Jamaica should secede from the West Indies Federation. Meanwhile the Inter-Governmental Conference would have completed its work. At a press conference at Federal House, Port-of-Spain, Manley declared that the People's National Party would solidly support Jamaica remaining in the Federation.[3] Shortly afterwards, Macleod, when visiting Jamaica, expressed his agreement to the holding of a referendum. This was necessary since there was no provision for it in the Jamaica Constitution.

These diverse episodes had one feature in common. Great Britain was always at some point involved, and often placed in an invidious position in regard to either a foreign nation or another member of the Commonwealth. Macleod visited Trinidad in June 1959 for discussions with political leaders. A defence pact between the Federation and Great Britain was signed, while a united policy in regard to the troublesome issue of the Chaguaramas base in Trinidad was adopted. Macleod also managed to secure agreement between the Trinidad Government and Opposition over the composition of a new constitution for that island. Thus the difficult task was pursued of launching a federation and at the same time extending the powers of its units by giving them wider constitutions. Though the Secretary of State was endeavouring to carry out Great Britain's avowed policy of steady advance towards self-government, it may be that Trinidad's new constitution, even if it advanced its status only to that already attained by Jamaica and Barbados, made the island government less accommodating.

In August 1960 the Federal Constitution was altered by Order in Council.[4] The Council of State was replaced by a Cabinet of

---

[1] *Hispanic American Report, op. cit.,* Vol. XIII, p. 316.

[2] Cargill also resigned his membership in the federal Democratic Labour Party.

[3] *Hispanic American Report, op. cit.,* Vol. XIII, p. 386.

[4] Given on August 3, 1960, and proclaimed by the Governor-General on August 16, 1960.

Ministers presided over by the Prime Minister. The Prime Minister, formerly elected by the House of Representatives, was now appointed by the Governor-General as being the person who in his judgment was best able to command the confidence of the majority of the members of the House of Assembly. Ministers would be appointed by the Governor-General on the advice of the Prime Minister. The Federal Government expressed to the Secretary of State for the Colonies its appreciation of the helpful and expeditious manner in which the British Government had acceded to the Federal Government's request for internal self-government.[1] Though the change might impose on the Governor-General, perhaps at a time of political crisis, the additional duty of selecting a Prime Minister, in fact it greatly reduced his political power and influence, since he no longer presided at ministerial meetings. The Federal Government took over full control of all matters within the constitutional responsibility of the Federation. Only defence and external affairs remained within the jurisdiction of the United Kingdom Government. Great Britain was implementing its policy of establishing a West Indies Federation with Dominion status. In a radio broadcast, Lord Hailes welcomed this "most important step towards West Indian independence and West Indian nationhood". Though the West Indies had experienced great difficulties and problems, unremitting efforts had been made to surmount and resolve them. The Governor-General also noted that this constitutional advance had lightened his own responsibilities, which to a corresponding extent had been placed on the shoulders of his Ministers where they rightly belonged.[2] The British Government probably felt that, having embarked on a policy of early Dominion status for the West Indies, it was wisest to confer Cabinet status at an early moment. Yet in the two and a half years which had elapsed since the Federation was inaugurated in 1958, it had become clearer that governmental difficulties and inter-island conflicts were increasing. In presiding over the Council of State, which had now become the Cabinet, a weak Prime Minister would replace a Governor-General who had for seven years as Chief Whip acted as the link between Churchill and his Parliamentary followers in the House of Commons.

[1] Federal Information Service, Port-of-Spain, Trinidad, August 3, 1960.
[2] Broadcast from Port-of-Spain, Trinidad, August 15, 1960.

CHAPTER VIII

THE COLLAPSE OF THE
WEST INDIES FEDERATION

If official views in Port-of-Spain and London remained optimistic over the success of the Federation,[1] there were many ominous signs of the beginnings of disintegration. More and more the basic weaknesses in the Constitution were appearing; still more serious, they were becoming evident to the public in Jamaica. The justness of Jamaica's complaints, especially over its under-representation in the Lower House, made the political assaults on the Federation all the more dangerous. In an editorial entitled "These . . . or Secede", the influential *Daily Gleaner*[2] set out a list of twelve conditions which it considered vital to the continuance of Jamaica in the Federation. These included proportionate representation, consultative machinery by means of a Regional Council of Ministers, the very gradual introduction of a customs union and internal free trade, denial to the Federal Government of the right to levy income tax, excise tax or consumption duties, and recognition of the right of unit govern- ments to raise overseas loans and of the right to amend the Constitution by a majority of the unit legislatures representing not less than two-thirds of the population of the area. The last provision would in effect have given to Jamaica a veto in regard to any change.

Meanwhile, the weakness of the Federal Government was be- coming more apparent. Significantly, Robert Bradshaw, Minister of Finance, announced in December 1960 that he would leave Federal politics shortly to return to island politics in St. Kitts. The frustration of attempting to finance a government with inadequate funds must have been considerable.

---

[1] In his Federation message from Port-of-Spain on February 22, 1961, to the peoples of the West Indies, Sir Grantley Adams said, "If we need to point once again to the progress we have made, it is only in an attempt to remind all West Indians of the solid achievements of the Federation."

[2] October 15, 1960.

Though Premier Eric Williams of Trinidad had suggested that the time was ripe for British Guiana to enter the West Indies Federation,[1] Wills Isaacs, Jamaica's Minister of Trade and Industry, declared that in no circumstances would he agree to Jamaica's remaining in a federation if a country which was Marxist-dominated were to enter it. Bradshaw next attacked Williams over statements which he had made at a Port-of-Spain press conference, adding that "if the Prime Minister is not inclined to join battle with the people who set out to embarrass him and his government, the Minister of Finance is not disinclined. Those people who do not like the complexion of the Federal Government, let them use their democratic and constitutional power to put the present government out of office, but do not sit by sniping at the Federal Government."[2]

These quarrels, while perhaps inherent in politics, were the more serious when they arose among political leaders likely to influence opinion in their own islands. They were matters over which Great Britain could exert little control, since with the continuous handing over of power, the authority of both the Governor-General and of island governors was inevitably diminishing.

An opportunity arose, however, to enhance the flagging prestige of the Federation when the thorny subject of the Caribbean bases, leased to the United States in the treaty of 1941, came up for discussion. In the words of Sir Grantley Adams: "Although constitutionally the United Kingdom would have been well within her rights to claim the revision of a treaty originally made by her, she nevertheless took the wise decision to give to the governments of the West Indies the right to speak for themselves and to negotiate new arrangements for the future. The generosity of spirit on the part of our British friends is, to my way of thinking, another sign of their resolve that the West Indies should even before the final moment of achieving independence participate fully in all the discussions and decisions which are an unavoidable commitment of any sovereign nation."[3] The negotiations resulted in the United States' giving up about 21,000 acres of its Trinidad base, though retaining for 17 years lands at the Chaguaramas naval station for defence and missile

[1] At a Port-of-Spain press conference, July 1960. *Hispanic American Report, op. cit.*, Vol. XIII, p. 455.
[2] *Daily Gleaner*, November 22, 1960.
[3] King's House, Jamaica, December 14, 1960.

tracking purposes.[1]   The successful outcome which made possible the establishment of a federal capital in Trinidad, was one of the few major triumphs of the Federal Government,[2] even if it may have been also partly due to the persistency of Williams' criticisms of the United States base. The agreement on the West Indies bases had left both the West Indies and the United States content.[3]   Great Britain, by its decision to place the negotiations in the hands of the West Indies, was also justified in feeling satisfied with the outcome.

International successes, important as they might be, had slight effect on the critics of federation.   At the annual conference[4] of his Jamaica Labour Party, Sir Alexander Bustamante made a forthright attack on federation to a crowded gathering.   He declared that anyone in Jamaica who supported federation was a traitor to his country.   He added that the island would have to give £3 million to the small islands in addition to the £4 million for expenses, if it remained within the Federation.

In March 1961 Harold Macmillan visited the West Indies. Addressing a joint session of the Federal Senate and the House of Representatives in Port-of-Spain, the British Prime Minister congratulated the Federal Government on the progress which it had achieved, including the Defence Bases Agreement with the United States, and the preparations being made to train staff for its future diplomatic representation.   Though he noted that there might still be lingering doubts in the minds of some people over the future of the Federation, "there were", he declared, "none in the minds of the British Government".   He concluded his speech, however, with these words: "It is your task now to resolve whatever differences remain among you about the future and the launching of the Federation.   You all belong to it.   It has made an encouraging start.   But you must go forward, as a united West Indian nation, to take your proper place among the nations of the world."[5]   The experienced and astute Prime Minister had clearly appreciated the latent dangers that

---

[1] The United States also released about 1700 acres in St. Lucia, while retaining 1000 acres, including Beane Airfield, and 900 acres in Antigua. In Jamaica, it released 23,000 acres. *Hispanic American Report, op. cit.*, Vol. XIII, p. 795.   Cf. *West Indies Federal Review*, Trinidad, January 19, 1961.
[2] "The agreement reached was a remarkable achievement of moderation and statecraft." *The Times*, editorial, March 25, 1961.
[3] John Crocker, "West Indies Bases Talks Leave Both Sides Content", *New York Herald Tribune*, January 8, 1961.
[4] Kingston, January 23, 1961.   [5] March 27, 1961.

existed to the survival of the Federation. Indeed, to express the support and encouragement of Great Britain during this critical period may have been one of the purposes of his visit to Trinidad and to Jamaica. Probably most observers at this time felt that Premier Norman Manley would win the referendum which was to be held in Jamaica to determine whether it remained in or seceded from the Federation, though opinions expressed were becoming increasingly guarded.[1]

The Inter-Governmental Conference which took place at Port-of-Spain in May 1961 reached agreement on most of the issues which had divided the islands. A revised system of representation largely abolished the acute disproportion of seats favouring the smaller islands in the House of Representatives. Considerable concessions had been made to meet the views of Jamaica, though some problems, including those of finance, remained. Comment was generally favourable, and the way was paved for a final conference in London with the Colonial Office to settle the amendments to the Constitution which would be

---

[1] Max Frankel writes: "Until recently, Prime Minister Norman W. Manley of Jamaica had personified the movement for union and freedom. But he, too, has been impressed by the arguments of anti-federalists. Thus while the smaller islands still argue for a strong central government and while many Jamaicans want no union at all any more, he has veered toward a middle course envisioning a weak federation—really, a confederation.

"The chances are that Mr. Manley's views will prevail, mainly because they rest on a close financial calculation of Jamaica's best interest." *The New York Times*, March 5, 1961.

"On the journey through the first three islands the visitor gets the impression that these common factors are strong enough to guarantee the success of an independent federation, although interest in it is not overwhelming. When he gets to Jamaica the visitor finds the atmosphere changed from one of indifference to one of distrust, resentment, even of anger.

"Nothing that is to be seen in the other islands prepares one for the strength of feeling that is to be found in Jamaica now. . . .

"Outside the Federal Parliament, it is only in Jamaica that strong feelings are aroused. Here people did not react so favourably to Mr. Macmillan's address to the Federal Parliament as they did in the other islands. To Jamaicans the British Prime Minister's warning that, to become effective, federation would have to be worked on a do-it-yourself basis means simply that it will be left to Jamaicans to carry it. 'Why should we slow down our own development for something that means nothing to us? What has federation got for us?' " *The Times* special correspondent in the West Indies, "Makeshift Pattern of Islands", April 4, 1961.

66

followed by the attainment of self-government.[1] Macmillan's advice to the West Indies to settle its differences appeared to have borne fruit.

The conference to approve the final draft of the West Indies Constitution[2] proved to be highly controversial. All the skill and tact of Iain Macleod, Secretary of State for the Colonies, were needed to pilot it through. He neatly summed up the problem which had proved so intractable in the past when he said, "The essence of the concept of federation is that the territories which seek to become associated wish to achieve union, but they do not seek complete unity." This was illustrated when the conference nearly collapsed following a proposal to remove income tax and industrial development from the exclusive jurisdiction of territorial governments in order to place them under the Federal Government. Macleod saved the situation with a compromise whereby both federal and unit governments would have power to legislate, provided there was unanimous consent from the territories. Though no territory appeared satisfied except Jamaica, agreement was reached, as it was over the formation of a customs union and the freedom of population movement which had been linked together for a period of years. Macleod, following the policy which Macmillan had pursued when in the West Indies, declared that Great Britain was ready to accept whatever constitutional safeguards or amendments the West Indies desired. Largely through his skill, agreement had been reached at the price of giving way to the demands of Jamaica. The new revised Constitution was incredibly weak at the centre; the Federal Government retained little

[1] "With agreement reached on the chief issues at the West Indies Inter-Governmental Conference, representatives will now be able to go to London for the discussions opening on May 31 with definite proposals on the Constitution and other matters relating to the structure of the West Indies Federation at and after independence." *The Times* Trinidad correspondent, May 18, 1961.

"After two weeks of patient negotiation, the leaders of the island territories of the British Caribbean have concluded the last major inter-governmental conference before they meet on May 31 in London to settle with Great Britain the terms of West Indies independence and full nationhood within the Commonwealth.

"The most important single factor uncovered at the recent conference in Trinidad is that the leaders of the West Indies today are statesmen of the calibre needed for stability in the Caribbean." A. L. Hendriks, "West Indies Near Federation Goal", *The Christian Science Monitor*, May 24, 1961.

[2] At Lancaster House, London, commencing May 31, 1961.

control over finances, while freedom of movement and a customs union were both phased over a period of nine years.

This debate posed the straight issue to the people of Jamaica: "Do you wish to share your future with your blood brothers across the waters—less expensively and with greater security—do you wish to make a rich future for us all, or do you wish to isolate yourselves from this rich area? That is what the people will have to decide in the coming referendum." With these words, Manley wound up the three days' debate in the Jamaica House of Representatives in which he recommended the House to accept the results of the West Indies Independence Conference.[1] Though the Government was assured of victory in a vote on party lines, everyone, including the British Government, knew that the real verdict of Jamaica would be given in the referendum which would shortly follow. On it would hang the life of the Federation.

Events now moved quickly. Though the referendum was regarded by many as being outside the realm of party strife, it soon became clear that it would be a fight between Manley's People's National Party and Bustamante's Jamaica Labour Party with their respective trade union allies.[2] Official opinion both in Jamaica and in Trinidad believed that Manley would be victorious, though the contest would be hard. The future of the Federation hung upon it. So too did the future of Manley, whom many saw as the next Prime Minister of the West Indies. On the other hand, it was inevitable, in a small community and with party machines at work, that local issues which had little to do with the referendum should begin to play their part. With a second term of office nearing its end, the People's National Party had lost much of the popularity which had carried it to victory in two successive elections.[3] The opposition was strongest in the country districts which considered that they had benefited much less from the Government than had the urban area of Kingston and St.

[1] July 12, 1962.
[2] The Trade Union Congress and the Bustamante Industrial Trade Union.
[3] ". . . this is perhaps the greatest struggle Mr. Manley and his band of loyal colleagues have yet had to face. And let no one fool anyone about it, it is a fight against the odds, against apathy, against a determined opposition, and against the natural insularity of Jamaicans grown proud in their own concept of nationhood, against a massive if little expressed resistance within the community for identification with anything that is not entirely Jamaican." "The Political Reporter", "Referendum, a Fight for Life", *The Sunday Gleaner*, August 6, 1961.

68

Andrew, where new industries had sprung up and large housing schemes including a university had been developed. When the first results of the voting were received from the Kingston and St. Andrew urban area on September 19, the "yes" votes led easily. But as the evening wore on, the "no" votes from the country districts crept up steadily, placing the fate of the Federation in the balance. When the final results were declared, the "no" votes exceeded the "yes" votes by almost 39,000 on a 60 per cent. poll. Of the electors, 46 per cent. had voted for Jamaica remaining in the Federation and 54 per cent. of them against.[1]

Though the referendum vitally affected Great Britain's West Indies policy, the British Government, following the lines which Macmillan had taken in refusing to comment on the referendum issue when he had visited Jamaica earlier in the year, remained a silent spectator. While keen disappointment was felt in London, comment was restrained, though there was a realization that the result must cause considerable confusion in British Caribbean policy.[2]

Bitter disappointment was felt throughout the other islands in the Federation. A different result had confidently been expected. To Manley it was a tremendous blow, though he at once expressed his acceptance of the decision which Jamaica had made. Refusing the demand of the Opposition for an immediate General Election, on

[1] In the referendum 256,261 persons voted "no" and 217,319 persons voted "yes". Of Jamaica's 14 parishes (a parish is equivalent in population to a very small British county), only Kingston, St. Andrew, St. Ann and Manchester had "yes" majorities. "The heaviest anti-Federation vote came from the important sugar parish of Clarendon, where all four constituencies recorded heavy "no" votes, the anti-Federation vote in this parish amounting to more than half the total majority against Federation. Part of this undoubtedly stemmed from the influence and prestige of Bustamante, who sits for a Clarendon seat." *Hispanic American Report, op. cit.,* Vol. XIV, p. 803.

[2] "Sorting out the mess created by Jamaica's departure will be a major task. . . . When the first sense of shock has abated, the other islands will have to consider what to do next, and it is the stand of Trinidad and Tobago that will be all important." *The Times,* September 21, 1961.

"Great disappointment is therefore inevitable. It is not merely that so much of the worry and expense of the long constitutional arguments about the Federation revolved around Jamaica's association with it. Even more important for the future is the fact that she will take with her out of the Federation just over half its population, as well as a significant part of its potential, if not yet realized, economic strength." *The Daily Telegraph,* September 21, 1961.

the grounds that there had been in the referendum no question of a vote of confidence in the Government, he made it clear that his Government would proceed with the preparations for Jamaica's attaining independence on its own.

With the main prop of the Federation knocked from under it, Adams had the unenviable task of trying to save it from collapse. He was far from admitting defeat and hurried to London for consultation. With Jamaica out, it was clear that the attitude of Trinidad, the richest of all the islands in the Federation, would be decisive. However, with a General Election approaching, Williams refused to divulge his views on this question, though he remarked to a large meeting in Woodford Square, Port-of-Spain, "There is no Federation today."[1]

The dismemberment of the Federation now moved forward rapidly, since the British Government had clearly accepted the referendum result as final. Williams won an overwhelming victory in the Trinidad and Tobago General Election in December.[2] He followed it up by announcing that Trinidad would seek independence on its own, though he added that his territory would be prepared to enter into political association on a unitary basis with any of the smaller islands which desired this. The Leeward and Windward Islands, however, seemed determined to form a federation of their own. The Colonial Office, frustrated by the collapse of its plan for federation, appeared ready to fall in with the views of the territories as they developed.

Once more Lancaster House, London, was the scene of a West Indies conference when Manley and Bustamante arrived with three representatives each to settle with Reginald Maudling, newly appointed Secretary of State for the Colonies, the future constitution of Jamaica. Unlike previous West Indies conferences, substantial agreement had previously been reached between the two political parties who had co-operated to provide a draft constitution. It followed the general pattern of modern Commonwealth constitutions, with a Governor-General, a Senate of 21 members to be appointed by the Governor-General, 13 being nominated by the Prime Minister and 8 by the

[1] October 6, 1961. Next day he announced that the Government of Trinidad and Tobago had agreed to take over British West Indian Airways from the British Overseas Airways Corporation, for a price of BWI $2,500,000 (£520,833).
[2] The People's National Movement was successful in 20 out of 30 seats.

70

Leader of the Opposition. The House of Representatives would consist of members elected from single member constituencies, each adult having a single vote. Boundary revision was provided for, but membership was limited to a maximum of 60. Two interesting provisions were protection from arbitrary arrest or detention and freedom of movement. These could only be changed by majorities in the Houses of Parliament, so arranged that a government could not overrule the opposition on a Bill concerning the entrenched clauses, since it controlled only 13 out of 21 Senate seats, giving it less than the necessary two-thirds majority.[1] The conference was quickly concluded.

The way was now open for a General Election in Jamaica which would precede the granting of independence. Voting followed the pattern of the referendum and though the margin between the votes polled by the Jamaica Labour Party and the People's National Party was small, the latter leading during the first two hours of the declaration of the count in the urban Kingston and St. Andrew area, the rural voters, disappointed with the difficulties which agriculture was encountering, secured the return of Bustamante with a substantial majority.

Great Britain's rôle in its three centuries of uninterrupted rule in Jamaica was now nearing the end. The granting of independence was fixed for August 6, 1962. Princess Margaret came to Jamaica to represent Queen Elizabeth II. Vice-President Lyndon B. Johnson brought the good wishes of the United States of America. During a week of celebrations, many were present who had played a part in the history of the island. Sir Kenneth Blackburne, the new Governor-General, had been asked to continue in office and had agreed to do so for a short period. This was a graceful compliment from Jamaica to Great Britain and a tribute to his success. Other former governors and senior civil servants were also there as the guests of the Jamaica Government. Yet the dominating figure was Prime Minister Bustamante, who at the age of 78 had altered the course of Jamaica and at the same time made almost inevitable the termination of the West Indies Federation. He believed fervently that it was the right course for Jamaica to follow.

At midnight on August 6 the Union Jack was hauled down while the British national anthem was played. There was a pause, and then to the strains of the new Jamaica anthem, the black, green and gold

[1] *Hispanic American Report, op. cit.,* Vol. XV, p. 139.

71

flag which the new nation had chosen was raised. The main ceremony in Kingston was repeated in all the island towns. In the cool
starlit night, three centuries of history passed by since Venables and
Penn had first raised the flag of England. Despite grave dangers,
Jamaica had never been conquered by any enemy. The expectant
crowd seemed to sense the drama, especially when the Union Jack was
lowered. Enthusiasm there was when Jamaica's standard was raised,
but it was an enthusiasm tempered perhaps by a feeling of awe for
what the future might hold.

Though Great Britain hoped that the West Indies Federation
might continue on a smaller scale under the leadership of Trinidad,
a visit to the Caribbean in January 1962 by Maudling failed as a
salvage operation. Williams had made it plain that after the secession
of Jamaica, Trinidad would also withdraw. On February 6, Maudling
announced in the House of Commons the end of the Federation. A
final visit to London by Adams in March achieved nothing. Trinidad
followed Jamaica into independence on August 30, 1962.

* * * * *

The main reasons for the failure of the Federation included the
distance between the islands and the poor and costly communications,
which made a highly centralized state difficult. The individualistic
history of the islands reinforced this. Unless the islands, large and
small, had been prepared to give up much of their local machinery of
government in favour of the centre, the Federation was likely to add
to the costs of administration. Barbados, for instance, which had
administered its own affairs reasonably well since 1652, could hardly
be expected to wind up its House of Assembly. In consequence,
right from the start, the objective of most of the islands was to whittle
down to a minimum the powers of the Federation. It had early
become apparent that Great Britain was prepared to grant a considerable measure of autonomy to territories within the Federation. In
the case of Jamaica, this had preceded the grant of autonomy to the
Federal Government. Thus the attraction of independence or
"freedom" was not necessarily linked to the forming of a federation.

The economic attractions of federation were extremely limited.
Geography was against federation. The population of under four
millions was ineffective because it was scattered. Air freight is very
costly, and goods have to move from island to island by sea. Most of
the islands produce the same products, and trade is oriented outwards

72

to Europe and North America. Though the best face was put on them, the trading possibilities of federation were never alluring.

Great Britain was aware of these problems. It may be that it should have insisted on a much more centralized constitution at the start. It was not without arguments, since it could have attached the offer of independence to the formation of a federation. Moreover, since it was assisting all but four of the territories with grants-in-aid, and all of them from Colonial Welfare and Development Funds, it would not have been unreasonable to have pressed for a more realistic approach by the Caribbean colonies. This might also have been considered in connection with the two mainland colonies.

The Colonial Office, however, was going through a difficult period. The West Indies constituted only a small part of its widespread problems, many of which involved the creation of new states. Its political science was stretched to the limit, while it had to further independence in many parts of the world against a background of increasing criticism of "colonialism". Its history in the West Indies had been a troubled one, and nowhere else had it met with more resolute opposition to its plans. Self-government was partially protected by the Campbell *v.* Hall decision in Grenada.[1] Though the Colonial Office had generally succeeded in replacing the elective system by Crown Colony government (despite its failure to do so in Barbados), it was this very Crown Colony system, however superior may have been its administration, which resulted in the territories having insufficient preparation for democratic government. At a time when Great Britain, from 1832 onwards to 1926, was step by step enlarging its franchise, the Colonial Office made little effort to extend the franchise in the colonies. The argument that many of the inhabitants were illiterate was not valid, since the extension could have been gradual. If the franchise had been extended to literates, it would have served at least to pin-point the weaknesses in the educational system.

Once the Federation had been launched, could it have been steered to success? Its defects were obvious, though at first the large islands, which had heavier financial burdens combined with electoral discrimination, did not perceive clearly what was happening. The matter had never been put to the voters at a General Election.

If the structure was weak, little was done to shore it up. Had the major political leaders of the West Indies agreed to support federation

[1] *Vide* Chapter III, p. 13.

73

wholeheartedly, it might have struggled through. Some, like Bustamante, had never believed in it. Others, like Manley and Williams,
who did believe in it, were not prepared to foresake the island governments in which they played so important a part, to enter federal
politics. Had it been possible to form a coalition Federal Government comprising the leaders, it might have been effective in steadying
popular opinion. It is not, however, easy to see how Manley and
Bustamante, or Williams and former Chief Minister of Trinidad
Albert Gomes could have worked together harmoniously at this time.

As it was, the weak and impecunious Federal Government headed
by Adams utterly failed to persuade an apathetic group of islands that
the Federation represented a dynamic new nation. Mistakes added
to the difficulties. The empty threat made by Adams of imposing
retroactive taxation may have been the turning-point in Jamaica's
attitude towards federation. At a later stage, when Manley went to
London to seek an assurance that Jamaica would decide by referendum whether it would remain within or stay out of the Federation,
Macleod may have acquiesced too easily.[1] The Constitution did not
provide for a referendum, and he might at least have delayed his
answer. He was strongly criticized over this by Gomes. Yet with
the experience in his mind of the troubles over the Central African
Federation and the difficult federal negotiations over Uganda, he may
well have considered that to force an unwilling Jamaica to remain
within the Federation would be unwise. He may also have felt that
Jamaica had grounds for complaint over the terms under which it had
entered the Federation. Macleod had only been in office some three
months, and his advisors at the Colonial Office may have under-
estimated the deep-seated opposition to federation which had been

[1] Though not an exact precedent, a comparison may be made with the
petition by the State of Western Australia to the Parliament of the United
Kingdom to introduce legislation for the amendment of the Commonwealth
Constitution Act to enable Western Australia to withdraw from the Federal
Commonwealth of Australia. A joint committee of the House of Lords and
the House of Commons reported that "the State of Western Australia, as such,
has no *locus standi* in asking for legislation from the Parliament of the United
Kingdom in regard to the constitution of the Commonwealth, any more than
it would have in asking for legislation to alter the constitution of another
Australian state, or than the Commonwealth would have in asking for an
amendment of the Constitution of the State of Western Australia". *Report
by the joint committee of the House of Lords and the House of Commons
appointed to consider the Petition of the State of Western Australia* (HMSO,
London, 1935), p. 5.

built up in Jamaica and which no measure of concession could assuage.

Had a referendum been taken in all the territories—or at least in the major ones—before the Federation was formed, it would have been an insurance policy for the future. This democratic instrument, which is found in the Australian Constitution on which the West Indies Constitution was to a considerable extent modelled, would have been of great value. Though there was always opposition in Jamaica to federation, it is by no means unlikely that a favourable majority might have been obtained in that island at a time when Manley was at the height of his power and before his government had suffered the inevitable loss of popularity which faces a democratically elected government after a period of years. In that event, a further referendum could hardly have been demanded.

Yet taking into account all these considerations, the success of federation depended on the West Indian leaders, just as it had done on the leaders of Canada and Australia on the one hand, or on those of the ill-fated Central American Confederation on the other. The test was one of statesmanship. The problem was a difficult and unpopular one. When the test came, the leaders did not seize the opportunity that was offered. Many were half-hearted. Others sincerely felt that federation was a mistake. With Great Britain, wisely, not prepared to force the issue, collapse was bound to follow. Even with the best of leadership, such were the flaws in the Constitution that it may have been impossible to avoid.

CHAPTER IX

THE POST-WAR BRITISH ECONOMIC POLICY IN THE CARIBBEAN

During the nineteenth and twentieth centuries the political and strategic importance of the Caribbean colonies had gradually faded; at the same time their economies had also declined. From the British point of view they had moved from being economic assets to liabilities. The British Government had had either to make good a colonial deficit, as public opinion both in Great Britain and, latterly, in the territories themselves, demanded that their parlous condition of living be ameliorated, or to ask Parliament to appropriate money for this purpose. In consequence, an ever-watchful Treasury pressed the Colonial Office to exert increasing control over those territories which had to be subsidized. This policy was apparent in those British Caribbean colonies which were grant-aided, even though this was tempered by the need to transfer a measure of authority, in view of the approach of self-government, and assuaged by the post-war policy of metropolitan expenditure to improve colonial conditions. With self-government being granted in other parts of the Commonwealth, clearly the Caribbean colonies had quickly to prepare themselves for it. Their publics were more sophisticated than those in some territories which were about to receive independence, and they had had experience in some cases in managing their own affairs. Air travel enabled more persons to go beyond the bounds of their own island. Many had served overseas during World War II. These factors helped to create a public opinion receptive to a change of status.

There was a strong reaction against the traditional policy that the British colonies should depend on importation for almost all manu-factured goods, and a growing demand for local industrialization. The success of "Operation Bootstrap" in Puerto Rico exerted a fascination over the rest of the Caribbean. Unfortunately the lengthy and difficult period, involving much hardship, during which Great Britain's process of industrialization had taken place, was usually forgotten in contemplating the apparent ease and speed with which this had been accomplished by the Government of Luis Muñoz Marín. Puerto Rico was United States territory. The movement of persons and goods between it and the U.S. mainland was unrestricted. More than that, the traditional American belief in the justness of no taxation without representation had enabled Puerto Rico to obtain the best of both worlds, namely, participation in the benefits which flowed from its association with the United States, combined with exemption from federal income and corporation tax. Even the excise duty collected by the Federal Government on Puerto Rican rum entering the United States was handed back to the island. Thus the Puerto Rico Government was in an excellent position to launch its plans for industrialization.[1] The wage rates, which were substantially lower than on the U.S. mainland,[2] made the establishment of certain industries within the confines of the island very attractive, since the whole of the United States was an open market.[3]

The American policy towards Puerto Rico was quite different from that of Great Britain towards its Caribbean territories, which was framed within the Ottawa agreements, concluded at the Imperial Economic Conference of 1932. There was no possibility of Great

[1] It created a Development Corporation and a Government Development Bank to further its policy. Earl Parker Hanson, *Transformation: The Story of Modern Puerto Rico* (New York, 1955), p. 200.

[2] Over a four-year period between 1955 and 1959, the Puerto Rico hourly wage rate remained at approximately $1·25 per hour below the continental United States' rate. Teodoro Moscoso, Head of the Economic Development Administration, illustrated this to the author when he visited Puerto Rico in 1959, using a graph which also showed the rising trend in both countries.

[3] Harvey S. Perloff, *Puerto Rico's Economic Future* (Chicago, 1949), p. 110. Cf. Ralph Hancock, *Puerto Rico: A Success Story* (Princeton, New Jersey, 1960), pp. 89-94.
"Thanks to the tax advantage, the island has made more progress in the past decade than during the entire preceding 54 years. . . . As a state, Puerto Rico would lose its favored status as a tax haven, would have to find new lures for the continued flow of vitally needed investment. Moreover, a large slice of the locally collected Commonwealth taxes now used to finance island projects would revert to Washington; Governor Muñoz estimates that the loss would run to $187 million a year, or 48 per cent. of his annual budget." *Time*, Latin America edition, August 3, 1962, pp. 14-15.
Eric Williams, Premier of Trinidad and Tobago, when addressing the British Caribbean Association in the House of Commons on May 31, 1962, commented that his country had the highest standard of living in the West Indies area except for Puerto Rico, "which has been very dependent on American subsidies". Cf. William H. Stead, *Fomento: The Economic Development of Puerto Rico* (Washington, D.C., 1958), *passim*.

77

Britain's giving financial aid to its West Indies and other colonies on a scale similar to that which the United States provided for its small territory of Puerto Rico. Even more important, Britain could not provide a comparable free and adjacent market. Unfortunately, politicians in the British territories and beyond were dazzled by the Puerto Rico success story. They often failed to analyze the reasons for its success. The Development Corporation they were able to copy; the pump-priming they had no means of matching, even if they gave tax concessions to new industries which in the long run would have to be paid for, at least partly, by the community. Free entry into the nearby United States could not be matched by Great Britain. Yet the dissimilarities tended to be glossed over. The disparity was enormous between the island market of little more than a million and a half persons in Jamaica, or merely double that figure if the whole of the Federated Territories were included, and that of the 172 million of much wealthier U.S. citizens to which Puerto Rico had access.

Notwithstanding, Great Britain, far from opposing industrial development in the colonies, began, in the post-war period, to promote it. The change in economic policy may be most clearly seen in the work of the Colonial Development Corporation.[1] The Labour Government which had been elected on a platform of expansion of state trading at home, considered that the rapid development of the resources of the Colonial Empire was possible with British financial assistance. In his first report, Lord Trefgarne,[2] first Chairman of the CDC, stated that "the Corporation was brought into being for the purpose of improving the standard of living of the colonial peoples by increasing their productivity and wealth".[3] The report pointed out significantly that, measured in terms of per capita productivity of the population and taking the net national product per capita in the United Kingdom as 100, the index of productivity in the colonies ranged from less than five in most African colonies to approximately 25 in the more developed West Indies colonies. Measured in terms of capital, the per capita amount invested in the most highly developed colonies was probably not more than 10 per cent. of the per capita investment in the United Kingdom, while in Africa it was less than 2 per cent. Though only approximate, these figures illustrate not

[1] It was created by section I of the Overseas Resources Development Act, 1948.
[2] Formerly George Morgan Garro-Jones, M.P.
[3] *Colonial Development Corporation, Report and Accounts 1948*, p. 6.

78

only the comparative absence of secondary industry in the colonies but also the low level of agricultural technique and mechanization.[1] The report well summarized the policy of Great Britain, calling for a united effort by colonial governments under the aegis of the Secretary of State, by private enterprise, by the Corporation and above all by the people of the territories concerned to overcome these handicaps.[2]

Great Britain was acutely conscious of its dollar deficit in the years following World War II. Since the sterling area pooled its dollar resources, Great Britain noted with anxiety that the average West Indian spent 40 per cent. of his income on imported goods, the bulk of which came from the dollar area. The Colonial Development Corporation believed that increased local food production combined with the manufacture of the simpler commodities would help to reduce the dollar deficit.

Though the Corporation came in for much criticism from the Conservative opposition, looked at in retrospect there was much to be said for its objectives. It had declared its desire to work in close co-operation with private enterprise, as in fact it frequently did, even if Lord Trefgarne's plea that it should have a measure of freedom "to venture and to act in circumstances of doubt"[3] may have led to substantial losses in some cases. However, few familiar with the hazards of agricultural development in the tropics expected to avoid serious set-backs from time to time. The purpose of the Corporation was to undertake projects itself or to provide others with development funds when this course seemed desirable, because of the lack of other avenues of finance.

The Korean War struck a hard blow at the Corporation, since the sharp rise in costs affected many of the developing projects on which it was engaged. This rise far exceeded the profit that came from the higher prices for those few of its enterprises which were already in production.[4] By 1951 an expenditure of £7,380,950 had been sanctioned for the Caribbean, including enterprises in the Bahamas, British Guiana, British Honduras, Dominica, Jamaica, St. Lucia,

[1] The report added that lack of capital had not been the only limiting factor. Unfavourable conditions of climate and soil, disease, undernutrition, ignorance and lack of incentive to work introduced elements of uncertainty into tropical agriculture. *Ibid.*, p. 6.
[2] *Ibid.*, p. 7.
[3] *Ibid.*, p. 8.
[4] Statement by Lord Reith, who had succeeded Lord Trefgarne as CDC Chairman. *Colonial Development Corporation Report and Accounts 1950.*

St. Vincent and Trinidad.[1] The Corporation, however, was beginning to show anxiety over finance, pointing out that it had no funds of its own, since the British Government had provided capital in the form of long-term redeemable loans at fixed interest,[2] while £4·5 million had been written off by the end of 1951. By 1952 the total deficit of the Corporation was £8,399,807.[3] The reorganization of the Corporation's work was now accelerated, with an emphasis on the greater sense of responsibility which had been furthered. As in the case of many new undertakings, the period of growing up had been costly. Perhaps the most significant factor in regard to the Corporation was that the Conservative governments of Winston Churchill, Sir Anthony Eden and Harold Macmillan continued to make full use of it, once again showing the basic unity of British policy towards its colonial territories.

In the post-war period, Great Britain continued to take much of the produce of the West Indies under preferred conditions. The growing and manufacture of sugar cane, which continued to receive shelter under the quota system that existed within the Commonwealth, employed the largest number of people in the British Caribbean. Although amalgamation into large units continued, with British-owned mills playing an active part,[4] topographical factors in the rugged Antilles limited the possibilities. There were cases where distance precluded the closing of a small factory since the cost of transportation of sugar cane to a longer but more distant factory would have made the venture uneconomical. Though progressive in their methods, the British Caribbean territories remained high-cost producers of sugar. The British policy of a price-negotiated quota

[1] *Colonial Development Corporation Report and Accounts 1951*, p. 2.
[2] *Ibid.*, p. 6.
[3] *Colonial Development Corporation Report and Accounts 1952*, p. 3. Lord Chandos, who as Oliver Lyttelton was Secretary of State for the Colonies from 1951 to 1954, is sharply critical of the constitution of the CDC on the grounds that no board of directors sitting in London could manage "a whole jumble of projects" from a rubber plantation in Borneo and a poultry farm in Gambia to an abattoir in the Falkland Islands and an hotel in Belize. "The right system would probably have been to form three or four development corporations, confined to specialist fields. . . . After the war, when I was Secretary of State for the Colonies, I had to wrestle—with the help of Lord Reith—with what he described as 'this *damnosa hereditas*' ". *The Memoirs of Lord Chandos* (London, 1962), pp. 201-2.
[4] Examples of concentration into larger mills may be seen in Jamaica, British Guiana, St. Kitts and Antigua.

80

for the Commonwealth, supplemented after the United States' diplomatic break with Cuba by a small American quota, was vital to the continuing prosperity of those territories.

Similarly, the West Indies banana industry, important both to Jamaica and to the Windward Islands, received protection in the British market.[1] The smaller industries were not overlooked. The Secretary of State re-affirmed the assurances of assistance which he had previously given over the safeguarding of the citrus industry, though he pointed out that he could not guarantee that the United Kingdom would take the whole of the export crop. To honour these undertakings, the British Government sent a fact-finding mission to the British Caribbean to examine the industries' present and future prospects.[2] The small but important lime-oil industry in Dominica, Jamaica, Trinidad and other islands, for instance, had its preference increased.[3]

As a means of strengthening the economic position of its Caribbean territories, Great Britain made full use of the Colonial Development and Welfare Acts.[4] Assistance from this source varied from territory to territory according to need. With its expanding revenue from oil, Trinidad was able to finance much of its development from its own resources. In other colonies, the situation was quite different. In

[1] In 1955, a Regional Economic Committee, comprising Norman Manley, Wills Isaacs, H. D. Shillingford and the Trade Commissioner, conferred over the Jamaica and Windward Islands banana industry. Great Britain negotiated with Brazil, then the main competitor of the West Indies in the United Kingdom market. As a result, the preference on colonial bananas was raised from 2s. 6d. to 7s. 6d. per cwt.

[2] *Report presented to the Comptroller for Development and Welfare in the West Indies by the Regional Economic Committee of the British West Indies, British Guiana and British Honduras for the period July 1954-December 1955* (Port-of-Spain, Trinidad), p. 13.

[3] In 1956, from 10 per cent. to 25 per cent.

[4] In 1929 the Colonial Development Act had provided a fund of £1 million a year to relieve economic depression in the United Kingdom and to stimulate agricultural and industrial activity in the colonial territories. It was superseded by the Colonial Development and Welfare Act, 1940, which provided £5 million a year, plus £500,000 for research, for the ten years 1941-1951. The 1945 Colonial Development and Welfare Act provided for £120 million (including £20 million carried forward in commitments under the 1940 Act) for the ten years 1946-1956. The 1950 Act increased the total provision of its predecessors from £120 million to £140 million for the five years 1955-1960. In 1959 a further Act extended the existing Acts to 1964 and made a further £95 million available. *The U.K. Colonial Development and Welfare Acts* (Central Office of Information, London, 1960), p. 10.

British Guiana, the Colonial Development and Welfare Fund provided one-quarter of the funds available, while the Leeward Islands, the Windward Islands and British Honduras relied mainly on it for most of their development.[1]

Helped by these measures and with a generally favourable commercial climate, assisted by energetic local government action, the economies of the two most populous Caribbean territories seemed to be making a satisfactory response. In Jamaica, "over the years 1950 to 1956 the gross domestic product rose at an average rate of 14·5 per cent. each year. In 1959, manufacturing represented 12·9 per cent. of the gross domestic product compared with 13·4 per cent. for agriculture."[2] While it may be that the industrial development had been deceivingly spectacular with Trinidad expanding its oil and Jamaica revolutionizing its financial position with the creation of a bauxite industry, the position of the British Caribbean from some angles still looked promising. It was becoming increasingly clear that more and more persons with university training would be required for this growing industrial economy.

Following the pattern which was being adopted of establishing new universities in British overseas territories, the University College of the West Indies was incorporated by Royal Charter in 1949.[3] The British Government had financed the buildings and equipment by an allocation from the Colonial Development and Welfare Fund. Further grants, benefactions and a public appeal sponsored by H.R.H. the Princess Alice, the first Chancellor of the College, provided further funds. The recurrent expenditure of the College was met during the first ten years by government contributions from British Caribbean territories after which it became the responsibility of the Federal Government.

[1] *The U.K. Colonial Development and Welfare Acts* (Central Office of Information, London, 1960), pp. 2 and 4.

[2] *Ibid.*, p. 24. The growth of manufacturing was illustrated by the fact that in 1956 about 32 per cent. of gross capital formation was in this sector, which included the very important investments of the bauxite companies.

[3] Following the recommendations of the Asquith Commission for Higher Education in the Colonies appointed by the Secretary of State for the Colonies in 1943, a subsidiary committee had been set up under the chairmanship of Sir James Irvine to consider the setting up of a university college, preliminary to the establishment of a West Indies university. The same pattern was followed in Uganda, when Makerere College at Kampala was also recognized in 1949 as a university institution associated with the University of London.

The fine setting in the foothills below the Blue Mountains of Jamaica dramatized the simple but effective lines of the modern architecture of the new College. The atmosphere was essentially that of a British university. Until full university status was conferred in 1962, it was associated with the University of London in the granting of its degrees. The red gowns worn by its students were a link with St. Andrews University, whose Principal and Vice-Chancellor, Sir James Irvine, had played an active part in the establishment of the University College.

Faculties of Arts and Sciences were established at Mona in Jamaica, together with a well-equipped teaching hospital. In 1960 the Imperial College of Tropical Agriculture at St. Augustine in Trinidad was incorporated into the University College of the West Indies to become the Faculty of Agriculture. A Faculty of Engineering was also established at St. Augustine.[1] The University College received university status in 1961. Plans for further expansion were announced, since many more West Indian students were studying at foreign universities than at the new University of the West Indies. Though the failure of the West Indies Federation had been a great disappointment to the University, it was already making an important contribution to the unity of West Indian life and its influence would undoubtedly grow rapidly as its graduates increased in numbers.

* * * *

Exports of sugar, traditionally the major product of the British Caribbean territories, had during the latter part of the nineteenth century swung away from Great Britain, which was importing cheap, bounty-fed sugar from Europe. Instead, the United States became an important market for West Indies sugar. Domestic United States sugar production was still insignificant, though the Hawaiian Islands were increasing their production, which since 1876 had entered duty-free.[2] The Spanish-American War, which resulted in the

[1] The Governor-General, Lord Hailes, described the handover of the Imperial College of Tropical Agriculture to the West Indies as a gift representing material assets valued at more than $10 million. "The union of two of the greatest centres of learning in the Caribbean", he said, "increases at one stroke and in unique degree the prestige and influence of the University College of the West Indies." *West Indies Federal Review*, October 1960.

[2] *The Economy of the West Indies*, ed. G. E. Cumper (Kingston, 1960), p. 234.

83

United States' annexation of Puerto Rico and its close relationship with Cuba, combined with heavy American investment in the islands' sugar industry, changed America's policy in regard to sugar, though the United States continued to be an important market for other products, including bananas. From 1901 sugar from Puerto Rico entered the United States duty-free. Cuba received a 20 per cent. tariff preference in 1903, while the Philippines obtained free entry for its sugar in 1914. At the same time, the production of U.S. domestic beet-sugar had risen tenfold, from 90,000 tons in 1900 to 940,000 in 1915. Meanwhile sugar imports from other foreign countries which did not receive special consideration had fallen steadily from 1·34 million tons to 160,000 during the same period, a decline which continued after World War I.[1]

However, up to the 1929-1931 slump the West Indies was selling nearly as much sugar to the United States as to Great Britain. The Ottawa agreements swung exports heavily once more towards Great Britain, while Canada continued to be a very important market for West Indies produce. Since World War II, increasing emphasis was laid on both the Canadian and the United States market for the West Indies' rapidly expanding bauxite industry. With the production of sugar probably nearing its economic limit and with the future of the banana industry (at least in Jamaica) uncertain, the outlook was difficult to forecast with confidence.

The upsurge in population throughout the Caribbean in the post-World War II period began to be reflected in increasing emigration to Great Britain, the only attractive source of employment where entry to citizens of the Commonwealth was free. Almost all other Commonwealth countries, including Caribbean colonies such as Jamaica, imposed various restrictions. Great Britain, as the centre of the Commonwealth, regarded the retention of this policy as almost essential. Moreover, expanding British industries were creating a demand for labour. British workers were sucked from the unskilled to the skilled jobs, leaving gaps to be filled by immigrants. To meet the shortage of labour, West Indians began to arrive there in numbers which, though fluctuating from year to year, tended to increase. A large proportion of the immigrants were at first skilled workers which the Caribbean could ill afford to lose. Apart from employment in

[1] Vladimir P. Timoshenko and Boris C. Swerling, *The World's Sugar* (Food Research Institute of Stanford University, Stanford, California, 1957), pp. 157-8.

84

factories, they were soon to be seen in increasing numbers as railway porters, bus conductors, and in similar jobs. There can be no doubt whatever that they were needed.[1] Yet there was opposition from a small minority of British citizens. Serious disturbances occurred in 1958 in Nottingham and London. Prompt and effective action was taken by the courts, including the award of four-year prison sentences on nine youths. Though there was some controversy over the severity of the punishment, it undoubtedly acted as an effective deterrent.[2]

Cheap air and sea travel added impetus to the migration to Britain, which might have been much greater if India and Pakistan had not imposed voluntary restrictions of their own.[3] In the first ten months of 1960, nearly three times as many immigrants arrived as in the whole of the year before.[4] Inevitably anxiety and criticism began to mount, particularly as overcrowding and the creation of new slums became more evident in cities such as Birmingham, Liverpool and Nottingham, and in parts of London. The obviously rising anxiety in Great Britain, reflected both in Parliament and in the press, presaged a change in British policy.[5] This was noted with alarm in

---

[1] "As it is, London could not run its hospitals, its public transport and much else without immigrants. This is equally true of other Western European countries: France has used its Algerians and West Germany the refugees from the lost provinces." "Multi-Racial Britain?" *The Economist*, December 30, 1960, pp. 112-14.

[2] For a full account of these events, cf. Ruth Glass, *Newcomers: The West Indians in London* (London, 1960).

[3] India refused passports to unskilled labourers; skilled workers were required to have a written agreement of employment from the future employer. Moreover, a sum covering one and half times the cost of passage had to be deposited with the Indian authorities to cover the cost of the emigrant's possible return. Pakistan required a deposit exceeding £180. When these restrictions were withdrawn shortly before the imposition of the British restriction on immigration, the numbers entering Great Britain from these two countries rose sharply. A measure of restriction operated in Jamaica, since application for a passport might take a matter of months, though this was ultimately remedied.

[4] 43,000 compared with 16,000.

[5] "There is first and foremost the proud tradition that all citizens of the British Commonwealth enjoy the right of unrestricted entry into the United Kingdom. The right is not reciprocal, and to some minds it is little more than a sentimental survival. But it stands as an isolated memorial to liberty in a world hag-ridden by documentation and permits." *The Times*, editorial, December 17, 1960.

85

the West Indies, particularly in Jamaica, which sent the largest number of emigrants to Great Britain.[1]

In 1961 opinion that some measure of restriction on immigration was necessary continued to mount, particularly within the Conservative Party. Back-bench Members of Parliament like Cyril Osborne[2] maintained a continuous pressure on the Government, while the *Daily Telegraph* pointed out that a rise in the total immigration from 2,000 in 1953 to 60,000 in 1960 could not be borne indefinitely.[3]

At the opening of the Lancaster House Conference in June 1961, Adams said, "This is not the time to talk about restricting West Indian entry into Great Britain. At the moment of independence, we need a period of time in which to deal successfully with the grave responsibilities of nationhood, without having to suffer the indignity of having a door that has traditionally and generously been kept open now slammed in our faces."[4] Macleod replied that he had no change to announce in the Government's position on immigration. Anxiety was, however, mounting among the West Indian leaders. At a meeting of the House of Commons, Williams strongly advocated the necessity of emigration to Britain from the West Indies.[5] Addressing

[1] "The latest news from the U.K. on migration is deeply disturbing for Jamaica. The open door policy for Commonwealth immigrants has helped to underwrite Jamaica's strenuous efforts towards economic expansion, and its continuance remains a vital link in the country's future planning." *Daily Gleaner*, December 20, 1960.

[2] After a full House of Commons debate, Osborne, who had introduced a motion calling for the control of immigration from all Commonwealth countries, withdrew it on the advice of David Renton, Under-Secretary of State for Home Affairs, who said that the Government was watching the situation with some concern but had not yet reached a conclusion. Hansard 634, col. 2018.

[3] February 18, 1961.

[4] London, May 31, 1962.
"Sir Grantley Adams, Prime Minister of the West Indies, has acknowledged the nature of the dilemma in a statesmanlike and perceptive speed...". *Daily Telegraph*, editorial, June 2, 1961.
A second editorial which commented on the weight of correspondence which the *Daily Telegraph* was receiving on the immigration issue followed a fortnight later. "The British people see immigration far more as an economic problem than as one of colour. . . . Many do not accept that the United Kingdom should be a receptacle for surplus populations. With the spreading realization that the West Indies alone have a surplus of about 100,000 persons per year, such thoughts are going to grow." *Daily Telegraph*, June 19, 1961.

[5] London, June 13, 1961.

a meeting of West Indian students, Manley declared that he did not believe that stresses and strains over housing and other internal disagreements were the real cause of the issue. He added that these claims did not conceal from him the underlying colour prejudice.[1] Speaking at Sheffield, Adams appealed to "the very large majority of liberal-minded people in Britain to assist in eliminating prejudice against West Indians".[2] Clearly the leaders of the West Indies now realized the risk of restriction on immigration and were endeavouring to persuade Great Britain to withhold or at least delay this blow. The subject continued to be ventilated at length in the British press.[3] The attitude of the British Government itself to this awkward problem which so vitally affected the West Indies was well summed up by the London correspondent of a Swiss newspaper who wrote: "Sous la pression de l'opinion britannique, le gouvernement de Londres sera peut-être contraint de recourir à des mesures restrictives du genre de celles dont il a déjà parlé au parlement. Il préférait cependant que les autorités fédérales fassent elles-mêmes quelque chose de positif pour freiner les départs de leurs îles d'hommes et de femmes qui s'imaginent trop volontiers que la fortune leur ouvre les bras en Angleterre."[4]

On November 1 the blow fell with the publication of the British Government's Commonwealth Immigrants Bill. Basically, it gave powers of control to the Home Office over the entry of immigrants from the Commonwealth, though it did not indicate the numbers who might still be admitted. Immigrants with a job to go to would

[1] London, June 13, 1961.
[2] June 4, 1961.
[3] "Sir Grantley Adams' words to West Indian immigrants at Sheffield yesterday must be read against the background of stabilities. . . . Of late the growth of immigration has behaved unexpectedly. The total coloured population is now reckoned to be about 300,000 and would have to reach 550,000 to constitute 1 per cent. The rate of West Indian immigration has been increasing from 2000 in 1953 to 16,400 in 1959 and to 50,000 last year.
"In the early months of this year the rate had doubled again, and a new factor had appeared in the sudden influx of numerous immigrants from the Asian parts of the Commonwealth. In fact, the total rate of immigration was five times as great. . . . The British Government have again made it clear that if they ever did have to exercise any control over the influx of Commonwealth immigrants, there would be no colour discrimination. This is cold comfort; 95 per cent. of these immigrants are non-white." *The Times*, editorial, June 5, 1961.
[4] *Journal de Genève*, June 10-11, 1961.

87

receive preference, as would skilled workers even without a job. An unspecified number of others would also be allowed to enter.

Though the reasons for control of immigration were cogent, the more so as Commonwealth countries were abandoning in some cases their former restrictions on emigration, the Bill caused great controversy in the House of Commons and in the British and overseas press. Should there be a marked industrial decline, unemployment among these newcomers might become critical. Moreover, in some city areas overcrowding had been seriously aggravated. Yet there were grave misgivings both in Parliament and in the country. Hugh Gaitskell and the Labour Party roundly condemned the Bill in the House of Commons. On the other hand, Conservatives, though regretting the measure, regarded it as necessary.

The more the immigrant problem was examined, the more awkward it became. Undoubtedly, the majority of British citizens considered that there must be a limit to the unrestricted entry of Commonwealth immigrants; and that the limit had already been reached. Though over-sensitive West Indian leaders had tried to pin colour prejudice to British policy, it is improbable that this was a major factor, though undoubtedly the appearance of West Indians made the numbers entering more obvious.[1] The passer-by in London, Birmingham or Liverpool could not readily distinguish an Irishman, but a West Indian or a Pakistani stood out.

Press comment was widespread both in Great Britain and the Commonwealth. *The Times* considered that "the passage of the Immigration Bill, which was bound to be controversial anyway, has been made more controversial by the thick atmosphere of humbug in which the Government have shrouded the measure".[2] To

[1] Opinion, however, on this was divided. "As far as the coloured Commonwealth is concerned, most of the damage must already have been done. In an age when it is acceptable to bar a man because he is poor or simply born in the wrong place and unacceptable to bar him because of his colour, the Bill has already incurred a colour stigma that it will carry to its grave." Gavin Lyall, "Immigration: Can the Bill Survive?", *The Sunday Times*, November 26, 1961.

[2] December 21, 1961. In an earlier editorial the newspaper had already termed the Bill "this unloved baby" and had added: "It would be best if the Bill could be thrown out altogether. If that is not practical politics, then twelve months at a time is long enough." It was referring to the shortening of the currency of the Bill from five years to one, after which it would require renewal.

88

the *Daily Telegraph*, the Bill would make "an inroad into one of the grandest of British ideals", namely an Empire or Commonwealth in which every subject was free to travel from end to end.[1] However, since almost every Commonwealth territory, including Jamaica and Trinidad, already imposed restrictions, the ideal was dead anyway.

Though in the House of Commons the Immigration Bill had a rough passage, to which its poor drafting had contributed, inevitably a Government with a substantial majority passed the measure into law. Equally, the reaction was highly critical both in the Federal Parliament and in the West Indies press. Probably the attack on the Bill, that it was discriminatory on grounds of colour, was unjustified. The anxiety created in Britain arose primarily from the numbers of immigrants who were arriving. The fact that they mainly came from coloured parts of the Commonwealth, which had a markedly lower standard of living than Great Britain, resulted in any effective measure of restriction falling most heavily on these countries. If the entry of Great Britain into the European Common Market, then under consideration, were eventually to result in giving priority to Common Market over Commonwealth citizens, the Commonwealth ideal would in addition suffer "enormous damage".[2]

The West Indies Governments protested in the strongest possible terms. Adams made no secret of his objections.[3] Press comment in the Caribbean was highly critical.[4] There was little that they could do except to plead that the restrictions should be reasonably applied.

[1] November 2, 1961. The newspaper added that erosion of the British ideal could have been detected when Canada, after World War II, enacted a separate citizenship of its own, not automatically open to all who shared the common allegiance to the Crown.

[2] *The Times*, September 11, 1962.

[3] For example, he sent a message to be read at a public meeting held by the Movement for Colonial Freedom in London on November 2, 1961, in the course of which he said: "Restrictions on migration from the Commonwealth to Britain will, therefore, in spite of pious assurances to the contrary, in effect, operate on a racial and colour basis.

"It is doubtful whether the Commonwealth can survive the repercussions which must follow implementation of the proposals. One thing is certain: it will never be the same again."

[4] "While the statistics were being tossed from head to head, an ugly element obtruded itself. Certain elements in Britain showed clearly that a great deal of the objection to West Indians was based on the difference of colour." *The West Indies Federal Review*, November-December 1961.

For this there was a large measure of sympathy in Great Britain. With doors to immigrants partly or wholly closed, both in Europe and in North America, it had become increasingly clear that the West Indies and especially Jamaica faced an unemployment problem of rising difficulty.

*   *   *   *

Great Britain's post-war economic policy showed a marked change from that of earlier years. It had accepted the inevitability of the desire of its Caribbean territories not only for political independence but for industrialization. More than that, through the Colonial Development and Welfare Fund and to some extent through the Colonial Development Corporation, it played an important part in the promotion of these plans, which were aided by the facilities which these territories enjoyed of raising money on the London market. Yet it was also a period of increasing interest in the Caribbean from other quarters. The bauxite industry, which had revolutionized the economy of Jamaica[1] and had greatly assisted that of British Guiana, had been pioneered by American and Canadian companies, who were consumers of the product. There was also increasing United States capital entering the Trinidad oil industry. The tourist trade, expanding in almost every one of the islands, depended mainly on North America. It was from there that much of the finance for the construction of hotels had come.

The proposed entry of Great Britain into the Common Market raised questions of the widest character. Until the terms of entry had been settled, it was impossible to predict what the ultimate effect would be on Britain's Caribbean associates, with their normally high-cost production. Over all hung the spectre of a population which was increasing far more quickly than most of the territories

[1] "Jamaica could perhaps now be appropriately called the 'bauxite island' and an aluminium ingot might well take pride of place on its heraldic shield. Nowhere is the rapid rise to predominance of the bauxite industry more clearly revealed than in the little table which shows the value of domestic exports between 1950 and 1957. There the startled observer can see that whereas no bauxite at all was exported until 1952, by 1957 the exports of bauxite and alumina accounted for not only almost half the total exports from the island (in money terms) but the annual export value of the mineral now is greater than the annual value of the island's total exports prior to 1953!" "Island in Transition: The Economic Survey of Jamaica", *The West Indian Economist*, editorial, Vol. I, No. 1, July 1958.

could absorb it. With Great Britain partially closed to immigration, the outlook was unpromising.[1]

* * * *

The Manley Government in Jamaica had pinned its faith largely on industrialization. The new trading estates outside Kingston made an impressive picture, but one that had to be studied in relation both to the cost of establishing the industries by the imposition of tariffs and to the cost of tax-exemptions, of which the burden, at least to some extent, fell on the public. In a poor community with low purchasing powers, a market of little more than a million and a half persons—or even double that figure if the West Indies Federation had endured—was an unattractive prospect for a modern industry, unless the public were prepared to underwrite the venture with heavy and continuing tariffs.[2] With autonomy being steadily extended, these decisions rested less and less with Great Britain.

Yet the substantial and well-publicized advances which had been made in some of the colonies were becoming overshadowed by the dangers that were threatening the basic agricultural industries, the mainstay of employment in every British territory. The post-war revolution in tropical agriculture may not, on the whole, have been

[1] "For many years the people of the Caribbean islands have had to seek employment overseas. The combination of a rapidly increasing population, an unstable agriculture, and a desperate lack of capital and trained personnel for promoting industrial schemes has resulted in a situation in which emigration or destitution are often the only choices open to them." Judith Henderson, "Race Relations in Britain", J. A. G. Griffith et al., Coloured Immigrants in Britain (Oxford University Press, London, 1960), p. 52.

[2] "To seek prosperity within an insulated national economy is a fallacy which arises by attaching an exaggerated importance to short run aspects of the problem and by ignoring the long run effects of these short run processes." Michael A. Heilperin, Studies in Economic Nationalism (Geneva, 1960), p. 177.

In a survey which he undertook at the request of the British Colonial Office, A. R. Prest brought out clearly the weakness of the economies of the Caribbean colonies, whose administrative problems he considered were more comparable to those of a local authority than with those of the United Kingdom Government. "We have seen that the British Caribbean consists of a number of small territories, with a long history of colonial rule but with rulers rapidly fading away as more and more independence is obtained. We have seen that these territories are often desperately poor, but even more desperately determined to copy Western social and economic patterns." A Fiscal Survey of the British Caribbean (HMSO, London, 1957), p. 19.

advantageous to the British Caribbean territories. Mechanization, the introduction of fertilizers, weed-killers and insecticides, together with rapidly rising wages aided by effective trade union organization in the sugar industry, had resulted in higher wages for some but in unemployment or underemployment for many others.[1] The extent of this was hard to judge, since unemployment statistics were not available. Ministerial pronouncements, however, indicated that unemployment was high.[2] With the production of sugar in the Commonwealth governed by quota,[3] and in most British Caribbean territories by the lack of additional unused first-class land which could be brought under the tractor, the future remained uncertain. Yet the numbers seeking employment mounted continuously. Despite the increasing employment afforded by the expanding tourist industry in most of the British islands, and by bauxite and oil, which had increased the revenues of Jamaica, British Guiana and Trinidad, the economic foundations in all territories were fragile.

[1] The Goldenberg Report recommended a crop bonus of 12½ per cent. to Jamaica sugar workers on all earnings during the 1959 crop period, and an increase in pay at the same rate from January 1, 1960, or from the beginning of the crop. *Report of the Commission of Enquiry on the Sugar Industry of Jamaica*, January 1960, p. 85. *The Hispanic American Report* commented: "This recommendation was accepted by both employers and unions. Many felt, however, that the large increase might lead to much marginal land going out of production, especially as it was believed that cane farmers would also have to concede substantial wage increases". *Op. cit.*, Vol. XIII, p. 33.

For a survey of the somewhat similar position in Trinidad, cf. *Report of the Board of Inquiry into a Trade Dispute in the Sugar Industry of Trinidad* (Government Printing Office, Trinidad, 1960).

[2] Edward Seaga, Jamaica's Minister of Development and Welfare, said in London that unemployment in Jamaica had reached 100,000 and that his island would have to export about 16,000 people a year to master the population problem. *Daily Gleaner*, July 2, 1962.

[3] The Commonwealth Sugar Agreement of 1951 between the United Kingdom and its sugar exporting colonies assured an outlet for 1,500,000 long tons of sugar known as "the negotiated price quota". A further sale of 800,000 tons was guaranteed by the United Kingdom at world prices with the addition of imperial preference. There was provision for the annual renegotiation of prices, while the agreement had a term of eight years which could be renewed annually. The effect of the agreement was that only about 250,000 tons of Commonwealth sugar was sold on the free market. In the post-World War II years, sugar purchases from the Commonwealth proved a convenient means for Great Britain to aid the colonies and at the same time to economize in the use of hard currency. Timoshenko and Swerling, *op. cit.*, pp. 327-8.

With pressure increasing to reduce or end the subsidies on foodstuffs which it had paid during and after World War II, Great Britain began to look ever more closely at its agreements with the West Indies. Reductions of orders for citrus products reflected its changed attitude. A high-cost producer of most commodities, the British Caribbean islands faced the prospect of mechanizing cane cultivation on its good level land and the risk of some of its secondary lands reverting from agriculture to pasture. There were some who wondered whether it might not be possible to grow more foodstuffs in the islands, thus reducing the import bill. Progress in this, however, appeared to be slow.[1]

A major cause of the collapse of the West Indies Federation had been the realization by many citizens of the Federation, as by many outside observers, that even with a customs union the market was limited, low in purchasing power and scattered. A single island with the same population, area, resources and skills as those of the Federation would have presented a much easier proposition, from an economic as well as from a political point of view.

The International Bank for Reconstruction and Development closed its 1952 report on Jamaica with these words: "Jamaica today is at a crucial stage of its political and economic development. In the near future, important steps in the direction of complete self-government will be taken. The success of this venture may well be jeopardized unless economic progress can also be assured. Jamaica can support its population under conditions of political and economic

---

[1] Interesting experiments have been conducted in Jamaica by the Yallahs Valley Authority and by the Christiana Area Land Authority in reclaiming eroded hillside land. In a very fair conclusion to a brochure which was issued to commemorate its first ten years, the Yallahs Valley Land Authority describes the problems of rehabilitating land eroded by poor cultivation or devastated by hurricane damage, frequently experienced in the territories under consideration. It also stresses the immense difficulties of changing the outlook of small farmers and of persuading them to adopt methods of soil conservation, very necessary in a mountainous area. *Yallahs Valley Land Authority, 1951-1961* (Kingston, Jamaica, n.d.). Notwithstanding the fine achievement of the Authority in rehabilitating this area, which lies within the parishes of St. Thomas and St. Andrew in Jamaica, much of it composed of steep hillsides ranging from sea-level to 5000 feet, the author, after visiting it in 1962, was left wondering whether the cost, which would be a continuing one, was justified by the agricultural production. As an experiment, though costly, it had been extremely interesting and carefully supervised.

93

stability only if an imaginative, far-sighted development program is vigorously prosecuted. In this task the people of Jamaica face a great challenge."[1] Ten years later, this challenge still remained to Jamaica and indeed to the whole Caribbean.

[1] Report by a mission of the International Bank for Reconstruction and Development: *The Economic Development of Jamaica* (Baltimore, Maryland, 1952), p. 149.

Chapter X

THE POST-WAR FRENCH POLITICAL AIMS IN THE CARIBBEAN

Differing fundamentally from British policy, French policy had continuously followed a pattern of centralization which had been first introduced in the seventeenth century. It had survived the controversies over slavery and even the dislocation of World War II. In theory it meant that citizens of the three overseas departments of Martinique, Guadeloupe and French Guiana were citizens of France. The concept was a generous one, since it implied the provision of education, welfare and development, and culture on the pattern of one of the world's leading nations. A common citizenship permitted freedom of movement between the overseas territories and metropolitan France. While history and logic influenced France in favour of centralization, the most liberal interpretation had been placed on civic rights. Long before Great Britain itself had enacted universal franchise, France had, at least in theory, extended it to its territories in the Caribbean, granting them direct representation in the French Parliament.[1] There were no restrictions on the movement of overseas citizens to the metropolis. The people of the Antillean departments were taught that they were French, an approach that was in some ways magnificent, even if, in practice, it proved difficult to carry out. Nationalism was to be not local but French.

Although the beginnings of this policy may be traced to the early days of French colonialism, a strong impetus had been given to it at various times, even if the concept of making Frenchmen of the inhabitants of these territories had proved more image than reality. The French Revolution had decreed emancipation, though Napoleon I had re-instituted slavery. The events of 1848 had finally brought about emancipation and had laid emphasis on the equality of citizenship, though the Second Empire had failed to fulfil these promises.

---

[1] In 1848 direct representation in the French National Assembly had been granted to Martinique and Guadeloupe, which had elected three representatives. Though suspended in 1854, this representation was restored in 1871. In 1875 adult suffrage for males was established.

95

France's empire continued to expand in the twentieth century, with additions after World War I from among the former colonies of Germany. Despite French reverses in World War II, its colonial empire emerged largely intact. The Caribbean was a small part of the French world-wide system, to which far-away Indo-China was to provide the first shock. France put forth all its might, but not even the sacrifices of its soldiers and legionaries as exemplified at Dien Bien Phu could hold back the upsurge of anti-French nationalism.

In 1946 Martinique, Guadeloupe[1] and French Guiana[2] were reorganized as departments. Instead of a governor, a prefect was appointed by the French Minister of the Interior. An elected General Council, with limited powers, was also established to deal with financial matters and the budget of the department. The administrative services were modelled on those of a French department, and the laws of metropolitan France became applicable to the Caribbean departments. However, the change in the system of government proved to be more difficult than had been anticipated. There had long been a small group of officials and clergy in the French Antilles who believed, rightly or wrongly, that changes should come about slowly, taking human nature into account. On the other hand, there were those who considered that reforms could take place quickly and that they could at once transform the territories. The conflict of views produced difficulties which were augmented by a lack of trained officials capable of dealing with French government departments.[3]

In the outcome, the authority of the prefects gradually increased until they became in effect more independent of the local authorities than the governors who had preceded them.[4] The General Councils had acquiesced in this. It was a measure of their ineffectiveness.

Within the Caribbean territories the system of progress moved slowly. Large estates continued in being, those in Martinique often

---

[1] Included in the department of Guadeloupe are the smaller islands of Marie-Galante, Désirade and Les Saintes, which are adjacent to the main island; and St. Barthélemy and the French half of St. Martin, which are situated farther north.

[2] La Guyane.

[3] The new departmental system was not fully in operation until the beginning of 1948. George Spitz, "La Martinique et ses institutions depuis 1948", *Developments towards Self-Government in the Caribbean* (The Hague, 1955), pp. 112-14.

[4] *Ibid.*, p. 114.

owned by French families who had resided for generations in the islands, and in Guadeloupe by French-controlled companies. Clearly several years had to elapse before the effect of assimilation could be fairly assessed. When General Charles de Gaulle visited the French West Indies in 1956, his speeches reflected the ideals and aspirations of France. He declared that even if the present was far from easy, the difficulties would not last for ever, adding: "C'est en toute confiance que je viens vous dire, avec la certitude la plus absolue, que la France vivra et retrouvera sa grandeur, sans laquelle elle ne serait pas la France. Vive la Martinique Française, vive la République, vive la France!"[1]

Yet all was not tranquil in the Antilles. Communism was active, linked to a demand to free the departments from colonialism, even if the municipal election at Fort-de-France in 1957 resulted in a resounding victory for the list of candidates endorsed by deputy Aimé Césaire, who had himself resigned from the Communist Party.[2] Illustrative of the underlying difficulties in the French Antilles was the municipal election at Le Moule in Grande-Terre, Guadeloupe, in 1953. Victory had been achieved by the Communist list. However, accusations of fraud were made and the island administration annulled the elections. A commission to run the small town was appointed.[3] The French authorities reacted strongly on this occasion just as did the British in suspending the British Guiana constitution in 1953[4] and in dismissing the Price Government in British Honduras in 1957.[5]

In December 1959 ugly riots broke out at Fort-de-France,

[1] Fort-de-France, August 14, 1956.
[2] At this election, Césaire's Union des Démocrates et des Progressistes Martiniquais obtained 82 per cent. of the votes cast, the Rassemblement du Peuple Français 9 per cent., and the Communists 4 per cent. Césaire's defection had caused a considerable stir, since he had been the party leader in Martinique. With views far to the left, Césaire, a strong opponent of colonialism and a critic of the departmental system in the French Caribbean territories, exercised great influence in Martinique, particularly in Fort-de-France.
[3] New elections were held at Le Moule in 1957, when the Communists obtained 2381 votes and the Rassemblement des Gauches Républicaines (RGR) list won 679. This resulted in 20 seats for the Communists and seven for the RGR. Once more the council was dissolved. *Le Monde*, September 5, 1957. Cf. *Combat*, August 26, 1957; *L' Humanité*, August 26, 1957.
[4] *Vide* Chapter XIV, p. 146.
[5] *Vide* Chapter XV, p. 164.

Martinique.[1] The immediate cause was a mere traffic accident in the city, yet the disturbances continued for several days. So gravely was the situation regarded by the French Government that the dispatch from France of the cruiser *De Grasse*, with French police on board, was announced, though at the last minute the sailing was cancelled since order had been restored. Police reinforcements had been sent from Guadeloupe.

If there appeared to be an official reluctance to face facts in France, the left-wing press had for long been highly critical of French administration in the Caribbean.[2] Inevitably, the Communist bloc made the most of those difficulties and, in liaison with the dissatisfied element in the Antillean departments, disseminated its criticisms.[3]

Riots in French overseas departments were not confined to the Caribbean, nor to any one cause. In the overseas department of La Réunion in the Indian Ocean, riots which had originated from protests by planters at the fixing of sugar prices by the French Government resulted in the sacking of the town hall of St. Denis. Damage was caused amounting to NF200,000. One man was killed and 40 injured.[4]

Much of France's difficulty in integrating and assimilating its Antillean departments undoubtedly arose from the breakdown of the policy of equality and progress, which has been enshrined in French thought since the Revolution, and was now confronted with the economic problems of the Caribbean. The author Victor Sablé summed it up when he wrote that the provision of new jobs had not kept pace with the improvement in public health, while the lack of openings for employment had become tragic. It was symptomatic

[1] *Le Monde*, December 24, 1959. Cf. *The New York Times*, December 25-26, 1959.
[2] On December 17, 1960, *L' Humanité*, the organ of the Communist Party, carried the banner headlines, "Trois choix offerts à la jeunesse: la misère, l'émigration, la caserne". It claimed that the youth of Martinique was looking towards Cuba.
[3] The Hsinhua News Agency, Peking, maintained a continuous attack. On June 28, 1961, for example, it quoted the political bureau of the central committee of the Martinique Communist Party, which had published a protest against the colonial régime and capitalism. The statement urged that working people and democrats should "frustrate the colonialist plot against class and its party". It called for a Martinique front to struggle for autonomy and to put an end to poverty and oppression.
[4] *The Times*, February 9, 1960. Cf. *Le Monde*, February 10, 1962.

that the rioters had been, for the most part, recruited from among the unemployed.[1]

Notwithstanding the restoration of order in Martinique, the causes of discontent had not been eliminated in the French Caribbean. In a letter to *The New York Times*, Mercer D. Tate considered that the report of riots should have caused no surprise. The major reason was the economic hardship and wage disparity in the island. He regarded Martinique as "a typical colonial holding in the nineteenth-century tradition", adding: "The paternalism of the mother country is such that business interests from other nations, including the United States, are almost totally excluded. . . . The free world can ill afford the luxury of a colonial domain for which the storm signals are so obvious."[2]

Although in comparison with happenings in other parts of the Caribbean the concern which France had shown over the Martinique riots of December 1959 may seem to have been unduly alarmist, the events continued to attract a great deal of attention in France and beyond. The internal situation in both Martinique and Guadeloupe was disquieting. The improvements in public health had dramatically accelerated the rise in the population. In both islands, as in other parts of the Caribbean, the virtual elimination of malaria had been of major importance.[3] Between 1960 and 1965 the population was expected to rise from 276,000 to 320,000 persons. Half of the Martinique population was under 20 years of age. Simply to avoid an increase in unemployment would require the creation of 15,000 new jobs during the 1960-1965 period.[4] Many of the young educated Martiniquais did not wish to do agricultural work. With over 400 scholarships a year given in Martinique for secondary or higher education in France, the number of intellectuals had grown

[1] The Radical-Socialist Party bulletin, quoted by *Le Monde*, January 14, 1960.

[2] *The New York Times*, January 1, 1960.

[3] "K. C. Liang, malariologist of the World Health Organization (WHO), which maintains a regional office in Caracas, commented on the progress of the campaign to eradicate malaria. In Guadeloupe no case of malaria had occurred during the past year, while in Martinique no case had been reported in the last few years. In French Guiana, an average of twenty cases per year had been notified for the coastal areas; the incidence had been much reduced." *Hispanic American Report, op. cit.*, Vol. XIII, p. 249.

[4] Claude Julien, "Un paradis plein de problèmes", *Le Monde*, May 2, 1960.

99

rapidly. Writing for *Le Figaro*, Max Clos commented, "Dans le domaine de l'éducation, le principe de l'assimilation a été appliqué sans réserves." These young people, inevitably discontented, had congregated in Fort-de-France seeking a more agreeable life. The population of the city had doubled in 15 years.[1]

The most serious feature was the growing feeling of resentment against the French system. The very nature of the assimilation of the overseas departments with France led to a far greater proportion of Frenchmen in official positions than that of British in Trinidad or in Jamaica.[2] Even to the visitor this was immediately apparent, for example in the number of police from France. This added to the racial tension, which was also evident in the Negroes' dislike of the "békés", or white Creoles, who occupied positions of importance as planters and merchants. Yet, as in other Caribbean islands, miscegenation had been so widespread that it mitigated the problems.[3]

[1] "Que se passe-t-il à la Martinique?" Paris, February 25, 1960. Commenting on this article, Daniel de Grandmaison asked, "Pourquoi faudrait-il que notre jeunesse pave les routes et accomplisse les durs travaux de l'agriculture, avant que l'on ait tout fait pour lui donner le métier auquel lui donne droit l'instruction—obligatoire ne l'oublions pas—à laquelle on l'a assujetie"? "Quelques problèmes", *Le Courrier*, Martinique, March 12, 1960.

[2] Writing at the time of the Martinique riots, Christian Crabot, former teacher of the Lycée Victor Schoelcher at Fort-de-France, attributed the poor state of Martinique to unemployment, racism and excessive centralization. "L'autre aspect du malaise martiniquais est d'ordre humain. Dans cette île où le souvenir d'esclavage, aboli en 1848, reste présente dans les mémoires, et où Victor Schoelcher est considéré comme un saint, dans cette population où, du Noir Africain au Blanc créole, toutes les nuances du métissage sont représentées, les relations humaines sont restées complexes, et la sensibilité antillaise est très vive.

"Or la 'départementalisation' a augmenté le nombre des métropolitains— ils sont environ cinq mille maintenant. Beaucoup arrivent ignorant tout du pays. Désorientés, ils ne cherchent pas à le comprendre, vivent en cercle fermé, tout en considerant le Martinique comme un purgatoire nécessaire à leur avancement. Leurs maladresses et leurs préjugés heurtent les Antillais." "Chômage, racisme et centralisation excessive sont à l'origine du malaise à la Martinique." *Le Monde*, December 29, 1959.

[3] Max Clos, who writes of "un racisme en cascade", also comments: "Plusieurs 'békés' m'ont assuré avec fierté et peut-être même une part de satisfaction inconsciente que, lors des émeutes de Fort-de-France, seuls les métropolitains avaient été molestés par la foule. Le fait d'être reconnu pour un 'béké' aurait constitué une sorte de sauf-conduit." *Le Figaro*, February 24, 1960.

Despite these problems, which also existed in the other French Antillean departments, probably a majority desired to retain close association with France. The vote in 1960 had been definite. Undoubtedly, the visit of de Gaulle in May 1960 produced a considerable effect. He envisaged the extension of the powers of prefects and general counsellors in the overseas departments.[1] It had proved difficult to administer these departments from Paris, some 5000 miles distant, in the same manner as metropolitan departments. Reforms which were announced included giving the prefects a co-ordinating rôle in regard to the heads of the different administrative services, who previously had been directly responsible to Paris. Prefects would also advise on staff changes and dismissals. General Councils would have their powers increased, including the allocation of funds provided for local expenditure.[2]

The malaise, however, was deep-seated; discontent continued. The transfer to the French Antilles of a number of officials who had served in Algeria caused further misgivings. To the people of Martinique and Guadeloupe they were identified with suppression in North Africa. Moreover, the success of the West Indies Federation, which at that time seemed assured, the advent to power of Cheddi Jagan in British Guiana, and the authority which Fidel Castro wielded in Cuba, together with the emancipation of Negro Africa, were closely watched by the citizens of France's Antillean departments.[3]

Camille Petit believed that what the people of Martinique desired

[1] Speech at Cayenne, French Guiana, May 2, 1960. This devolution of power which de Gaulle described was no new concept. When the departmental system was first effectively established in Martinique, Guadeloupe, French Guiana and Réunion in 1946, provision was made for adjustment to their needs of laws passed in metropolitan France. In 1954, a Minister of State was created in charge of the overseas departments. The French Constitution of 1958 further emphasized that the administrative organization could be adjusted to meet the special position of the overseas departments. Thus from the outset, the problems of the overseas departments had been recognized by France.
[2] Guy Lasserre comments, "Si le renforcement du rôle de coordinateur du préfet est un mesure hautement souhaitable, il ne s'imposait peut-être pas de lui donner dans d'autres domaines des pouvoirs accrus. Il faut prendre garde de ne point ressusciter le 'gouverneur'." La Guadeloupe (Bordeaux, 1961), Vol. II, p. 1063.
[3] Philippe Decraene, "Dans l'intention de prévenir des revendications politiques", Le Monde, October 4, 1961.

was not separation from France, but the same social advantages as were enjoyed in the metropolis, including family allowances on the same scale, the tackling of the problem of destitute youth, and the setting up of pilot industries by the State in the overseas departments, protected against competition from the metropolis.[1]

Obviously concerned at the rising discontent in French Antillean departments and French Guiana, the French Government, in December 1961, put forward an interesting solution. It proposed to make a change in the training of conscripts, which had for several months presented difficulties, since there were insufficient military duties to be discharged in the territories. This prevented the whole contingent's serving locally. A proportion therefore was drafted for service with metropolitan units in France. The young West Indians were ill-adapted psychologically and technically for service in the metropolitan militia and disliked their period of service.[2]

An army bulletin announced the details of the new plan, which was named the Nemo scheme for General Nemo, Commander of the Antilles-French Guiana forces. The statement faced the issue frankly, stating that demographic pressure in Martinique and Guadeloupe, where economy rested essentially on the cultivation of sugar cane, involved a substantial agricultural proletariat and large landowners. On the other hand, French Guiana with its industrial and agricultural possibilities remained a veritable desert.[3] The Nemo scheme would be adapted to the special needs of these departments. It envisaged that as part of their training for citizenship the young conscripts, many of them serving in engineering units, would work on road construction, including tourist routes, the erection of buildings for small farms, and similar projects. The original cadres would be formed in French Guiana, which the French Government planned to develop by using settlers from the French Caribbean islands. This

[1] "La Martinique, département français des Antilles", Le Monde, May 11, 1961. Camille Petit was Mayor of Grand-Rivière, Martinique, Conseiller Général de Fort-de-France, and member of the Social and Economic Council of Martinique.

[2] "Tous les jeunes Antillais seront appelés pour un service militaire adapté", Le Monde, December 12, 1961. In Great Britain, however, there were examples of West Indians voluntarily serving with British units, apparently happily. They had not, of course, been conscripted.

[3] Bulletin d'information du Ministère des Armées (Paris), December 21, 1961.

preliminary work would be extended to the other two Antillean departments.[1]

The plan was an interesting one, since it aimed at stressing the value of manual work to unemployed city youth; the population would continue for many years to depend on agriculture for a large part of its employment, as it had done in the past. It was the Government's reply to the problem of unemployed youth, which some felt was sapping the morale of the country. The Nemo scheme was open to the criticism that it constituted semi-forced labour, and it may have raised doubts in the minds of those who recalled youth training in totalitarian countries. Yet it was democratic, in so far as it aimed at creating Frenchmen by breaking through racial barriers.

To the parties of the left, however, the obstacle to progress was the departmental status of these territories. Césaire expressed this forcibly, contending that in a world which was ridding itself of colonialism, the French Antilles were among the few remaining colonies. Fundamental change was needed, and the adoption of a bold policy of industrialization.[2] However, a majority both in the overseas departments and in France still favoured the link with the metropolis.

The cantonal elections of June 1961 brought little change in the composition of the General Councils of the Antillean departments. The majority of the electors had expressed their desire to keep their territories' status as departments of France, which had been a main electoral issue.[3] There was, however, an important and influential body of separatist opinion. Martinique, out of 12 contested seats, returned 6 supporters of Césaire on a separatist ticket, though in French Guiana there was a decline of support for deputy Justin

[1] "Au cours de la première phase (1962-1963) les travaux prévus aux Antilles seront les suivants: perfectionnement du réseau routier et notamment amélioration du réseau touristique pour favoriser l'industrie hôtelière, reconquête de terres à défricher, construction d'habitations en Guadeloupe; notamment cent quarante-cinq fermes-types seront construites et cédées à des conditions avantageuses aux jeunes Antillais, afin de favoriser la création d'une petite propriété.

"En Guyane, on prévoit l'achèvement de la route côtière de Saint Laurent-de-Maroni à Saint Georges-de-l'Oyapok, . . . et la construction de villages." *Le Monde*, December 23, 1961. Cf. *ibid.*, December 12, 1961.

[2] "Crise dans les départements d'outre-mer ou crise de la départementalisation?" *Le Monde*, March 29, 1961.

[3] *Hispanic American Report, op. cit.*, March 29, Vol. XIV, p. 513.

Catayée, who was defeated.[1] Though in French Guiana the pro-
Communist Union Populaire Guyanaise lost support, in Guadeloupe
the Communists won 5 out of 18 contested seats.

Apparently concluding that only a noisy minority wished to end the
departmental system in the Antillean departments, the French
Government adopted a stronger policy.[2] It interdicted the Front
Antillais et Guyanais pour l'Autonomie.[3] This was followed by the
expulsion of nine teachers, including the head of the Ecole Normale
from Guadeloupe to France.[4] Edouard Glissant, a well-known
Martinique author,[5] who had protested against the suppression of the
Front Antillais et Guyanais, was also shortly afterwards expelled from
Guadeloupe. While admitting the menace of Communism in the
French Antilles, these steps, for which no reasons were given, seemed
very drastic on the part of the French Government. Even more
surprising was the small volume of protest in France or in its overseas
departments, in contrast with the outburst of criticism in the House
of Commons and the British press when a few months later a
Jamaican girl who had been convicted of shoplifting in Great Britain
received a deportation order to return to Jamaica.[6]

[1] Voting was, however, close between the moderate Mouvement Populaire
Guyanais, which favoured French Guiana retaining its departmental status,
and Catayée's Parti Socialiste Guyanais, which favoured a special status for
the territory. Le Monde, June 7, 1961.
Catayée had for long pressed for substantial modification of the departmental system for French Guiana in order to permit its more rapid development. "Le trait dominant de ces élections reste l'éclatante victoire de M.
Vignon, ancien Préfet de la Guyane, sur le Député Catayée à Iracoubo,
obtenue dès le premier tour." Match, Guadeloupe, editorial, June 20, 1961.

[2] It may also have been heartened in its analysis of opinion in the three
Caribbean departments by the heavy support of de Gaulle's policy in the
referendum on Algeria in April 1961.
"At a dinner for parliamentary representatives of the overseas departments,
Michel Debré, French Prime Minister, thanked the guests of honor for
showing their attachment to France in the cantonal elections." Hispanic
American Report, op. cit., Vol. XIV, p. 616.

[3] Le Monde, July 21, 1961.

[4] Under the Ordinance of October 15, 1960, which allowed the prefects
of overseas departments to send back public servants whose behaviour was
such as to disturb the orderly running of the community.

[5] Winner of the Théophraste Renaudot prize of 1958 for his novel La lézarde.

[6] The case was debated in the House of Commons, and received great
publicity in the press. Finally, Henry Brooke, the newly appointed
Secretary of State for Home Affairs, withdrew the expulsion order. Parliamentary Report, The Times, July 24, 1962.

$\longrightarrow$ Combined with a toughening policy in Paris was a strong effort to reduce the inequalities, both in social services and in other payments, which existed in the Antillean departments in comparison with metropolitan France. Following serious strikes in Martinique in March 1961,[1] an increase in family allowances had been declared. On his return visit to the Caribbean, Jean de Broglie, Secretary for the Overseas Departments, announced at a Paris press conference measures to improve economic and social conditions in the overseas departments. These included an increase of 6 per cent. in the guaranteed minimum salary for trained workers, while family allowances were increased by 30 per cent. Special economic aid was put forward, while a new post was created in the prefecture of each department to deal with economic affairs. In March 1962 Pierre Sudreau, French Minister of Construction, toured the French Antilles.[2] Plans were announced for the building of over 2000 houses a year in Guadeloupe. France was combining a policy of firmness with one of carefully planned expenditure towards its Antillean departments.

Yet the French experiment appeared to be meeting with increasing resistance. Perhaps the greatest difficulty was that it had been launched during a period when colonialism was under heavy attack in many parts of the world. Even if some of the attacks ignored the advantages of association with richer and more developed nations, a world movement towards independence was taking place, often

---

[1] Three persons were killed and twenty-five, including six police, injured. *Hispanic American Report, op. cit.*, Vol. XIV, p. 226.

Another aspect of the grievances in the French Antilles against differentiation in wage rates was voiced by the workers' union of the Compagnie Générale Transatlantique when on strike in Martinique and Guadeloupe. They complained of the inequality of allowances and conditions of service between local employees and staff from metropolitan France, and particularly of the cost of living allowance of 40 per cent. of salary paid to the latter. *Ibid.*, p. 514.

"Nous poursuivons la campagne pour que le personnel de cette compagnie de navigation obtienne satisfaction. Nous avons toujours défendu dans les colonnes de cet organe l'égalité des droits de nos travailleurs avec le peuple de France. . . . Ces intolérables discriminations doivent disparaître en terre française." *Match*, June 8, 1961.

[2] His visit had been well received. "L'homme d'état ne s'est pas contenté de lire des rapports ou d'écouter des renseignements. Il a voulu voir par lui-même pour se faire une opinion sur l'état actuel de l'habitat à la Martinique." *Le Courrier*, editorial, March 10, 1962.

without regard to the size of the units. An outward mark of dissatisfaction were the strikes, riots and deportations of French citizens from Guadeloupe. Within was the volume of opinion, still a minority, which was strongly opposed to the departmental system for the West Indies territories of France. The arguments of the critics were fortified by the rates of wages and of payments in some social services in the Antillean departments, which were substantially below those in France. In other directions, France had provided fine educational and medical services. Yet they may only have served to exacerbate the problems of the educated Negro who could find no suitable employment; and a rapidly rising birth-rate engendered still more problems.

At first, France had hoped to brush aside opposition. Clearly the policy had failed. After General de Gaulle's visit in 1960, France instituted a two-pronged drive to override criticism and to raise social services towards the standard existing in France, combined with economic expansion and the Nemo scheme. The young colonials would be oriented towards the metropolis. Much would depend on the handling of the recruits. Tact and imagination would be needed. Striking success might be achieved, but a fiasco could endanger France's ties with its ancient colonies.

Underlying everything was the weak economy of the three departments. To change that, if it could be changed, would require a very heavy capital outlay. At a price, France could make the necessary adjustment in the social services.[1] It could hardly, however, undertake permanently the financial support of a growing number of unemployed persons. To some of the island politicians the solution was the termination of the departmental system. Then the territories might or might not remain associated with France. No one ventured to suggest what power, if France withdrew, would take its place to subsidize the sugar and the bananas which were the mainstay of the two major Antillean departments. No one had yet shown how the departments would be more successful economically on their own, with Haiti as an alarming example of what might happen. Their

---

[1] ". . . mais elle est très coûteuse pour les finances nationales, tout en ne fournissant pas de solution constructive aux grands problèmes économiques et sociaux dont souffrent les îles." Luc Fauvel, "Les conséquences économiques et sociales de l'assimilation administrative des Antilles françaises", *Developments towards Self-Government in the Caribbean, op. cit.*, p. 197.

association with France had been very long, and the imprint of French culture and language had been far more marked than in any of the former African colonies of France. In assessing the stresses and strains which were appearing in the French Caribbean departments, the underlying strength of the links had also to be considered.[1] The answer would finally rest on whether the majority of the people believed that the advantages of association with France outweighed those of self-government.[2]

[1] Writing at the time of General de Gaulle's second visit to the Caribbean departments, the Paris correspondent of *The Guardian*, Manchester, wrote: "Guadeloupe and Martinique are undoubtedly the most French of France's overseas possessions, but they are still seeking a status that fits their situation. From being colonies with parliamentary representation in Paris before the war, they became at their own request Overseas Departments after the war, but have since asked for greater decentralization." May 3, 1960.
Nine out of ten senators and deputies for Martinique and Guadeloupe signed a joint declaration stating that considerable progress had been made since the introduction of the change of status setting up overseas departments under the law of May 19, 1946. Only Aimé Césaire, deputy for Martinique, did not associate himself with the statement.

[2] "If one may assume that what is good for the mother country is also good for Guadeloupe and Martinique, one rests his hope for the islands' future on the wisdom of the French to know what is best for themselves. If one believes that occasionally what is good for metropolitan France may be bad for her Caribbean islands, then one finds little solace in their representation in Paris. French Caribbean dissatisfactions in the near future will doubtless focus upon the boundary line which is drawn between national policies laid down in Paris and local policies decided in Basse-Terre and Fort-de-France." Franklin D. Parker, "Political Development in the French Caribbean", *The Caribbean, op. cit.*, p. 104.

CHAPTER XI

THE POST-WAR FRENCH ECONOMIC
POLICY IN THE CARIBBEAN

The basic reason for the underlying discontent in the French
Antillean departments, which burst out from time to time in strikes
and riots, was the growing national self-consciousness of the population. Martinique and Guadeloupe remained monuments to the
monoculture of earlier colonial days. The benefits of French
medicine and education were increasing and were raising a population
for whom there seemed to be few employment openings except work
in the sugar-cane fields, an industry that was fast reducing its labour
requirements as in other parts of the Caribbean. One of the results
of assimilation with France had been an increase in real wages. This
had often resulted, among low-paid workers, in a shorter period of
work. Owners of sugar-mills tended increasingly to reduce labour by
mechanization, even if this had been less extensive than in some other
countries.[1] An extension of social services might mitigate the
problem; it could not resolve it.

Perceptive writers like Daniel de Grandmaison criticized the
blindness of the French régime, which appeared to be unaware of the
dangers that were arising.[2] The opponents of the French departmental system, though in a minority, were active. Aided by the
much smaller Communist group, they found plenty of discontent to

[1] What in Jamaica had taken place as a result of a substantial increase of
wages arising out of an arbitration award (*vide* Chapter IX, p. 92) occurred
in Martinique and Guadeloupe as a result of government action. In each
case, the rapid increase of wages had not been accompanied by a sufficient
general expansion of production. While clearly mechanization was desirable,
the effects in both the French Antilles and Jamaica seem to have resulted in
increased unemployment, or underemployment, which would appear to
bear out the theory of Friedrich A. Hayek that, as a general rule, wage fixing,
whether by unions or by authority, will make wages higher than they would
otherwise be only if they are also higher than the wage at which all willing
workers can be employed. Cf. *The Constitution of Liberty* (London, 1960),
pp. 269-71.
[2] Daniel de Grandmaison, "La verité sur le tourisme", *Le Courrier*,
November 11, 18, 25, 1961.

fan among the low-paid and often unemployed or underemployed workers.

As in the British and Dutch islands, political development in the French Caribbean territories was closely linked to economic conditions. The resemblances were many, though France maintained a much tighter grip on the trade of its Antillean departments than did Great Britain or the Netherlands on the trade of their respective dependencies. The tradition of *l'exclusif* had been continued into the post-World War II period. The position of the French Caribbean territories had tended to become increasingly difficult. The very sheltered nature of their commerce had in some ways retarded the progress which the competition of a more open economy often impels. A striking example existed in the sugar industry of Martinique, where small mills still predominated, though large central factories which processed cane from a number of estates and small farms had become increasingly a characteristic of the Caribbean sugar industry in the twentieth century. This development could be observed in Cuba, the Dominican Republic, Puerto Rico and Jamaica in the Greater Antilles, and in Trinidad and British Guiana. Even in the Leeward Islands, the numerous sugar-mills of former days in St. Kitts and Antigua had given way in each case to a single central factory. Often the ruined shells of the abandoned mills of an earlier period silently testified to the change that had taken place. Guadeloupe, with flat land on Grande-Terre and more capital available, as a result of French ownership of many estates, had been better placed to modernize its sugar industry than mountainous Martinique, with its small creole family properties. Progress in the French islands could not, however, compare with the advance which had been achieved in some enterprises in other parts of the Caribbean.[1]

[1] The author, who has had experience as a director of sugar-mills in Jamaica and British Honduras, visited Martinique and Guadeloupe in May 1962 immediately after seeing sugar operations in two leading districts in Jamaica and British Guiana. The less efficient transport, a vital factor in the economical production of sugar cane, was very noticeable in the case of the French islands, as was the smaller size of the units. Against this, it should be borne in mind that mechanization normally means a reduction of labour on a sugar estate. There is therefore the argument that if France is prepared to subsidize the sugar industry in its overseas departments, there may be no immediate purpose in mechanization with the existing surplus of labour. The production of rum, often sold as a branded article, may fit in with small units.

France's policy had been applied also to bananas[1]. The importance of this industry, which unlike sugar cane affords employment all the year round, had been appreciated by the metropolitan power which had allocated a quota to the French Caribbean, threatened by the competition of French Africa. The construction of good roads, vital in transporting bananas to the port of shipment, had for long been a feature of French administrative policy. This had enabled bananas to be successfully grown for export in mountainous districts such as the west part of Basse-Terre in Guadeloupe, where sugar cane could not be economically grown under modern conditions.[2]

The French islands prospered less than did the British and Dutch during World War II owing to the uncertain policy of the Vichy Government.[3] Lacking the developed mineral wealth of Trinidad, Jamaica, British Guiana or Surinam, or the advantages of oil refining in Curaçao and Aruba, the French Caribbean progressed slowly. There was not the encouragement of American and Canadian capital

Moreover, mountainous Martinique is not well suited for concentrating production in a few large centres. The cost of transporting sugar cane long distances and over mountain ridges may be prohibitive. As Lafcadio Hearn so well describes it: "Except for the transportation of sugar and rum, there is practically no communication by sea between the west and the north-east coast—the sea is too dangerous—and thus the populations on either side of the island are more or less isolated from each other, besides being further subdivided and segregated by the lesser mountain chains crossing their respective territories." Certainly Martinique would never present an easy proposition for large-scale concentration of the processing of sugar cane. *Two Years in the French West Indies* (New York, 1890), pp. 123-6.

[1] Bananas from Martinique and Guadeloupe are shipped to Dieppe, and those from Africa to Bordeaux.

[2] In the same way, Jamaica, which had for long grown a substantial part of its banana production in hilly areas, constructed a useful network of roads. A former governor of the island once commented to the author that the road system was "too good for the island". He meant that, but for the valuable banana export trade, such an expenditure would not have been justified.

[3] The governorship of Admiral Georges Robert (1940-1943) had proved to be a period of great hardship for the French Antilles. Unlike many other French leaders in the colonies, he acknowledged the Vichy Government. In consequence, the allied powers imposed a measure of blockade against these islands, which brought them to the verge of starvation. Sugar became increasingly difficult to export to France. The few French merchantmen in operation were often seized by Great Britain or held up by the United States. Finally, on the express orders of Germany, both Premier Pierre Laval and Marshal Pétain ordered Robert to sink the French warships and

which had begun to appear in the British and Dutch territories for the development of industries and tourist hotels.

As in so many other Caribbean islands, the growth of population advanced apace. France, however, unlike Great Britain, did not restrict immigration from its overseas departments. In 1962 there were about 150,000 Antilleans in France of whom a substantial number worked in Paris. Many found employment as officials and teachers.[1] Factory labour was required in France, but much of this came from Algeria and Europe, favoured by the shorter distances. Cost of travel was a limiting factor in emigration from all the Caribbean islands. With stringent control of the entry of non-Commonwealth labour, these sources of supply were not open to British employers. Moreover, the emigration from the British Caribbean to England had come predominantly from Jamaica, an island more industrialized than the French Antilles. The emigrants tended to be those who were skilled or semi-skilled workers, more numerous in Jamaica than in Martinique and Guadeloupe.[2] The immigrants were drawn essentially from the more ambitious members

the French gold (*vide* Chapter VI, p. 37)—orders he did not carry out. As a result of the American blockade of the French islands, imports of foodstuffs had practically ceased, while sugar and rum, the mainstay of the islands, could hardly be exported. During this period, Puerto Rico and the British and Dutch islands were enjoying a measure of prosperity. By backing Vichy instead of General de Gaulle, Robert had caused Martinique and Guadeloupe to pay a heavy price. Cf. Amiral Georges Robert, *La France aux Antilles de 1939 à 1943* (Paris, 1950), pp. 149-50 and 169.

[1] "Près de 5000 Guadeloupéens seraient fonctionnaires en métropole, dont 600 dans les seuls services hospitaliers de la Seine." Philippe Decraene, "Terres françaises des Antilles", IV, *Le Monde*, October 11, 12, 13, 14, 1962. Decraene also points out that in Guadeloupe there were only 400 officials from France, including 27 departmental heads, out of 4129 officials in the territory.

[2] A feature of emigration from Jamaica had been the acceleration of the process by widespread newspaper advertisements of travel agencies. There was nothing comparable in the French Antillean press. Cheap travel by steamship and rail via Genoa to London was much used, while the airlines advertised cut-rate fares. Moreover, the immigrants, once established in their new country of residence, played a major part in encouraging and assisting their friends and relatives to join them. For a small territory like Jamaica, the emigrant trade (two-way, since many returned home each year) was a business of some account. Enterprising manufacturers even started the export of Jamaica canned goods such as ackees (a fruit) for the Jamaica emigrants in Great Britain.

of the population, even if they had to be content with unskilled work on arrival in England.

Professor Luc Fauvel points out that the French system of family allowances had been introduced from 1930 to encourage a rise in the birth-rate to counteract the losses incurred in World War I. The system had no relevance to conditions in the overseas departments. He considered, however, that the industrial regions in France could provide immigrants with employment, but added that it remained a question of who would pay the cost of their transportation and settlement in France.[1] He emphasized the heavy cost to the metropolis of extending a complete system of social security to the Antilles.[2]

Plans were at long last put forward to develop the French Antilles. Funds were allocated by France for land drainage, and the development of small-holdings in Guadeloupe and Martinique. The difficulty of these schemes, as Jamaica had found in its land settlement experiments, was the cost involved.[3]

Certain features were becoming apparent in agriculture, in the French Antilles as in other tropical countries. The intense competition in exports kept the prices of most commodities low, except when they were supported artificially by tariffs, preferences or subsidies. The successful operations were those which had large areas of first-class flat land combined with highly mechanized operations. There appeared to be, however, scope for vegetable growing and the raising of chickens and other products for domestic consumption. Developments of this kind, combined with a tourist industry which the French departments had so far failed effectively to develop, might help to alleviate the problem of unemployment. At a later stage the European Economic Community might even bring about new prosperity to the overseas French territories, though equally it might reduce France's ability to subsidize and protect its not too efficient colonial enterprises. Despite all the criticism of France by its overseas departments, the position remained that the French market was crucial to the export of subsidized sugar and of quota-protected bananas.[4] Should the separatists succeed in their

---

[1] Luc Fauvel, *op. cit.*, pp. 183-4.   [2] *Ibid.*, p. 185.
[3] *Vide* Chapter IX, p. 93n.
[4] "Incapables de s'étendre, leurs faibles dimensions les ont bien condamnées à jamais à ne plus compter dans le monde économique, fût-ce pour les productions même dont elles avaient jadis le monopole. Ce n'est pas que la consommation du café, du sucre, de toutes les denrées coloniales ait cessé de

endeavour to break away, the problem of unemployment might yet become even greater.

*   *   *   *

With an area of 34,740 square miles and the population of a small market-town,[1] French Guiana had not progressed under Bourbon, Imperial or Republican Governments. For more than three-quarters of a century French Guiana had been governed according to the provisions of a senate decree of Napoleon III, passed in 1854. In 1930 the country was divided into Guiana and the territory of Inini, which comprised the hinterland.

The experiment of making French Guiana an overseas department in 1946 had failed to change the pattern. Less than 11 square miles of land were under cultivation.[2] In 1950, Bren-Sirquard described the problems of the country pessimistically, referring especially to the lack of communications. He even considered that the closing of the convict settlement had removed the only source of labour for developing the colony, since all previous attempts at colonization had failed.[3] Maurice Vaussard had found a visit equally depressing. He pointed out that French Guiana's population, which had been 60,000 in 1875, had fallen to about half that figure. The mining of gold in adequate quantities had failed. In a whole century, a total of only 150 tons had been extracted: at the close, production had greatly fallen from its peak.[4] Most of the country remained a primitive jungle with few communications apart from canoes on the rivers, which were often interrupted by rapids as in Surinam or British

---

faire des progrès. Mais par le fait même de leur vulgarisation, ces productions ne sont plus rémunératrices qu'à condition d'être produites en quantités énormes, comme le café au Brésil ou le sucre à Java, et par suite de leur faible étendue, de leur organisation social surtout, la Martinique, la Guadeloupe et la Réunion ne sont nullement outillées pour une production de ce genre." J. Tramond and A. Reussner, *Eléments d'histoire maritime et coloniale* (Paris, 1924), p. 341. Tramond and Reussner were writing of the second half of the eighteenth century. Their conclusions apply with even more force today, and may be extended to cover many of the non-French Antilles.

[1] About 32,000.
[2] 6700 acres. James, *op. cit.*, p. 856.
[3] "Au chevet de la Guyane", *Le Monde*, March 21, 22, 23, 1950.
[4] Maurice Vaussard, "La Guyane peut-elle renaître?" *L' Aube*, May 9, 10, 11, 1950.

Guiana.[1] It remained to be seen whether the Nemo plan would be more successful than former development schemes, involving the transportation to French Guiana of labourers, ranging from political prisoners in the eighteenth century to convicts in the nineteenth century. Professor Eugène Revert took a somewhat less pessimistic view of French Guiana than some other writers, though he admitted that only by the discipline of a settled policy could French Guiana find prosperity.[2]

*   *   *   *

The critics, however, continued to blame all the ills of the territories on the departmental system.[3] Perhaps the basic difficulty was that both the Antillean departments and France itself were becoming disillusioned. France had parted company with its former colonies in Indo-China and in Algeria. Though the Caribbean association was a long one, imaginative and sympathetic statesmanship would be needed on both sides to preserve it.

The novel concept of one of the most perceptive and logical nations in the modern world, was that the ancient Caribbean colonies which Colbert had first sought to integrate into France should end up as French departments on a parity with those of the metropolis; it was a daring modern experiment in political science. The probability of its success was not supported by history. However, a revolution in communications had taken place in the second half of the twentieth

[1] An interesting account of a journey up the Maroni river, which separates French Guiana from Surinam, and then by canoe from Maripasoula in French Guiana to Belém do Pará in Brazil was written by Guillaume Chenevière describing the 1958 expedition led by Henry d'Ormond and entitled "Un Genevois et un Français dans la jungle Guyanaise", *La Tribune de Genève*, July 4-5, 7, 17, 1959.

[2] "La population a commencé d'augmenter par excédent des naissances, mais de manière très insuffisante. Il n'y a pas encore un habitant par trois kilomètres carrés. On trouve de l'or, mais le temps des placers individuels est aujourd'hui révolu. Il y a les bois, l'élevage, l'agriculture. Chacune de ces activités peut donner d'excellents résultats. Mais il faut choisir. Il peut être fait beaucoup, mais au prix d'une stricte discipline et c'est à ce prix seulement que ce vieux pays finira par trouver la prospérité et les richesses que les vicissitudes de la colonisation lui on jusqu'à présent refusées." Eugène Revert, *Le Monde Caraïbe* (Paris, 1958), pp. 151-2.

[3] "Aujourd'hui ma conviction est que pour la politique antillaise de la France l'heure de la révision déchirante est arrivée." Aimé Césaire, "Crise dans les Départements d'Outre-Mer ou Crise de la Départementalisation?" *Le Monde*, March 29, 1961.

114

century which had in effect brought the Caribbean nearer to France. Theoretically, a striking difference in climate suggested that the economies of France and the French Antilles were complementary, not competitive.

The offer to the Antillean departments of a common citizenship in the context of a democratic world implied a measure of equality, especially in State services. Yet the enormous disparity in wages presaged danger to the experiment, at least so far as social services were concerned.

With more limited territorial responsibilities overseas, the United States had succeeded, through the use of massive financial support, in enabling Puerto Rico, fully prepared to make use of its opportunities, to attain the highest standard of living in Latin America.[1] For a less wealthy France with far wider territorial responsibilities, the problem was much more onerous. The task of lifting the Caribbean departments to the level of a French department might prove to be insupportable.[2] Caribbean post-war planning in Paris had been different from that in Washington, London and The Hague. The challenge to France remained as did the challenge to the other powers. The results of France's carefully planned policy of assimilation would be watched by the world. In the outcome, economies would play a decisive part in the attempt to solve the problems of the French Caribbean.[3]

[1] Per capita income in 1961 was $571.00. Yet despite the United States' heavy subsidies to Puerto Rico in tax remission and in the removal of customs duties, the island had not yet reached the income level of the poorest state in the United States.

[2] Guy Lasserre considered that the adjusted departmental system reduced the immediate rather than the deeper causes of the malaise in the Antilles. "Il ne faut point perdre de vue que si les Antilles sont françaises, elles sont aussi autre chose que la France, et qu'elles ont leurs problèmes spécifiques hérités d'un milieu géographique tropical et de trois siècles d'histoire coloniale. Tout notre ouvrage n'en est que la démonstration. Or, le monde d'aujourd'hui étant ce qu'il est, les Antilles se placent tout naturellement dans le camp du 'tiers-monde' et leur sympathie, qui est grande pour une certaine image de la France—sinon toujours pour la métropole—, va aussi vers les jeunes Etats indépendants qui ont secoué la tutelle coloniale. Cette attitude est un fait géographique, au même titre que le relief ou le climat: il faut en tenir compte." Guy Lasserre, op. cit., Vol. II, p. 1065.

[3] "A l'analyser froidement, la situation actuelle de la Martinique et de la Guadeloupe paraît grosse de dangers pour un avenir proche. Leur prospérité dépend uniquement des cultures d'exportation, canne à sucre et bananes. On peut prévoir le moment où les sucres et les rhums qui n'ont

In a penetrating criticism, Professor Fauvel concluded that although assimilation encouraged an increase of population in territories already overpopulated, it did not provide the means for emigration to France and by increasing wage rate, it had created a new problem to industrial diversification,[1] adding, "le seul fait que 'la colonie' soit devenue 'département' ne changeait pas les capacités productives des divers groupes sociaux".[2] Even if official policy in France and in its Antillean departments still remained confident of ultimate success of assimilation through the departmental system, the volume of pessimistic opinion was significant.[3]

---

d'autres acheteurs que la Métropole et l'Union Française, vont se trouver en concurrence avec les produits similaires de France même. Il peut en résulter soit un effondrement des cours, soit le retour à de strictes mesures de contingentement." Eugène Revert, *La France d'Amérique* (Paris, 1955), p. 247.

[1] Fauvel, *op. cit.*, p. 197.   [2] *Ibid.*, p. 177.

[3] "La structure sociale antillaise est complexe. L'élément moteur de l'évolution, la classe ouvrière et paysanne, est maintenant convaincue que l'assimilation constitue une impasse, que seule l'autonomie lui permettra de réaliser ses conquêtes sociales. La petite bourgeoisie de couleur, se rend-elle aussi compte qu'elle n'est qu'une pseudo-classe dont le développement véritable est impossible au sein d'un système dominé par une économie extérieure. Elle se découvre une vocation nationale. La grande bourgeoisie elle-même est quelquefois atteinte par les mesures de discrimination que l'économie dominante pratique à l'égard du sucre et de la banane. L'exemple le plus récente en est la position officielle des betteraviers pour que le marché français et algérien soit réservé exclusivement au sucre de betterave, alors que ce marché absorbe à lui seul 75 per cent. de la production sucrière de la zone franc.

"Objectivement, une solidarité réelle, même limitée dans son étendue à certains domaines, se crée donc entre les différentes classes de la société antillo-guyanaise et ce fait positif joue en faveur d'un changement radical de statut. Dans les luttes à venir la ligne de partage des forces suivra sensiblement celle des intérêts, d'après l'idée que s'en font les hommes et les groupes. L'assimilation ou une formule voisine sera défendue par ceux qui pensent que le système actuel permet un maintien ou un développement de leurs affaires, par certains hommes politiques appuyés sur la fraude et la finance, par les sociétés sucrières et les grands usiniers-propriétaires à qui l'impérialisme aura pu faire une place dans un monde et à travers une époque où leurs privilèges égoïstes se sentent de plus en plus menacés.

"L'Autonomie sera la plate-forme de la classe ouvrière et paysanne, de la moyenne et petite bourgeoisie, et des éléments intelligents de la grande bourgeoisie qui comprendront que leurs intérêts essentiels peuvent être garantis s'ils savent s'adapter à temps à la marche irréversible de l'Histoire." Paul Niger, "L'assimilation, forme suprême du colonialisme", *Esprit* (Paris, April 1962), pp. 531-2.

CHAPTER XII

THE POST-WAR NETHERLANDS
POLITICAL AIMS IN THE CARIBBEAN

The Netherlands Antilles is divided into two groups, the Leeward Islands (a term that has fallen out of use), which consist of Curaçao, Aruba and Bonaire, and the Windward Islands, comprising St. Eustatius, Saba and the Dutch portion of St. Martin, which are situated over 500 miles away, confusingly among the British Leeward Islands. With a population of under 5000, the Windward Islands are of small importance in the twentieth century, though in the eighteenth century St. Eustatius was a major trading centre in the Caribbean.[1] The small Negro and white population speaks English, though Dutch is the language of the administration.

Of much greater importance, Curaçao and Aruba, which lie between 20 and 38 miles off the Venezuelan coast and some 200 miles from the Lake Maracaibo oilfield, have a population of about 200,000. In these islands together with Bonaire, the language most spoken is Papiamento, which is a mixture of Spanish, Portuguese, Dutch and English. It is increasing and newspapers are published in it. The official language, however, which is taught in the schools, is Dutch. The islanders are good linguists, many speaking in addition Spanish and English.

Political parties have not followed the pattern of the Netherlands. They are dominantly organized on island lines. Curaçao, with its substantial population (126,000), has two main parties. The National People's Party, led by Dr. Moises Da Costa Gomez, draws its strength from the Negro population in the country districts and is relatively conservative. The Democratic Party of Dr. Efraim Jonckheer is somewhat more radical. Personal attachments to the leader are strong, with a situation recalling that of Sir Alexander Bustamante and Norman Manley in Jamaica, just as the division of parties between the country and the town in Curaçao has also appeared in Jamaica.[2] With separate political parties, Aruba has tended to hold

[1] *Vide* Chapter II, pp. 6 and 10.
[2] *Ibid.*, Chapter VIII, pp. 68-69 and p. 71.

117

the balance between the parties of the more populous island.[1] The Windward Islands, which also has its party, returns one member. Surprisingly, the Netherlands Antilles Parliament has been largely composed of officials who, after election, continued to draw their salaries; there were no salary payments for Members of Parliament. The system is a little reminiscent of the British Parliament in the eighteenth and early nineteenth centuries, when ambitious British naval and army officers sometimes combined with their official post a seat in the House of Commons. The practice appeared, however, to function satisfactorily in the Netherlands Antilles.

In Aruba and Bonaire there was a much greater Amerindian element in the population than in Curaçao, which was dominantly Negro. As a result of the rapid expansion of the oil refineries, a shortage of labour in Curaçao and Aruba had occurred, which had been filled by immigrants from the Netherlands Windward Islands, Surinam and the British islands in the West Indies, attracted by the high rates of wages paid, though in later years a contrary trend had developed. There was a tradition of racial harmony based on the past which had continued to be manifested.[2]

Fronting the Atlantic to the north and pressed between French Guiana to the east and British Guiana to the west, Surinam is practically sealed off by impenetrable jungle from Brazil, which forms its southern boundary. As in British Guiana, the use of its rivers is limited by rapids to the lower reaches. The population of over a quarter of a million is concentrated in the flat area of the north where the Dutch have demonstrated their skill in the use of waterways and the construction of canals. The heterogeneous population of the country includes Creoles,[3] Hindustani comprising Hindus and

[1] After World War II, Aruba expressed a desire for independence to free itself from what it called the domination of the more populous Curaçao. The Netherlands Government decided, however, that it must remain within the Netherlands Antilles political structure. This attitude may be contrasted with that of the British Government, which permitted the secession of first Jamaica and then Trinidad from the West Indies Federation. *Vide* Chapter VIII, pp. 72 and 74.

[2] Dr. H. Hoetink contributes a valuable study to this. *Het Patroon van de Oude Curaçaose Samenleving* (Assen, 1958).

[3] "Within the Creole group, the collective name used in Suriname for the coloured and Negroes, there have also been considerable changes since the end of the nineteenth century. The Creole middle class has shown a great deal of social mobility. The top level of the class has been reinforced by an increase in the number of Creole intellectuals, while at the same time

118

Moslems from India, Indonesians, Bush Negroes, Europeans, Chinese, Amerindians and other small groups. Outside the regularly occupied areas are some 37,000 Bush Negroes whose forebears took to the woods, and Amerindians. The colours of the national flag— black, brown, red, white and yellow—denote the main racial composition of the population. Two-thirds of the Creoles live in Paramaribo, the capital, which they dominate. By reason of the system of voting, which has operated in their favour, they have played a major part among the elected representatives. Creoles, Hindustani and Javanese have organized parties on racial lines, but there has not been the bitterness which has characterized politics in British Guiana. Dutch is the official language of the administration and is taught in the schools. Instruction is modelled on that of the Netherlands, where many Surinamers complete their studies.

The vicissitudes of war had resulted in the Caribbean territories being the only part of the tripartite Kingdom of the Netherlands to remain free from invasion throughout World War II. This had renewed their significance, though the Dutch Government had transferred its headquarters to London, and not to Batavia in 1940, or to Willemstad or Paramaribo in 1941. Communication considerations had ruled them out as the possible seat of the Dutch Government. The failure of the Netherlands to find a solution for the Indonesian problem, if indeed a solution was possible, had profound repercussions on the Netherlands Antilles and Surinam. In the first place, it increased their importance to a Netherlands which, even if it was becoming disillusioned and disappointed over the loss of its colonial empire, still believed that its prosperity was closely linked to the trade which it had conducted with its overseas territories. That a small well-organized country, though lacking large natural resources, might be highly prosperous without colonies had not yet been widely recognized, though the Netherlands and afterwards Belgium were soon to prove this.[1] The reaction in the Netherlands

a fairly large number of Negroes have entered the class. On the other hand, it has undergone a continuous drain of its strength because a large number of its members have left for the Netherlands and the Netherlands Antilles." R. A. J. van Lier, "Social and Political Conditions in Suriname and the Netherlands Antilles: Introduction", *Developments Towards Self-Government in the Caribbean* (The Hague, 1955), p. 127.

[1] "If we wish to characterize the financial and economic developments in the Netherlands during the year under report—July 1, 1959, to June 30, 1960—a 'record year' may simply be spoken of. In nearly all sectors

to the break with Indonesia was that the relationship with the remaining colonies must be placed on a more solid basis if it were to continue. With the belief in a written constitution reinforced by a long and distinguished legal tradition, immense pains were taken to draft an instrument which would govern future relationships between the three remaining parts of the Netherlands Kingdom. At the same time, the disaster in Indonesia had sharply emphasized the rise of nationalism, which was also exemplified by the establishment of Burma in 1948 as an independent country outside the British Commonwealth, and by the collapse of French rule in Indo-China. The constitutional situation which existed in the Netherlands Caribbean territories after World War II was increasingly unsatisfactory, though there were significant differences between the Netherlands Antilles and Surinam. In 1865, before universal suffrage had been introduced in the Netherlands, it had been decided that the Netherlands Antilles should have a colonial parliament composed of officials and members nominated by the Government. Though the Netherlands Legislative Assembly protested that this solution was inadequate taking into account the relatively high level of education of both the white and coloured population in these islands, the Netherlands Government's proposal was accepted. A strong argument for the measure was that, in a period when a property qualification was considered to be basic, only 200 persons out of 20,000 in Curaçao would have been entitled to vote. The official Dutch view was that nomination of members by a governor, which in practice meant conferring on him plenary control, would result in better government than that by an oligarchy of merchants and property owners. Moreover, with sea communication between Curaçao and the other Dutch islands slow and uncertain, elected representatives from these islands would have found it difficult to attend in Willemstad.[1] The British Colonial Office held almost identical views, which were the basis of the Crown Colony system of

of Dutch economic life, historic peak figures were reached. For both industrial production and Dutch exports attained new highs, while simultaneously the national income and prices on the stock exchange rose to record levels." *Hollandsche Bank-Unie N.V.*, *Annual Report 1959-1960* (Amsterdam, 1960), p. 39. The economic recovery of the Netherlands had been spectacular.

[1] Hans G. Hermans, "Constitutional Development of the Netherlands Antilles and Surinam", *The Caribbean, op. cit.*, p. 58.

government, essentially a system of nomination as opposed to election, with full control in the hands of a governor directly responsible to London.[1] With a measure of reason, the metropolitan powers feared that a small oligarchy might be less liberal than an administration controlled by a home-appointed governor. Both the British and Dutch Governments had failed to appreciate the need for gradual extension of the electorate in the colonies even if they were both adopting this method at home.

Though the 1865 regulations gave the Netherlands Antilles no measure of self-government, Surinam received a colonial assembly of 13 members, of whom 9 were elected by some 800 voters.[2] "In both colonies there ruled a governor appointed by the Crown. There was no executive body, but only an advisory council, also appointed by the Crown and usually consisting for a part of administrative officials."[3]

After World War I, criticism against this undemocratic form of government began to mount, as it did in the British territories, though protests were not yet strongly voiced.[4] In 1936 the Dutch Government had attempted to grant an extension of autonomy, but had in fact mainly increased the governor's powers, which were less closely directed from The Hague than previously. Thus, while the control of the Netherlands had been lessened, there had not been a corresponding liberalization in the political structure of the territory. Though a majority of seats in the colonial assembly were elective, political opinion evolved slowly.[5] Queen Wilhelmina had, during the war, given the promise that a partnership would be established between the Netherlands and its overseas territories. The complicated task of translating generalities into a precise document was undertaken against the background of the acute difficulties which had arisen in Indonesia. Though discussions with Surinam and the Netherlands

[1] *Vide* Chapter III, pp. 13-14.
[2] Hermans, *op. cit.*, p. 58.
[3] J. H. A. Logemann, "The Constitutional Status of the Netherlands Caribbean Territories", *Developments Towards Self-Government in the Caribbean, op. cit.*, p. 49.
[4] "In the twentieth century the tide began to turn against such autocratic systems of government. It goes without saying, of course, that the persons called upon to take part in the colonial governments had for long taken offence at their lack of independence in action and that voices had often been raised in protest." *Ibid.*, p. 49.
[5] Hermans, *op. cit.*, pp. 60-1.

Antilles had commenced in 1946, eight years elapsed before they were completed, an indication of both their complexity and the amount of care which had been bestowed on them. A temporary measure of self-government was given to Surinam and to the Netherlands Antilles in 1948. This was further revised for Surinam in 1949 and for the Netherlands Antilles in 1950.[1] Professor Logemann noted that "the clear change in the political climate was plainly reflected in the great impatience with which the people of Surinam and the Antilles awaited the granting of autonomy in internal affairs."[2]

In April 1952 a round table conference was held at The Hague to settle the juridical basis for the new commonwealth, with representatives from the Netherlands Antilles and Surinam. Doubtless with the Indonesian difficulties in mind, Prime Minister Willem Drees said in his opening address that the meeting was being held not to close a conflict but to open an epoch of intensive co-operation. Notwithstanding this, the conference nearly collapsed, since Surinam and the Netherlands Antilles complained that the Netherlands was offering inadequate guarantees for the self-determination of the area. They were also apprehensive that the Dutch wished to retain too much power to interfere in the Caribbean territories.[3]

Agreement was finally reached at a further conference in 1954 and signed by Queen Juliana and by the Prime Ministers of the three countries. The new Charter for the Kingdom of the Netherlands reflected the prolonged attempts of the negotiators to find a means of reconciling the rising nationalist sentiment in the Netherlands Antilles and Surinam with the desire of all parties not to sever the tie which united them. It was an ingenious series of compromises which seemed to be workable.

The Charter was an intricate and subtle document designed to combine the desire of Surinam and the Netherlands Antilles for the maximum of self-government and appearance of independence with their wish to remain part of the kingdom of the Netherlands. With

[1] "Two years later, in 1948, the Dutch drastically revised the colonial constitutional law (*staatsregeling*) granting universal suffrage to all men and women on the same basis as in the Netherlands. In Surinam and the Netherlands Antilles, the political parties which had campaigned for autonomy were not satisfied." *The Times British Colonies Review—Summer 1962*, p. 19.

[2] Logemann, *op. cit.*, pp. 50-1.

[3] *Manchester Guardian* diplomatic correspondent, June 3, 1952.

the recent severance of Indonesia from the Netherlands in the minds of all parties, the wish that this failure should not be repeated was probably the major factor in preventing the negotiations from breaking down during these years of complex discussion. Close integration on the lines adopted by France was unacceptable, since the establishment of Surinam and the Netherlands Antilles as Dutch provinces would have involved too much metropolitan control.[1] The practical difficulties of such a solution were soon to be exemplified in the French Caribbean departments.[2] Wisely it was decided to reduce Kingdom matters to the minimum. They alone were to be the subject of discussion and decision by all three members of the Tripartite Kingdom of the Netherlands. Contributing to this decision was the distance from the Netherlands of its two partners, more than 4000 miles away, and the difference in population between the Netherlands with 10 million persons and of Surinam and the Netherlands Antilles with less than half a million between them.

The vital part of the solution was the setting up of a Council of Ministers composed of the Netherlands Ministers together with the two Ministers Plenipotentiary appointed one by the Surinam and the other by the Netherlands Antilles Governments.[3] In practice, it meant that whenever matters affecting Surinam or the Antilles came before the Dutch Cabinet, the respective Minister Plenipotentiary had the right to participate on an equal footing with the Netherlands Ministers.[4]

[1] "Naturellement, l'idée se présenta immédiatement de faire de Surinam et des Antilles Néerlandaises les douzième et treizième provinces des Pays-Bas, s'ajoutant aux onze provinces déjà existantes. Toutefois, cette idée fut aussitôt écartée, car la structure des provinces néerlandaises, provenant d'un processus d'évolution historique, n'aurait pu parfaitement convenir à Surinam et aux Antilles Néerlandaises. Quel que soit le domaine de l'administration que l'on envisage, il n'est pour ainsi dire pas de réglementation en vigueur dans les provinces, qui soit également applicable à Surinam et aux Antilles. Tout bien pesé, il n'existe pas de points de concordance entre ces territoires et les provinces néerlandaises, tandis que les divergences sont très importantes." W. H. van Helsdingen, "La Charte du Royaume des Pays-Bas", *Revue juridique et politique de l'Union Française*, (Paris, 1956), p. 649.

[2] *Vide* Chapters X and XI *passim*.

[3] Charter for the Kingdom of the Netherlands, 1954, Article 7.

[4] Surinam and the Netherlands Antilles were also entitled to representation in the Council of State, a permanent advisory body, presided over by the monarch, which is consulted on new legislation and on administrative problems.

Certain matters, including foreign affairs, defence, citizenship with naturalization, and the Amendment of the Constitution, so far as they affected Surinam and the Netherlands Antilles, were specified as being essentially Kingdom matters.[1] The Governments of Surinam and the Netherlands Antilles had the right to act in matters other than those mentioned as being Kingdom affairs. Moreover, before any final vote was taken by the States General, on any proposal for a Kingdom statute, the Minister Plenipotentiary, if he expressed his opposition, could request the Chamber to postpone discussion until the following meeting. Provision was made for Surinam and the Netherlands Antilles to apply for membership in international organizations.[2]

The Charter stated that the Netherlands, Surinam and the Netherlands Antilles were to conduct their affairs autonomously, while the interests of the Kingdom were of common concern.[3] The State constitutions of Surinam and the Netherlands Antilles were set up within the Kingdom of the Netherlands.[4] Major amendments, including articles relating to human rights and freedoms, the powers of the governor and the administration of justice, had to be submitted to the Kingdom Government,[5] a clear, if subtle, indication of the limits of autonomy in Surinam and the Netherlands Antilles.

To compare their status vis-à-vis the Netherlands with that of Canada or in a Caribbean context with that of Jamaica or Trinidad in relation to Great Britain, would be misleading. It was clear that since they did not handle their own foreign affairs, armed forces or citizenship, they had not achieved full independence. Yet in practice they had gained much. At all points they had to be consulted and on occasion might even delay Kingdom legislation even if they could not prevent it. The cost of organizing a foreign service would have been very heavy on such small countries. In practice, the Netherlands attached a representative of Surinam or the Netherlands Antilles to missions where this seemed to be appropriate. Surinam and the Netherlands Antilles enjoyed the benefit of Netherlands defence, a factor of possible importance for territories more vulnerable from the sea than from the land.[6]

[1] Charter for the Kingdom of the Netherlands, 1954, Article 11, paragraphs 1-5.
[2] *Ibid.*, Article 28. [3] *Ibid.*, Article 41. [4] *Ibid.*, Article 42. [5] *Ibid.*, Article 44.
[6] Most of Surinam's land frontiers received natural protection from the exceptionally rough and difficult nature of the terrain.

Surinam and the Netherlands Antilles had achieved a position of far greater influence in Dutch affairs than had Puerto Rico with its single observer at Washington. The Netherlands, Surinam and the Netherlands Antilles were each declared to be kingdoms in their own right, with the stipulation that the sovereign of the Netherlands was sovereign of all three parts. In this, there was an approach to the status of a British dominion in its relation to Great Britain through the sovereign.

The Kingdom of the Netherlands, however, had much closer bonds than the British "Commonwealth Club", from which unilateral resignation was permissible, as the Union of South Africa was later to show. The *Netherlands News* commented that the new statute represented the result of several years of patient and sometimes difficult negotiations.[1] The result was an ingenious compromise which eliminated some of the criticism of colonialism and yet retained for the overseas territories links with the Netherlands which provided them with a foreign service and security forces, beyond their reach as small individual units. It had avoided the fragmentation of sovereignty which was to become a feature of the British Caribbean.

In both the Netherlands Antilles and Surinam, power was vested in a single chamber legislature.[2] Each received a cabinet system of government with a Premier and Ministers responsible to Parliament. Though political parties did not develop on the lines of the Netherlands, the influence of the Netherlands system of election, with party lists, led to a number of parties being established. This supported the conclusion of Sir Robert Ensor, who considered that the Dutch system of proportional representation, copied by other countries, had led to the proliferation of parties.[3]

[1] *Netherlands News* (Netherlands Embassy, London), July 21, 1954.
[2] The Netherlands Antilles Parliament consisted of 22 members (12 from Curaçao, 8 from Aruba, 1 from Bonaire and 1 from the Windward Islands). Surinam elected 21 members, of whom 10 were returned by Paramaribo.
[3] "In 1918, while the first war was still in progress, Holland, which under second ballot suffered from the usual multiplicity of parties and had seen the Belgian system working well next door, decided to instal proportional representation. She copied the two existing models, but with, as was supposed, an improvement. Regarding it as unjust that any votes should seem wasted, the theorists devised a plan whereby the votes left over in each constituency were collected into a 'national pool', from which by again applying proportional representation further members were returned to the parliament. This plan was adopted, its sponsors not appreciating that the feature which it removed from the Belgo-Swedish system was really the

In Surinam, the varied population had, perhaps inevitably, stimulated the growth of politics along racial lines. However, a strong spirit of compromise existed, which thus avoided the asperities that were to appear in British Guiana.[1]

Following on the establishment of the Kingdom of the Netherlands under its new Charter, Queen Juliana, accompanied by Prince Bernhard, made an official visit to the Netherlands Antilles and Surinam. The purpose was to seal the bond between the three parts. In the course of her tour, the Queen said at Willemstad, "We are attending a symbolical manifestation of your independence, which at the same time means a fully autonomous and equal partnership with Surinam and the Netherlands."[2] At Paramaribo, she declared, "You are part of the Kingdom of the Netherlands, which must henceforth be fully aware of the fact that it consists of three independent, equal, associated parts."[3] Though success had eluded the efforts of the Netherlands Government in Indonesia, and had led to the severance of all political ties, the handling of the Netherlands West Indies problems had been very successful, and had been concluded in a much more friendly atmosphere.[4] The visit of Queen Juliana to the Caribbean was the first occasion when a Netherlands sovereign had visited a Netherlands territory; it had been well-timed. As had been

---

keystone. For the creation of a 'national pool' took away all incentive to keep the number of parties small. Indeed, it went to the other extreme and opened the door wide to 'splinter' parties." *The New Cambridge Modern History* (Cambridge, 1960), Vol. XII, p. 79.

[1] At the General Election of June 25, 1958, the opposition parties, ten in number, gained an overwhelming victory, winning 19 out of 21 seats. All parties which had supported the former government, except the Indonesian Farmers' Party, were wiped out. The National Party, with 10 seats, was the largest group. Severinus D. Emanuels became Premier of a coalition government.

[2] At a special meeting of the Legislative Council of the Netherlands Antilles, October 18, 1955.

[3] At a special meeting of the Legislative Council of Surinam, October 28, 1955.

[4] Robert M. Hallet, "Queen Juliana's Visit Cements Caribbean Ties", *The Christian Science Monitor*, November 2, 1955.

At a royal reception at Nickerie near the frontier with British Guiana, on November 4, 1955, the Queen received Sir Patrick Renison, Governor of British Guiana, who read a message from Queen Elizabeth II affirming the long-standing friendship which existed between the British and Dutch peoples throughout the world.

demonstrated in the British Commonwealth, the rôle of the sovereign could be of major importance as a bond between the different parts. Immense care and patience had been devoted to the constitutional agreements between the Netherlands, Surinam and the Netherlands Antilles. Though the interpretation of the 1954 agreement was further discussed at a round table conference at The Hague in June 1961, when problems of foreign policy were considered, Dr. Severinus D. Emanuels, Premier of Surinam, made it clear that his country wished to retain its association with the Netherlands and to recognise Queen Juliana as head of the Surinam State, although Surinam sought greater control over its own foreign policy. The prolonged consideration given by the three partners to the problem of their future constitutional relations appeared to have met with success.[1] Links of a very special character appeared to join these countries together, just as canals and bridges were a feature of Dutch life.[2] The Netherlands and its partners in the Tripartite Kingdom had made an original contribution to finding a solution to the problems of colonialism.

[1] "Part of the members of the Surinam delegation to the Round Table Conference that was held in Holland have returned home. Judging from the interviews which some of them had with reporters of the local press and radio broadcasting companies, it is evident that the Surinam delegation considers that the conference was a success." *Surinam News in Brief*, Government Information Office, Paramaribo, June 26, 1961.

[2] "Delegates from the Netherlands Antilles have intrigued listeners here with their calm account of the autonomy which the Dutch isles have enjoyed since 1954. . . . Without fanfare, and almost without any of the heroic adjectives that coat Puerto Rico's 'bold and unique' Commonwealth status, it seems the Dutch-tutored inhabitants of Curaçao and its sister islands enjoy a degree of autonomy that many an impatient Muñoz-follower frets for.

"Both the Dutch isles and Puerto Rico have a similar control over their internal affairs, but the Dutch subjects have a far stronger say in their foreign affairs than has Puerto Rico." Harold J. Lidin, "Political Patterns", *San Juan Star*, September 8, 1961,

CHAPTER XIII

THE POST-WAR NETHERLANDS
ECONOMIC POLICY IN THE CARIBBEAN

On the whole, World War II had proved to be a period of prosperity for the Netherlands West Indies. Though far removed from the major theatres of war, the great refineries at Curaçao and Aruba had played a very important part in the supply of oil products to the Allies, who were often in desperate straits due to the virtual closing of the Mediterranean and in consequence the normal supply routes from the Middle East.[1] Not only did they provide employment for about half of the population of Curaçao and Aruba, but they drew labour from other parts of the Caribbean and Surinam, attracted by the high wage scale. The transformation of the two arid islands was amazing. The necessity to import substantial quantities of water emphasized this,[2] though local supplies were also supplemented by distillation from salt water.[3]

The commencement of Curaçao's success had stemmed from the trading skill of the Dutch, who had used to full advantage the fine harbour at Annabay. The Shell Oil Company, Anglo-Dutch controlled, had shown the value of Dutch enterprise in Curaçao in 1917.[4] Its example may have been a determining factor in the decision of the Standard Oil Company of New Jersey to use Aruba as

[1] Robert K. Shellaby quotes Governor P. A. Kasteel of the Netherlands Antilles as saying, "As indispensable a link as there was to the United Nations' chain of victory, the refineries emitted more than half the oil necessary for the war effort." "Dutch Speed Twin Goals in West Indies", *The Christian Science Monitor*, May 20, 1947.

[2] As an example, the Norwegian tanker *Ora* left Belfast on March 8, 1949, carrying three million gallons of Irish water for Curaçao, which was suffering from a drought. The tanker returned with oil, whose film was steamed off before the tanks were filled with water. The call in the future would be a regular one. Water was also shipped for Aruba from Kingston and New York by tankers of the Standard Oil Company.

[3] The award was announced on February 15, 1956, of a £1·25 million contract to a Glasgow firm for the construction in Aruba of a sea water evaporating plant to distil 1,792,000 gallons of fresh water per day.

[4] *Vide* Chapter V, p. 29.

128

the site for a refinery, controlled by a subsidiary, the Lago Oil Company. These were tributes by both an international and an American company to the integrity, efficiency and solidity of Dutch colonial administration. By its policy towards the Antilles, the Netherlands had made an immense contribution to improving the lot of an area scantily supplied with natural resources. After the Charter of the Netherlands had come into force, Dutch influence continued. Though the judicial system was now largely separated from that of the Netherlands, Dutch legal principles and traditions remained, which were an encouragement to both Dutch and foreign investors. Moreover, the Netherlands, which had made a remarkable recovery after its disaster in Indonesia and had become one of the most prosperous countries in post-war Europe, was able to supply at least a substantial part of the finance needed by the Antilles.[1]

Notwithstanding an area almost five times as large as the Netherlands, and 140 times as large as the Netherlands Antilles, Surinam's plantation system of agriculture had progressively decreased since the abolition of slavery in 1863. The importation of Hindustani and Indonesian labourers on contract had not proved an effective substitute. The plantation produce of Surinam was competing against the new East Indian estates which were being developed with cheaper labour. Moreover, the opening of the Suez Canal in 1869 had resulted in a large increase in shipping between Europe and the East Indies, which placed Surinam at an increasing disadvantage in regard to freight rates. In consequence, many plantations were gradually abandoned. During the twentieth century there was a continuing change over to small peasant holdings.[2] From a technical point of view, less-efficient agriculture resulted, unfortunately

[1] In January 1961 it was announced that the Netherlands Government had agreed to guarantee a loan of $33,375,000 for development work in Curaçao and Aruba. Curaçao proposed to improve its harbour, which already ranked seventh in the world in annual tonnage handled.

[2] "Suriname was traditionally a country of plantations, and continued to be so till the beginning of the twentieth century, when the plantations had to make way for small-scale agriculture. The progressive deterioration of the plantation system caused the white estate owners and their managers to leave in great numbers. Only those slave owners who were Jewish and whose families had been in Suriname since the beginning of American settlement remained. They no longer functioned as planters, however, but became traders. The white upper class was henceforth to consist of officials sent out from the Netherlands and a few members of the Jewish group." Van Lier, op. cit., p. 126.

emphasized by the revolution in tropical agriculture which took place in the post-World War II period. The small size of many of the holdings contained the seeds of future difficulties.[1]

On the other hand, the small farmer by his acquisition of land, which was more readily available and easier to cultivate than in the overcrowded Antilles, had a stake in his country which the plantation labourer could never have. The peasant farmer could also grow a substantial part of his own food. From this angle, the considerable area of level land in Surinam proved to be of real advantage. Gold mining, begun in 1876, had proved disappointing, as it had in the neighbouring territories of French Guiana and British Guiana.[2]

By far the most successful industry in modern times was bauxite mining[3], the production of which had risen from under 400,000 tons in 1938 to over 1,000,000 tons in 1941 and to over 2,000,000 in 1950. With little overburden to be removed and with a high grade of ore, there was the additional advantage that the workings were near enough a suitable river to be loaded directly on to ocean-going vessels. Reserves were ample.[4] Mining was carried on by two large concerns.[5] By 1950 bauxite accounted for 80 per cent. of the exports of Surinam.[6] Some 3000 workers were employed in this industry.

Though much smaller and less spectacular than the mining of bauxite, the timber industry was also growing in importance. New timber factories were opened on the Surinam river just outside Paramaribo by the Bruynzeel Company to process hardwood for

[1] "The extremely small size of the holdings necessitates methods of production which result in very low returns. To this can be added that the per capita quantity of capital goods (agricultural machinery, cattle, etc.) available in agricultural production is exceedingly low. All in all the new pattern of agricultural production, which grew at the cost of plantation farming, accounts for the very low income per capita in the agricultural sector. Owing to the preponderance of this sector in the economy (population) the national income per capita too becomes meagre." R. M. N. Panday, *Agriculture in Surinam 1650-1950* (Amsterdam, 1959), p. 218.

[2] *Vide* Chapters XI, p. 113 and XIV, pp. 150-151. Surinam produced just over 4950 ounces of gold in 1960.

[3] Begun in 1922.

[4] Estimated to be 50 million tons in 1952.

[5] The Surinam Bauxite Company, a subsidiary of the American Alcoa Mining Company, and the Billiton Mining Company, a Netherlands enterprise.

[6] As in the case of Jamaica, the rapid development of bauxite had transformed the economy of the territory. *Vide* Chapter IX, p. 90.

shipbuilding purposes, civil engineering structures, wagon construction and the Netherlands railways.[1] To the Netherlands this development was attractive since it could pay in Surinam guilders without drawing on its exiguous supply of hard currency, just as Great Britain through the medium of the Colonial Development Corporation was also encouraging new enterprises which were designed to save dollars.

However, with a rapidly rising population, none of these projects seemed likely to solve the economic problems of the country. The Surinam Government received in 1951 a report from the Surinam Planning Bureau which set forth a list of developments to be included in a Ten Years' Program which was under consideration for the development of the country. The report in turn was submitted to the International Bank for Reconstruction and Development, which was invited by the Governments of the Netherlands and of Surinam to make an economic survey of Surinam.[2]

In October 1951 the Bank sent a mission to Surinam and its report was published the following year.[3] On the whole, its guarded comments on Surinam's administration were favourable, which suggested that the policy of the Netherlands towards this territory had been enlightened. In a period when freedom of exchange had not yet been attained, it expressed the desirability of avoiding Government controls as much as possible.[4] It also commended the operation of the Surinamsche Bank, which, besides being the largest commercial bank in the country, also carried out the functions of a central bank.[5] The Mission, however, sharply criticized the governmental control of

[1] Paramaribo is the centre of the saw-milling industry. It has some 16 mills while there are small mills at Nickerie and in other districts.

The modern installation of the Bruynzeel Company, which has an experimental laboratory in the Netherlands, has been instrumental in important recent developments in the production of plywood. Prospects are considered good for an expansion of this industry. *Surinam, Recommendations for a Ten Year Development Program. Report of a Mission organized by the International Bank for Reconstruction and Development at the request of the Governments of the Netherlands and of Surinam* (Baltimore, Maryland, 1952), pp. 167-8, 179 and 196.

[2] The Charter of the Kingdom of the Netherlands was not signed until 1954 so that the Netherlands Government was entitled to take part in these matters.

[3] *Surinam, Recommendations for a Ten Year Development Program, op. cit.*

[4] *Ibid.*, p. 90.

[5] *Ibid.*, p. 92. In 1956 the Centrale Bank van Suriname was established as the bank of issue for the country, with the sole right to issue banknotes.

131

foreign capital entering the country, which was permitted only if the Government was satisfied that the proposed venture was likely to succeed.[1]

In the Ten Year Development Program which it advocated, the International Bank, though not going into detail, expressed the view that the bauxite industry in Surinam could be expanded for the production of aluminium. Since Surinam at that time was the largest producer of bauxite, the possibilities of so doing were considerable, provided that a suitable supply of electricity was available.[2] The best site appeared to be at Brokopondo, where a dam could be placed across the Surinam river.

The feasibility of the scheme would turn on a long-term contract between the Surinam Government, which would promote the electrical development, and a consumer of electricity. In due course, agreement was reached between the Surinam Government and the Aluminum Company of America whereby its subsidiary company "Suralco" agreed to construct a hydro-electric plant at Affobakka on the Surinam river.[3] It would also erect an alumina plant and an aluminium smelter with a capacity of 40,000 tons of aluminium annually. The site of the dam, about 70 miles from Paramaribo, necessitated the creation of a lake of 600 square miles, approximately the size of the Dutch province of Utrecht.

This very large project was mainly a United States enterprise, though the hydro-electric installation would revert to the Surinam

[1] "Due to the fact that, in the past, private business ventures have often proved unsuccessful, Surinam has unfortunately acquired a bad reputation in investment circles. In an attempt to avoid any repetition of these failures, the Government permits foreign capital to enter the country only if satisfied that the proposed private undertaking has a reasonable prospect of success. The Mission believes, however, that it is neither appropriate nor desirable for the Government to pass judgment on whether a proposed private industrial endeavor is likely to prove profitable; nor is the Government well equipped to perform any such function. While we agree that foreign capital wishing to enter Surinam should be registered, that the prospects of new foreign enterprises should be carefully studied, and that an opinion on such prospects should be given to the investors by the Government, we strongly recommend that the intervention of the Government should go no further." *Ibid.*, p. 95.

[2] To manufacture one pound of aluminium from alumina requires approximately ten kw-hours of electric energy.

[3] The estimated cost was about $60 million. The production of electricity would be one billion kw-hours annually, which was 50 times the existing consumption in Paramaribo.

Government after 75 years.[1] It was another example of the increasing financial interest of the United States and might be compared with the American investments in bauxite in Jamaica and British Guiana.[2] Transport and agricultural projects were receiving financial support from the Prosperity Fund which the Netherlands Government had set up.[3] As a result of the genius of the Dutch in developing inland waterways, the navigable rivers had been put to good use. Bauxite was loaded at Moengo and Paranam for direct shipment to Trinidad[4] and United States ports. Food for Paramaribo and stone, gravel and sand for construction and road building were moved normally by water. There was also coastal traffic from Nickerie and Coronie to the capital. Timber was floated or brought on rafts from the forests of the interior to Paramaribo. Among the projects advocated by the report of the International Bank was the widening and deepening of the Saramacca Canal, the cost of which would be partially financed from the Netherlands Prosperity Fund.[5] Other plans involving Netherlands assistance were also put forward.

* * * *

Though the Netherlands Antilles were more prosperous than most

[1] The Surinam Government was responsible for providing the necessary land for the Brokopondo development, along with access roads, and for removing the population and buildings in the reservoir areas.

When the author visited the project in April 1962, some 2000 persons were employed, accommodated in a large temporary camp. He was informed that Suralco would use 95 per cent. of the power generated.

In May 1962 Suralco announced that the Brokopondo dam at Affobakka would be completed in March 1964, six months ahead of schedule.

[2] An interesting sidelight was the use of 60-cycle electrical equipment, standard in the United States, compared to the existing 50-cycle equipment in Paramaribo, which would have to change over to the American standard when it received electrical power from the Brokopondo installation.

It was another example of the competition in the Caribbean, as in Latin America, between European-controlled electric installation, which usually preferred 50-cycle equipment, and American-financed projects, where 60-cycle was normal. This of course affected all equipment which would be installed in the supply area.

[3] A grant of 40 million Netherlands guilders was allocated to this fund, payable in annual instalments of 8 million guilders during the years 1947 to 1951.

[4] At Port-of-Spain the bauxite ore was transhipped.

[5] This project was designed not only to improve inland transport on a vital waterway linking Paramaribo with Uitkijk; it would also improve the drainage of an important area near the capital. It was a good example of Dutch skill in hydraulic engineering.

133

other Caribbean territories, Curaçao and Aruba were aware that their economies rested on a vulnerable foundation, since all of the oil on which their great refineries depended had to be imported. With Venezuela, the principal source of supply,[1] experiencing a period of political difficulties combined with rising nationalism, far-sighted diplomacy was required. The existence of a tradition of smuggling from Curaçao to Venezuela did not improve relations.

Jamaica and some of the smaller British islands, as well as Puerto Rico, and Cuba in the pre-Castro days, presented an example to the Caribbean of the great possibilities of the tourist trade. With their experience in handling ships, Curaçao and Aruba were well equipped to handle cruise traffic. The very low import duties made Willemstad and Oranjestad almost "free ports", and thus attractive shopping centres. However, as more and more people travelled by air, it became necessary to cater also for these potential tourists. This involved heavy capital expenditure on building hotels, an enterprise which was successfully carried out. With considerable imagination and good taste, the historical buildings and fortifications at Curaçao were made centres of attraction for visitors. Here, too, the influence of the Netherlands could be detected. Lacking the historical attractions of Curaçao, Aruba concentrated on diversifying its industry, though it also developed its tourist trade.

Curaçao and Aruba were also improving their harbour facilities and endeavouring to attract industry to offset the reduction in employment, very noticeable in Curaçao, which had resulted from a slackening in the oil refining industry and the efforts made to economize in the use of labour through automation.[2] In Aruba, the policy of industrialization was already bearing fruit.[3]

---

[1] Curaçao imported Middle East oil to blend with the Venezuelan oil.
[2] "In 1958, the Shell plant here had a payroll of 9376 and the Lago plant one of 5529. At the end of last year the Shell payroll had shrunk to 6561 and Lago's to 3954. Most of those cut off the payroll were heads of families. There was no significant drop in production in the two plants in the period of increasing layoffs. A matter of great concern is that as automation techniques increase the payrolls will dwindle still more. . . .
"The unemployment problem is of still more concern because the population increase is slightly over three per cent. a year and about 65 per cent. of the present population is 16 years old and under. . . .
"The principal difficulty here and in Aruba is that, although the Government had industrial development plans for the principal islands, the automation advances in cracking crude oil developed still faster than the so-called

The expansion of social services, including the establishment of old-age pensions and the improvement of the formerly inadequate water supplies with the installation of costly distillation plants, was significant. With the resulting improvement in health conditions including the elimination of malaria, the population expanded in all territories. Yet the very success of this far-sighted policy, initiated by the Netherlands Government and continued by the Netherlands Antilles, raised problems of employment which might one day become acute, even though there was still a cushion of foreign labour in the oil refineries, part of which was sent home in 1960 when the industry became less prosperous.

The entry of the Netherlands into the European Common Market had initially resulted in a struggle with France over the free entry of oil products from the Netherlands Antilles. The result appeared to be favourable to the Dutch. The value of the quota which the Netherlands Antilles received might turn on whether or not Great Britain, with somewhat similar claims for preferential treatment for Commonwealth oil, entered the organization.

*   *   *   *

The Netherlands Caribbean countries faced problems enough, but the outlook seemed somewhat better than in the British or French territories. Certainly Curaçao and Aruba might be paralysed if their oil supply from Venezuela were to be cut off. Yet in the second half of the twentieth century ever fewer countries were able to survive without international trade. The Suez crisis had demonstrated the vulnerability of even the leading nations of Western Europe to any interruption in their oil supplies.

Surinam, which had avoided an economy of large plantations, had developed a multi-racial society with a substantial proportion of

---

Ten-Year Program. The Government had already begun to harbor improvement, electricity and water distillation plans for which 225,000,000 guilders ($121,500,000) had been apportioned. . . .

"There has been a squeeze between a rising population and a shrinking tax base. . . ." Paul P. Kennedy, "Automation Cuts Payrolls in Curaçao and Threatens the Economy", The New York Times, October 8, 1962.

³ In June 1962 construction began at Barcadera in Aruba on the $20 million ammonia fertilizer plants to be operated by the Antilles Chemical Company and Aruba Chemical Industries, both associated with Standard Oil of New Jersey.

peasant farmers, who might prove a stabilizing factor. The Broko-pondo scheme opened up the possibility of a well-planned industrial development which for the first time harnessed on a significant scale water power, available but largely undeveloped in all three Guianas.

In education and social services, the Netherlands policy was being continued by the autonomous governments at Willemstad and Paramaribo. The cultural influence of the Netherlands remained very strong, despite the marked American influence in Aruba, and the use of Papiamento as the unofficial but most-spoken language in its Leeward Islands,[1] and that of English in its Windward Islands.

With the wise decision not to seek full independence, which could have proved costly and might have reduced the substantial advantages which they continued to receive from the Netherlands, Surinam and the Netherlands Antilles seemed settled in an interesting experiment as junior but active partners in a firm of great political and commercial traditions with reasonable prospects of successful advance. The Netherlands, relieved of its problems, first in Indonesia and then in West New Guinea, was well placed to devote a portion of its surplus capital arising from its expanding home economy to investment in the Caribbean countries of the Tripartite Kingdom.

At the same time, the Netherlands Antilles and Surinam were becoming more Caribbean-minded.[2] They were directly represented in the Caribbean Organization in Puerto Rico, which had replaced the former Caribbean Commission in Trinidad. Though strong commercial links remained with the Netherlands, yet cultural links were perhaps even stronger, since the educational system was closely linked to that of the Netherlands, combined with the use of Dutch as the official language in all territories, even if in the Netherlands Antilles Papiamento flourished and might increase.

Like the British, the Dutch had delayed too long the extension of self-government in their Caribbean territories. Yet, at the end, the setting up of the Tripartite Kingdom was a considerable piece of juridical draughtsmanship. Even if it appeared to grant independence with one hand and yet withhold with the other, the constitution seemed to be acceptable to all parties and to be workable. While no

[1] Papiamento is a mixture of Dutch, Spanish, Portuguese and English with some African words.
[2] Joanna Felhoen Kraal, "Principles of Administration in the Netherlands West Indies". *Principles and Methods of Colonial Administration, op. cit.*, p. 74.

exact parallel could be found to this constitutional association, there were plenty of precedents in the British Commonwealth for unlikely solutions continuing to function smoothly.

The Netherlands Antilles and Surinam were also becoming steadily more concerned with international trade. The expanding Surinam bauxite industry depended largely on United States enterprise, as did the oil refining industry in Aruba, while the administration of the refinery industry in Curaçao had been transferred from the Netherlands to London. Venezuela remained the basic source of supply for the industry of the two islands, supplemented in the case of Curaçao by small quantities of other oil for purposes of blending. Strong commercial ties, however, remained with the Netherlands, reinforced by cultural links.

Chapter XIV

BRITISH GUIANA

Though normally regarded as one of the British Caribbean colonies, British Guiana requires separate consideration. A part of the continent of South America, it is nearly twice the size of Cuba (the largest island in the Antilles) but has only about one-tenth of Cuba's population.[1] It is more than 20 times the size of Jamaica, the largest of the British islands, with only one-third of Jamaica's population. Historically, it was developed by the Dutch.

The originally Dutch trading posts of Essequibo, Demerara and Berbice had been occupied in the seventeenth century and considerably expanded in the middle of the eighteenth century, when settlers including some from Barbados established plantations. It was a period of rapid development of the sugar industry, concentrated on the strip of swampy sea-coast which fringed the territories. The Dutch, many of whom came from Zeeland, were able to make use of their traditional skill in the construction of polders.[2] Meanwhile the population increased sharply with the importation of African slaves, some of whom were brought from the Dutch and British Antilles.

In contrast to Surinam, which was at first a British colony but was later ceded to the Netherlands,[3] these colonies were to become British. Discouraged by Admiral Rodney's capture and destruction of St. Eustatius,[4] and alarmed at the presence of six British privateers which had captured 15 Dutch merchantmen in the Demerara river, the Dutch colonies of Essequibo and Demerara capitulated on generous terms to a demand from the Governor of Barbados in 1781. They were, however, captured by the French the following year and recovered by the Netherlands at the Treaty of Paris in 1783.

---

[1] In area British Guiana is 83,000 square miles, and its estimated population in 1960 was 575,270.

[2] A piece of low-lying land reclaimed from a sea or river and protected by dikes.

[3] In exchange for an area comprising the present city and part of the State of New York, under the Treaty of Breda in 1667.

[4] *Vide* Chapter II, p. 6.

Reoccupied by a British expeditionary force from Barbados in 1796, they remained in British possession, apart from the brief interlude following the Peace of Amiens (1801-1803), when they were returned to the Netherlands.

The Dutch colonies had been at first administered mainly by the Dutch West India Company through a Council of Policy and Justice which dated from the end of the seventeenth century. The system of company control was modified in 1743 by the creation of a College of Kiezers (electors) who were militia officers and, as such, representatives of the planters for whom militia service was obligatory. The College of Kiezers had the duty of nominating representatives to the Council. Thus the planters had secured some measure of representation.[1] After an unfavourable report on the administration of the West India Company in 1792, the United Colony of Demerara and Essequibo was established under the States-General of the Netherlands.[2] Berbice was a separate colony.

"By the terms of the capitulation of 1803, the rights and privileges of the people were guaranteed, and the result was that the former Dutch constitution (and Roman-Dutch law) long continued to exist, with little change, under the British flag.[3]" The legislature was unusual. It consisted of two bodies, one of which was a Court of Policy of four official members, and of four unofficial members chosen by the Kiezers, who were elected representatives of the planters. The other was a Combined Court, composed of the Court of Policy with six representatives added by the Kiezers. The Combined Court controlled taxation and finance, much as did the Houses of Assembly under the old British colonial system.[4] In-fluenced by its difficulties with the colonial legislatures during the eighteenth century, Great Britain may have been the more ready to try out a different system. In any case, the Dutch system was continued after the final cession of Demerara, Essequibo and Berbice by the Netherlands to Great Britain in the Treaty of London in 1814. The ceded territories became the colony of British Guiana in 1831 with Georgetown (formerly Stabroek) as the capital.

[1] There had for long been conflict over the revenue which was supplied by the Company ("the company chest") and that levied on the settlers ("the colony chest"). As in other colonial conflicts, the colonists demanded control of the taxes which they paid.

[2] Raymond T. Smith, *British Guiana* (London, 1962), p. 24.

[3] Burns, *op. cit.*, p. 608.

[4] *Vide* Chapter III, p. 12.

During the nineteenth century, British policy towards British Guiana was similar to that which it followed in its Caribbean islands. The abolition of the slave trade was followed by the emancipation of the slaves after a period of apprenticeship.[1] The fear that large numbers of Negroes would move into the bush, as happened under slavery in Surinam and at an earlier date in Brazil, was unfounded.[2] However, with land more readily available than in the Antilles, Negro villages grew up, often by the purchase of abandoned estates.[3] This ultimately created a labour shortage, which was met by the introduction of indentured labourers from India, who lived on the plantations during the period of their service in conditions little different from those of the slaves whom they had replaced.[4] Many of the freed slaves continued to take seasonal work during the cane harvest. Without this co-operation, despite the large-scale introduction of East Indian labour, the cane crop could not have been harvested. The goodwill and assistance of Great Britain in arranging for this supply of labour had been vital to the continuance of the plantation economy, which in French Guiana had collapsed.[5] Great Britain was pursuing the same policy as it was in Trinidad, and also in Mauritius.

Major constitutional changes were introduced in 1891 when the franchise, which had been slightly widened in 1850, was still further extended. The College of Kiezers was abolished, and election to the Court of Policy became direct. Since the Negro population was increasing, and the white population diminishing as a result of a period of adversity for the sugar industry, the balance of power in the Court of Policy changed, despite a franchise that was still relatively narrow. The rising influence of the middle-class negroes accentuated the differences between the Court of Policy which voted taxation, and the Executive Council which the Governor controlled. With the colony hard hit by further depression in the sugar industry after

---

[1] Emancipation took place in the British colonies in 1834; in the French colonies in 1848; in the Netherlands colonies in 1863; and in Brazil in 1888.
[2] For Surinam, cf. James Rodway, *Guiana: British, Dutch, and French* (London, 1912), pp. 77-9. For Brazil, cf. Herring, *op. cit.*, p. 113.
[3] Smith, *op. cit.*, pp. 39-40.
[4] The period of indenture, at first limited by Order in Council to three years, was revised in 1837 to five years. The British Government overruled the British Guiana Court of Policy, which had provided for a seven-year indenture period. Smith, *op. cit.*, p. 43.
[5] *Vide* Chapter IV, pp. 23 and 113.

World War I, the Secretary of State for the Colonies appointed a commission to investigate the causes. It produced a critical report,[1] stressing the weakness of a government which did not have control of finance. The report called for fundamental changes in the Constitution.

The elected members, "solid middle-class Guianese", claimed a greater share in running their country.[2] This, however, was disregarded. A new constitution was forced through in 1928 in which the Court of Policy was abolished in favour of a legislative council comprising the Governor, Colonial Secretary, Attorney General, 8 nominated officials, 5 nominated unofficial members, and 14 elected members. In addition to having a government majority in the legislative council, the Governor was also given powers to override it. An executive council of 12 was set up, composed of officials, 3 nominated unofficial members, and 2 of the elected members of the legislative council, who were also nominated by the Governor. Apart from extending the franchise to women, the highly restrictive voting qualifications were retained.

The effect was to increase the influence of the British-controlled sugar industry and commercial enterprises, which received representation on the executive council, while the power of the Guianese middle class, which had been exercised through the restraining influence of the veto in the former Combined Court under the old constitution, was weakened.

The dual system of a Court of Policy and a Combined Court which the British had taken over from the Dutch had certainly proved difficult to apply.[3] To destroy it, however, was short-sighted, since the declared objective was to prepare the colony for eventual self-government modelled on the British parliamentary system. Bermuda, probably the most successful British colony in the Western Hemisphere, was to prove that, notwithstanding the similar duality which existed in its Constitution, government could function successfully. It is curious that the British Parliament, which had widely extended

[1] *Report of the British Guiana Commission, April 1927*, Cmd. 2841.
[2] Smith, *op. cit.*, p. 55.
[3] "The fundamental weakness in the Dutch system of administration was the separation of powers; the official majority in the Court of Policy was responsible for governing while the unofficial majority in the Combined Court controlled the purse. This same weakness was the main defect also in the British islands with Houses of Assembly." Parry and Sherlock, *op. cit.*, p. 208.

the British franchise in 1918 and had given votes to women on equal terms with men in 1926 for the first time, should have acquiesced in the retrograde British Guiana Constitution. It was a period when reforms were already under way in India. Stanley Baldwin, the Prime Minister, was as far from being a reactionary as was L. S. Amery, the Secretary of State for the Colonies. British Guiana, however, was a remote colony which only a few Members of Parliament ever visited. The Colonial Office, convinced that it could govern better, had its way. In the short run it may have been correct. Yet in the case of British Guiana, the miscalculation of the time left to prepare for self-government was disastrous. By its action in delaying the political training of enough Guianese to run the country at the top level, Great Britain may have unwittingly prepared the way for the racial antagonisms and violence which were later to arise.

* * * *

If the remoteness of the British, French, and Netherlands Guiana colonies was a major reason for their survival, the exploration and development of the South American continent inevitably raised questions over territorial limits, just as it had done between Spain and Portugal at an earlier date. No country in Latin America had been more successful than Brazil in extending its boundaries, whether in the south and south-west, where it had secured territory from Paraguay, or in the Amazon basin, where it had pushed forward its western boundaries far beyond the limits of the Treaty of Tordesillas.

Brazil gained independence in 1822, eight years after Great Britain's possession of the three Dutch colonies of Demerara, Essequibo and Berbice had been confirmed at the Treaty of Paris in 1814. Both sides needed time to settle down; neither country, at first, evinced any interest in boundaries. However, in 1835 the Royal Geographical Society of London organized an expedition led by Robert Schomburgk, who followed the rivers Essequibo and Rupununi to the vicinity of Mt. Annai, which had traditionally been considered to be the extreme south-west boundary of the British colony. He carried out a reconnaissance of British territory in the south prior to examining the Pacaraima chain which dominated it to the north. Schomburgk, though a German, continued his explorations on behalf of Great Britain, leading a second expedition in 1838 to Pirara, a point of convenient communication between the basins of the Essequibo and Amazon. This led to a diplomatic dispute

142

between Brazil and Great Britain over the boundaries of British Guiana.[1] After half a century of intermittent wrangling over this unpromising territory, both parties agreed to request the King of Italy to arbitrate. In an interesting finding, the arbiter laid down that the discovery of traffic routes in unannexed territory did not establish sovereignty, which required effective occupation. Each of the contestants had occupied only a part of the territory. He therefore selected as a boundary the Mahú-Tacutú line which he considered equitable. Basically, this represented a diplomatic success for Great Britain. It was a great blow to Joaquim Nabuco, Brazil's negotiator, who appeared to have failed in comparison with the series of Brazilian successes which had been achieved in boundary disputes by the Baron of Rio Branco.[2] The British thus kept control of the corridor leading from the Essequibo to the Amazon basin, thereby gaining an entry to the latter, while the Brazilians received no entry to the Essequibo basin.[3]

Meanwhile, the settlement in 1899 of the boundary dispute between Great Britain and Venezuela, with which President Grover Cleveland of the United States and Joseph Chamberlain, British Secretary of State for the Colonies, had been concerned, in the outcome had also been favourable to Great Britain.[4] Both disputes illustrated the great importance attached by Great Britain to preserving and extending the boundaries of its overseas territories, even when they appeared to have no strategic or commercial value.[5]

[1] Gordon Ireland, *Boundaries and Conflicts in South America* (Harvard University Press, Cambridge, Massachusetts, 1938), pp. 152-8.

[2] This British success may have led Nabuco to reorient Brazil's traditional pro-British policy in favour of the United States when he went to Washington in 1905 as Brazil's first ambassador. Carolina Nabuco, *Life of Joaquim Nabuco*, trans., ed. Ronald Hilton (Stanford, California, 1950), pp. 298-304.

[3] Paul Fauchille criticized the King of Italy's judgment for being too favourable to Great Britain. "Le conflit de Limites entre le Brésil et la Grande-Bretagne et la sentence arbitrale du Roi d'Italie", *Revue Générale de Droit International Public*, Vol. XII (Paris, 1905).

[4] *Vide* Chapter III, pp. 16-17.

[5] Professor Samuel Flagg Bemis comments, "At that moment Great Britain in 'splendid isolation' stood before the world without allies, without friends among the great powers, on the verge of a war crisis with the United States over the paltry issue of a jungle boundary of Guiana, involving a principle which meant so much to the American mind, so little to the British Empire." *A Diplomatic History of the United States* (New York, 1957), p. 420.

Though in 1943 the elected members in the Legislative Council were increased in number so that they had a majority and though the substantial property requirement was reduced and the franchise extended to women, the 1928 Constitution remained with the Governor in control of the Executive Council and with very wide reserve powers. However, further constitutional revision took place in 1953 with the important introduction of adult franchise at the age of 21 years, and of a House of Assembly of 24 elected members and three *ex-officio* members.[1] An Upper Chamber, the State Council, was set up with six members nominated by the Governor, and two by the majority and one by the minority party in the House of Assembly. The property or income requirements for elected members were abolished. Provision was made for an executive Court of Policy consisting of the Governor and the three *ex-officio* members as in the former constitution, together with seven ministers, six of whom were to be elected by the Lower House and one by the State Council. Thus Great Britain was slowly following its traditional policy of political advance with an elected Lower House and a nominated Upper House, which already existed elsewhere in the British Caribbean.

However, the orderly progress planned by the Colonial Office, and sponsored by successive Secretaries of State in their recommendations to the British Parliament, was rudely interrupted. Dr. Cheddi Jagan, who had been educated in the United States at Northwestern University and had married an American, returned to British Guiana in 1943. The son of an East Indian sugar-estate driver, Jagan, assisted by his wife Janet, threw himself into the political life of the colony. His timing was excellent. The impoverished East Indian section of the population, concentrated in the sugar estates and in the rice-growing villages (in contrast to the Negro population which dominated Georgetown and the mining industry), was beginning to take an increasingly active interest in politics: it was also growing rapidly in numbers. This was partly due to striking advances made

---

While Professor Bemis is right in his assessment of the relative value of the issues at stake in this dispute, the point of view of Joseph Chamberlain and the large body of public opinion in Great Britain, which at the end of the nineteenth century he represented, was very different. In 1962 President Rómulo Betancourt of Venezuela revived the boundary dispute with British Guiana.

[1] The Chief Secretary, Financial Secretary and Attorney-General.

towards the eradication of malaria in the colony in the post-World War II years. The consequent improvement in the general health of the East Indian section of the population led to greater energy and may have been partly responsible for an increasing interest in politics.

Jagan secured election to the House of Assembly in 1946.[1] Thus when the sweeping reforms in the 1953 Constitution were enacted, he was excellently placed as a politician already known in the colony. In 1950 the People's Progressive Party had been formed. It aimed at drawing support from both the Negro and East Indian sections of the population. Besides the Jagans, its leaders included Linden Forbes Burnham, a well-known Negro barrister, and Ashton Chase, a leader of the Georgetown Negro dockworkers. The party was believed to have Communist sympathies. Through its newspaper *Thunder*, capably edited by Janet Jagan, it soon became one of the most effective political bodies in the colony. By concentrating on the poverty of the mass of the people and "the alleged exploitation of labour and natural resources by the sugar kings and bauxite barons",[2] a suitable electoral cry was set up which appealed to both Negroes and East Indians. Moreover, People's Progressive Party committees were set up in the villages with the thoroughness of an old and experienced party organization.[3] The Jagans had succeeded in inculcating the People's Progressive Party Organization with the methods advocated both by Mr. Taper and Mr. Tadpole, even if the Party's objectives were hardly those referred to by Disraeli in *Coningsby*. Though the politically-minded Caribbean had exhibited the effective use of political organization—democratic and undemocratic—by Muñoz Marín in Puerto Rico, by Fulgencio Batista and Fidel Castro in Cuba, by Sir Alexander Bustamante and Norman Manley in Jamaica, by Eric Williams in Trinidad, and by Rafael Leonidas Trujillo in the

[1] The 1943 lowering of the franchise requirement resulted in over 17,000 Indians, less than one-third of the total electorate, becoming qualified to vote.
[2] Morley Ayearst, *The British West Indies* (New York, 1960), p. 118.
[3] Describing the Jagan system of organization, Professor Morley Ayearst writes: "The chairman is often a local notable and sometimes does little but lend the prestige of his name. The driving force is usually the secretary, chosen for his ability and enthusiasm. He is constantly in touch not only with all local party activities, but also with the Secretary-General, Mrs. Jagan, who keeps him informed of the directives issued by the high command." *Ibid.*, p. 117.

Dominican Republic, the Jagans must be rated high as regards the efficiency of their methods.

At the 1953 General Election the People's Progressive Party gained a substantial victory against divided opposition. Their task was simplified, since out of the 130 candidates for the 24 seats, 79 were independents. The People's Progressive Party polled more than half of the votes, winning 18 of the seats. Though the total majority of votes obtained was small, the result, under the British system of voting which tends to emphasize the victory of the largest party, was decisive. The People's Progressive Party had the constitutional duty of nominating the ministers.

Perhaps surprised at the size of their victory and prepared for opposition rather than government, the People's Progressive Party ministers may have realized for the first time the extent of their powers. Placing party interest first, they aimed at dominating the Civil Service and independent boards which played a vital part in the administration of the country. Rejecting an invitation from Jamaica to send two representatives to participate in the welcome to Queen Elizabeth II on the occasion of her visit to that island, they proceeded to introduce a Bill to repeal the ordinance which had been passed in 1953 to restrict Communist literature imported by the People's Progressive Party.[1] They also proposed the creation of an auxiliary police force to be placed under the control of local government authorities instead of that of the Colonial Secretary. In the Executive Council, the six People's Progressive Party ministers formed a united front against the Governor and the *ex-officio* ministers. To sum up, the British system of government, which essentially depends upon compromise, goodwill and understanding, was undermined to the point where the colony's administration was near collapse. How much this was due to inexperience and lack of preparation for office and how much to a desire to make government unworkable is a matter for conjecture. Advised of this situation by the Governor, the Churchill Government reacted strongly. The Governor declared a state of emergency; the Constitution was suspended; the People's Progressive Party ministers were dismissed from office; the legislature was prorogued.[2] In its place, a nominated single-chamber legislature

---

[1] *Ibid.*, p. 120.

[2] On October 8, 1953. For an account of the British Government's reasons for this action, which included the reports of its intelligence services, cf. Chandos, *op. cit.*, pp. 427-30.

was set up.[1] The British intervention had been dramatic. Its effect was difficult to forecast. Cheddi Jagan and his wife Janet received sentences of imprisonment.

After a period of what was in effect a caretaker government of Civil Servants with the addition of nominated members, new elections under a revised constitution were held in 1957. The political situation had, however, undergone a substantial change due to a break between Jagan and Burnham after a struggle in 1955 for the control of the People's Progressive Party, which as a result was split. In the 1957 General Election, the first to be held since the suspension of the Constitution in 1953, the Jagan group won nine seats in the rural areas, while the Burnham group won three seats in Georgetown. In consequence, the Governor nominated candidates to give Jagan a working majority.

In March 1960 Great Britain made a further attempt to prepare for the introduction of democratic self-government into British Guiana. The divergent views of the People's Progressive Party, which was reluctant to enter the West Indies Federation, and the People's National Congress,[2] which favoured entry, made agreement difficult. At one point Jagan walked out of the conference which was held in London. Finally, however, under strong protest, he accepted Great Britain's proposals.[3]

Under the new Constitution, which would come into effect after a General Election the following year, a two-chamber legislature was provided for. The 13 Senate members would all be nominated, while the Legislative Assembly of 35 members would be wholly elective. Full internal self-government was instituted. Defence and

[1] Professor Ayearst comments: "From the beginning the new ministers retained the attitude of an opposition rather than a government vis-à-vis the officials. In his initial speech in reply to the Governor's address, Dr. Jagan attacked the Constitution, the officials and the State Council. In their months of office, the ministers did relatively little to tackle the immediate problems of the Colony but rather sought to obtain, first of all, absolute party control of all independent boards and commissions and of the civil service. Their view of democracy was the Communist one: that a party allegedly representing the proletariat should admit of no checks whatever upon its policies and would be justified in using any means to destroy all effective opposition." *Op. cit.*, p. 120.

[2] This name was adopted by the section of the former People's Progressive Party which followed Burnham and was mainly composed of Negroes with its strength in Georgetown.

[3] *Hispanic American Report, op. cit.*, Vol. XIII, p. 185.

external affairs, however, remained with the Governor. Statutory Commissions were set up to make recommendations to the Governor in regard to the judiciary and the Civil Service. The Governor in many cases was required to consult the Premier. Control of the police rested in a commission. The Governor would appoint a member of the Legislative Council as Premier and, apart from his reserved functions, would act on the advice of his Council of Ministers.

On his return to British Guiana, Jagan continued to criticize the proposals, at the same time demanding independence for British Guiana.[1] The Colonial Office, however, remembering the crisis of 1953, had advanced its policy with caution: it refused to be hurried.

In the General Election which was held in August 1961, Jagan's People's Progressive Party won 20 seats, thus gaining a clear majority. The People's National Congress, led by Burnham, won 11 seats, and the United Force, headed by Peter D'Aguiar, 4 seats.[2] Jagan's victory had once again demonstrated that arrest and imprisonment in a British territory was a sure way to power. The pattern could be traced from India to Jamaica, Ghana and Cyprus. More significantly, the election had crystallized the dangerous split between the electors of East Indian and those of African stock. Apart from D'Aguiar's participation, the Negroes who were mainly in the urban areas had supported the People's National Congress. Jagan's support came for the most part from the Hindustani agricultural labourers. The concept of multi-racial harmony, which had seemed possible when Jagan and Burnham had co-operated politically, had vanished. It was an additional blow to the West Indies Federation.[3]

[1] At the second Inter-American Conference for Democracy and Freedom in April 1960, at Maracay, Venezuela, Dr. Jagan, Narine Singh and Ranjee Chandi Singh presented a resolution which demanded that British Guiana be declared a free nation, and that if necessary a plebiscite be held under the United Nations to decide the wishes of the people.

[2] The United Force was supported by conservative and business interests.

[3] "Dr. Jagan's victory in the British Guiana elections confirms the steady pattern of Guianese politics. In the first elections under universal adult suffrage, held in 1953, his People's Progressive Party, representing then both the major races in the country, won three to one. Thereafter Mr. Forbes Burnham split the party, carrying into opposition the majority of the Negroes and solidifying not merely a racial division but also to some extent a division between town and country. . . .

"Yesterday's results are not likely to forward the cause of Guianese entry into the Federation. Basically, the Asian population see their interests best

148

Because of Jagan's sympathy towards the Communist viewpoint, the British Guiana general election had aroused world-wide interest. The strained situation which existed between the Western Powers and the Communist bloc, aggravated in the Caribbean by the tension between the United States and Cuba, added to the importance of the event.

Strengthened by his second electoral victory, Jagan was in no mood to compromise. He hurried to Washington to demand financial assistance on pain of turning to the Communist bloc, if it was refused.[1] President Kennedy cautiously agreed to send a commission to British Guiana to advise on the possibility of aid. Opinion in the United States showed great anxiety lest British Guiana should follow the Cuban lead and open a door to Communism in Latin America. Britain, also approached by Jagan, promised limited assistance.

Faced with severe financial problems, Jagan called in as adviser Nicolas Kaldor of Cambridge University, who had advised both Ceylon and Ghana on their problems. As a result, in February 1962, Jagan introduced an austerity budget which drastically increased taxation both on rich and poor. Since its impact appeared likely to fall most severely on Georgetown, the only large urban area, it was bitterly resented. The racial political cleavage which had been evinced in the 1961 General Election was thus further stimulated. Both Burnham and D'Aguiar, who, though rivals, dominated Georgetown politics, were highly critical of Jagan's budget. With heavy rises envisaged in the cost of imported goods, the Negro population displayed its anger towards the Government. Ultimately some business premises in the centre of the city, owned by Indians believed to have supported Jagan, were set on fire by the mob. The conflagration spread rapidly, destroying a substantial area in the business centre of Georgetown. So serious was the situation that, at the request of the Jagan Government, British troops from Jamaica and Great Britain and British warships were sent to restore order. The

---

served as remaining the dominant element in an independent British Guiana, not in joining a negro-dominated West Indies. Dr. Jagan himself has never appeared as intellectually opposed to federation. As leader of a united British Guiana he might well have carried it with him into the Federation. As leader of a majority group of the population only, and a group fundamentally opposed to the concept, he can hardly attempt to." *The Times*, August 23, 1961.

[1] *Hispanic American Report, op. cit.*, Vol. XIV, pp. 903-4.

damage was estimated at £10 million. Thus Great Britain, which had despatched troops to British Guiana in 1953 when it had dismissed the first Jagan Government, was responsible in 1962 for rescuing the third Jagan Government from the fury of its opponents. At least Harold Macmillan's Conservative Government in Britain had demonstrated, despite its probable suspicions of Jagan's flirtation with the Communist bloc, that it was no less determined than the Churchill administration had been nine years previously to support the Constitution which it had been responsible for setting up.

* * * *

The economic policy of Great Britain in British Guiana followed the same pattern as in other Caribbean territories. Based on sugar, the economy fluctuated with the complications arising from the abolition of slavery. A slow improvement was brought about by the introduction of East Indian indentured labour. Discoveries of gold and diamonds in the 1880s had provided a speculative interlude, as had the gold rush in French Guiana a quarter of a century before. But the workings never developed on a large scale.

Though commenced at a later date, bauxite mining proved highly successful. The Demerara Bauxite Company[1] established an operation at Mackenzie on the Demerara river, which continued to be a major source of revenue to the colony.[2] Bauxite mining in British Guiana, however, was more costly than in Jamaica since the overburden to be removed tended to be greater. It was possible, however, that the extensive water power available in British Guiana might be harnessed to produce electricity for the processing of bauxite ore on the lines of the Brokopondo scheme, which was being completed in Surinam.[3]

As in other British Caribbean territories, the Colonial Development Corporation[4] endeavoured to assist the expansion of British Guiana. In the period following World War II, when the winning of gold for the sterling area was considered by the British Government to be of special importance on account of the weak position of sterling, the Colonial Development Corporation had been under pressure to assist the expansion of the British Guiana Consolidated Goldfields and its

[1] Associated with the Aluminum Company of Canada.
[2] Reynolds Metals Company also produced bauxite on the Berbice river in British Guiana.
[3] *Vide* Chapter XIII, p. 132.   [4] *Vide* Chapter IX, pp. 79-80.

subsidiary, the Potaro Hydro-Electric Company. With a fixed price for gold, and a rise in costs of 120 per cent. in a decade, the well-intentioned help of the British Government through the medium of the Colonial Development Corporation resulted in a heavy loss.[1]

Agriculture remained the main provider of work. The highly organized British-controlled sugar industry had succeeded in making the most of a difficult proposition. Much of the land growing sugar cane had originally been reclaimed from the sea. Moreover, when the tonnage of cane fell, fields could be fallowed by leaving them from six to nine months under water. This unusual and carefully planned system alone made possible the growing of sugar cane in British Guiana. Nevertheless, capital expenditure was heavy and costs high. The British policy of subsidizing and assuring a market for Commonwealth sugar cane had saved the industry in British Guiana as in other British Caribbean territories.[2]

If sugar cane was the industry of the larger plantations, rice growing was the mainstay of the peasant farmer. Interspersed with cane plantations were East Indian villages growing rice. A major problem for British Guiana was the disposal of the crop. Among the few economic attractions of entering the West Indies Federation was the possibility that Trinidad, with its large East Indian population, and other territories would purchase rice from British Guiana. However, Great Britain's policy of a West Indies Federation had been unacceptable to British Guiana, while Trinidad had been one of the architects of the Federation's downfall. Rice was in fact purchased by the West Indies Government, largely for consumption in Trinidad. Disagreements, however, over conditions of sale had been frequent. British Guiana had latterly turned to Cuba and Czechoslovakia as additional outlets for rice, as for other commodities.

To Great Britain, British Guiana had been a great disappointment. Though the dream of Sir Walter Raleigh that England should have a domain in Guiana had been fulfilled, it had at the end faded, like the hopes of that intrepid but ill-starred individual. Ten times more extensive than the British West Indies islands, British Guiana had been intended as an outlet for the surplus population of the Antilles

---

[1] The Colonial Development Corporation wrote off £1,200,000 over what it stated had always been a marginal project. *Colonial Development Corporation Report 1958*, pp. 7, 29-31.

[2] *Vide* Chapter IX, pp. 80-81.

when federation had first been mooted. For that reason as well as others, it had refused to join, thereby contributing to the failure of the venture. The dominant East Indian population probably feared the addition of large numbers of West Indian Negroes, which would have altered the racial balance. This, however, would be to overlook the other difficulties of a small and poor country of some 600,000 persons seeking independence. Encouraged by Jagan and his party, the impoverished territory sought independence in the form of a republic within the Commonwealth at the earliest moment and apparently regardless of the cost. The gaps in the unity of British Guiana, far from closing, had widened. The ruined central area of Georgetown bore mute evidence of the ferocity of the passions which had been aroused.

The clamant need was for a measure of co-operation between the races, expressed through the medium of the political parties. Yet even if that were achieved, no one had shown how a country, whose population filled a narrow strip of territory partially reclaimed from the sea and protected by dikes, could support its costly economy, which depended upon highly competitive export markets. Great Britain was aiding British Guiana's sugar economy under the Commonwealth Sugar Agreement.[1] Whether this Agreement, which had a currency of eight years, would be affected if Great Britain entered the Common Market was impossible to forecast. Premier Eric Williams of Trinidad had issued a warning.[2] Though the cultivation of rice yielded only a scanty living to the peasant producers of British Guiana, at least there was likely to be an outlet for it even if sales to Communist bloc countries might cause misgivings in the United States as to whether it should afford aid to British Guiana.

The interior of the country remained empty of people and un-developed apart from the important bauxite industry, itself subject to competition from other countries. The large reserves of water power in the rivers of the interior might be utilized for the production of the aluminium. The distance from Georgetown and the populated coastal belt to the majority of the sites available for hydro-electric development made further undertakings in this field unlikely for

[1] *Vide* Chapter IX, p. 92, note 3.
[2] Addressing the Convention of the British Caribbean Cane Farmers Association in Trinidad on August 23, 1962, Williams said: "If you people think you are safe with the Commonwealth Sugar Agreement, you had better start thinking again. You have got to fight."

some time. Moreover, an effective industrialization of British Guiana seemed remote. Even in regard to the production of aluminium, Surinam was likely to achieve a dominant position in the Guianas with its Brokopondo scheme nearing completion.[1]

Forests were an asset, but poor communications were a limiting factor in their exploitation.[2] Cattle ranching had been developed mainly in the remote Rupununi district, but only with modest success. The pastures were poor and the distance from a market a severe handicap.[3]

Great Britain had endeavoured to prepare British Guiana for self-government. If the introduction of the unrepresentative Crown Colony system of government in 1928 had been a mistake, followed possibly by another error when the Constitution had been suspended in 1953, Great Britain had made a sincere attempt in the 1961 Constitution to accelerate the granting of autonomy which would quickly lead to independence, following the pattern used in other former colonies. Notwithstanding its misgivings over Jagan's apparent leanings towards Communism, Great Britain, by the dispatch of troops in 1962, had restored order in faction-ridden Georgetown, thereby saving the People's Progressive Party Government from imminent collapse. To bring about racial harmony, however, was beyond Great Britain's power. Pressure for independence, a policy to which Great Britain was committed, seemed likely to result in its early grant. In that event, the Republic of Guyana, which the People's Progressive Party sought to create within the British Commonwealth, would have the task of solving the problems of its future.

[1] *Vide* Chapter XIII, pp. 132-133.
[2] Assistance had been given by the Colonial Development Corporation.
[3] The report of a mission organized by the International Bank for Reconstruction and Development which visited British Guiana in 1953 could hardly have been more discouraging over the livestock situation at that time. It pointed out that the Rupununi savannahs could only carry about 10 to 15 cattle to a square mile. The animals had either to be slaughtered and carried by air to Georgetown or driven to Tawama on the Berbice river, a distance of 200 miles. In the coastal areas conditions were also unsuitable for cattle. "During the rice season they are put into poorly drained backlands, marshes and conservancies, behind the polders. The lands are swampy and cattle are commonly seen deep in water and nibbling un-nutritious grasses." *The Economic Development of British Guiana* (Baltimore, Maryland, 1953), pp. 174-5.

CHAPTER XV

BRITISH HONDURAS

Even more than British Guiana, British Honduras requires separate consideration. A territory of 8688 square miles in Central America, it is bounded on the north and north-west by Mexico, on the west and south by Guatemala, and on the east by the Caribbean sea. About one-third of its population of about 90,000 persons live in Belize, the capital. Its historical origins are wrapped in uncertainty.[1] When logwood for dyes[2] was a highly desirable product, adventuresome British entrepreneurs, perhaps more buccaneers than traders, established a precarious foothold on the Mexican coast. Under pressure from the Spaniards, the centre of their activities was moved from the west to the east side of the Yucatán peninsula. With Jamaica, the nearest English territory, more than 600 miles distant, Britain's interest was limited. However, by the Treaty of Paris in 1763 it obtained rights to cut logwood, though the territory to which the concession applied was extremely ill-defined. Throughout the eighteenth-century wars with Spain, Britain managed to retain its foothold on the Bay of Honduras in an area which the Spaniards had not settled. The logging rights were later extended to the cutting of mahogany. Spain, however, jealous of its American Empire, resolutely limited the rights of the British settlements to those of a

[1] E.g. the Godolphin Treaty concluded between Great Britain and Spain in 1670 confirmed to Great Britain "sovereignty, dominion, possession and propriety in all the lands, regions, islands, colonies and places whatsoever, being or situated in the West Indies or any part of America, which the said King of Great Britain and his subjects do at present hold or possess . . .". There is disagreement as to whether Great Britain had or had not a settlement in British Honduras at that time.

[2] As early as the sixteenth century, logwood (*Haematoxylon campechianum*) was imported for dyeing by Europeans. The buccaneers often captured Spanish ships laden with logwood which sold well in London. Later they are believed to have organized logwood cutting on shore, when logwood became scarce. The logwood industry reached its peak in the second half of the nineteenth century after which it was largely replaced by synthetic dyes. Samuel J. Record and Robert W. Hess, *Timbers of the New World* (Yale University Press, New Haven, 1943), pp. 276-7.

usufructuary character. The very fact that this was stated or implied in succeeding treaties may have weakened the claim to sovereignty which Great Britain built up through long years of effective occupation. As sovereign, Spain claimed, and occasionally exercised, the right of inspection. The victory of Great Britain and its colonists at St. George's Cay in 1798 cannot be said to have established any right of sovereignty by conquest even if it did lead to a lessening of Spain's interest in the British settlement.

At the close of the Napoleonic Wars, a weakened Spain, which was soon to be immersed in revolutionary colonial wars, was less and less interested in what seemed to be an unproductive and unhealthy area, minute in relation to its vast and turbulent domains. Even at the height of its power, however, Great Britain continued to avoid claiming sovereignty. Though it had not demanded large territorial concessions at Vienna, as the premier industrial nation it had a significant stake in preserving the sanctity of treaties. Belize was tiny in relation to Britain's large and scattered empire. A strictly correct attitude was shown towards its resolute if troublesome former ally of the Peninsular war, even if Great Britain might secretly encourage the rebellious colonists in Spanish America and shut its eyes to territorial encroachments by its own colonists, who constantly sought new forest areas to replace those which they had cut out.[1]

Although Great Britain gradually began to establish government in the Belize settlement, it had not yet claimed sovereignty there.[2] The Clayton-Bulwer Treaty of 1850 between the United States and Great Britain, which included a declaration that neither party would exercise dominion over any part of Central America, further

[1] The cutting of mahogany was closely linked to the expansion of British settlements in Honduras. The British railway boom in the 1830s and 1840s led to a strong if short-lived demand for this wood. By the 1786 Treaty with Spain, the British settlers were permitted to cut mahogany between the River Hondo in the north of Belize as far south as the River Sibún. However, since mahogany could only be transported by water, and in a period when no mechanical haulage was available, logging was confined to areas adjacent to rivers. Only trees relatively close at hand could be utilized. Moreover, since mahogany grows sparsely interspersed with other forest trees, a large area was soon cut out in a logging operation confined to this timber. This had a basic influence on the continuous expansion of the Belize settlement.

[2] A Supreme Court was established by Act of Parliament in 1819, and the Slave Emancipation Act of 1833 had been extended to the settlement. Local government with district magistrates was set up prior to the 1859 Convention with Guatemala. Thus there was a curious dichotomy in the British attitude.

complicated matters. So ambiguous was the wording of its first article that before it was ratified, Bulwer and Clayton exchanged declarations on the meaning, making it clear that British Honduras was not included in the treaty.[1] This treaty was not, however, an American declaration of British sovereignty over the territory, and did not prevent additional controversy at a later date.

Guatemala, a successor state to the United Provinces of Central America, was torn between, on the one hand, its fears of the interference of the United States arising out of the conflicting activities of Cornelius Vanderbilt and William Walker,[2] and on the other, its apprehensions of the continued encroachments of British logwood cutters.

If the Clayton-Bulwer Treaty had been imprecise, the Anglo-Guatemalan Convention of 1859 was even more baffling. Probably neither the British negotiator Charles Lennox Wyke nor the Guatemalan Pedro de Aycinena felt certain of his ground. Great Britain's objective was clearly to secure recognition by Guatemala of its sovereignty over British Honduras within defined boundaries, a recognition which Spain had never given. Guatemala, a new and weak country, wished to secure itself against the interference of two powerful states, and had every reason to be apprehensive of the traditional activities of the acquisitive Baymen, as the men of Belize were called. A further complication was the fact that the boundary of the British settlement in the north and in the west probably as far as the Sibún river was with Mexico and not Guatemala, though this too had never been defined in that rough and thinly-populated territory.

Wykes, a capable negotiator, kept in mind the need for securing definite boundaries for the Belize settlement which would be recognized by Guatemala. Great Britain's position in Central America, which had been maintained both by its successes in war

[1] Bemis, *op. cit.*, p. 251.
[2] Vanderbilt had organized a profitable system of transport between the Atlantic and Pacific oceans in Nicaragua at a time when this route was the most rapid means of travelling from the eastern United States to California, then in process of expansion. Walker, also an American, succeeded in becoming for a short period (1855-1857) virtual dictator of Nicaragua. The whole episode aroused apprehension in the weak Central American republics in regard to the intentions of the United States. Cf. Bemis, *op. cit.*, pp. 327-33; Julius W. Pratt, *A History of United States Foreign Policy* (Englewood Cliffs, New Jersey, 1955), p. 291; Thomas A. Bailey, *A Diplomatic History of the American People* (New York, 1958), pp. 277-8.

further afield and by the enterprise of its citizens locally, appeared to be weakening. The Clayton-Bulwer Treaty had already doomed its rule over the Mosquito coast.[1] Against mounting United States criticism, an agreement with Guatemala was imperative if the Belize settlement was to be retained. In furtherance of Britain's policy, Wyke did not hesitate to exceed his instructions by proposing to Aycinena that Great Britain should co-operate with Guatemala in establishing a route "between the fittest place on the Atlantic Coast, near the Settlement of Belize, and the capital of Guatemala". A cart-road was suggested. The purpose of this unpromising project through jungles and over mountains from sea level to Guatemala City, which stands at an elevation of 4877 feet, was to re-establish trade between Great Britain and the Guatemalan capital, which had suffered from the easier route to the pacific port of San José, and thence to the West Coast of the United States.

The cart-road was never built, nor is it likely, if it had been, that it would have proved a lasting stimulus to Anglo-Guatemalan commerce. No starting-point for the new trade route had been specified in the Anglo-Guatemalan Treaty of 1859. Afterwards, when the Colonial Office came to the conclusion that its terminus, which was to be in Guatemalan territory, was more likely to hurt than to help the commerce of Belize, it became critical of the project. No sum to be expended by either party had been specified in the Treaty, though it was generally surmised that the share of Great Britain would be £50,000 or more. This was by no means an excessive sum for the greatest commercial country in the world to pay for what might be regarded as a substantial acquisition of territory, even though this had been glossed over in the Convention of 1859 probably through fear of contravening the Clayton-Bulwer Treaty. Great Britain had secured boundary definitions for what was the future colony of British Honduras. It failed, however, to carry out whatever obligations were imposed or implied in Clause VII of the 1859 Treaty, the clause which deals with the building of the road.[2]

[1] The Mosquito coast (Mosquitia) was a loosely defined area on the Caribbean coasts of Honduras and Nicaragua. The Bay Islands, of which the largest is Roatán, in the Bay of Honduras, were also in the British sphere of influence.

[2] Professor Bemis comments, "The history of Belize is a fine example of how successful buccaneering can lead to territorial encroachments, to settlements, to a sphere of influence, to a protectorate with expanding boundaries, and to actual sovereignty." *Op. cit.*, p. 247.

The long, drawn-out wrangle illustrates the somewhat confused policy of Great Britain at this time. The Foreign Office clearly showed awareness of Great Britain's obligation to implement the treaty; however, the Colonial Office was lukewarm, while the Treasury made financial objections, suggesting that the implementation of the treaty obligation was impracticable since Parliament would not sanction the expenditure. The tortuous dispute, ably described by Professor Humphreys,[1] died down only to be revived in the form of claims for sovereignty over British Honduras by President Jorge Ubico and later by President Juan José Arévalo. In the latest phase it almost led to a diplomatic rupture in our own times between Guatemala and Great Britain in 1962, following which a conference between the two countries took place at Puerto Rico which, though it did not settle the dispute, created a more favourable atmosphere for a settlement.[2]

While the Guatemala issue remained in dispute, trouble flared with Mexico in 1865 during the imperial régime of Maximilian. Claims were made by Mexico on the whole of British Honduras up to the River Sarstoon. For good measure, Mexico also asserted its right to the Guatemala province of Petén. Energetic protests were made by Great Britain, while the Indians on the northern frontier of British Honduras, traditionally hostile to the Mexicans and disturbed by rumours of territorial changes, showed hostility to both parties. Incursions into northern British Honduras occurred in 1870 and 1872 when Indians crossed the frontier at the Hondo river and approached Orange Walk, where a counter-attack was necessary. Meanwhile, diplomatic relations between Great Britain and Mexico had been broken off in 1867 and were not re-established until 1884. It was a period of confusion, with Great Britain, Mexico and Guatemala in dispute over these inhospitable lands.

Gradually Great Britain began to institute government in Belize, though it still hesitated to appoint a governor; prior to the Anglo-Guatemalan Convention of 1859, the status of British Honduras remained in doubt.[3] Probably the *de facto* possession of the territory

[1] R. A. Humphreys, *The Diplomatic History of British Honduras* (London, 1961), pp. 109-32 and 151-66.
[2] *Hispanic American Report*, op. cit., Vol. XV, p. 329.
[3] William J. Bianchi comments, "There can be little question that neither the British authorities in the home office, nor the subordinate officers in Jamaica or the settlement of Belize, considered Great Britain as the true sovereign with power to exercise jurisdiction until after 1859." *Op. cit.*,

158

by Great Britain, ill-defined as its boundaries were, would have implied that sovereignty had been acquired, had it not been for the express usufructuary rights set out in the Treaty of Paris in 1763 and confirmed both by subsequent treaties and by the actions of the British Government up to the middle of the nineteenth century. The loss by Spain of Mexico and Central America further confused the position. Great Britain in its policy towards British Honduras had not been disposed to acknowledge the doctrine of *uti possidetis* which had been generally accepted by the Latin America successor states to Spain. Among supporters of the doctrine itself there was disagreement as to whether a successor state assumed the treaty obligations of the former Spanish Colonial Empire, such as those in Belize.

Great Britain, however, took the opportunity of demarcating the northern frontier of its colony. Ultimately, its policy of establishing sovereignty over British Honduras was partially crowned with success when a treaty was signed in 1893 with Mexico which defined the boundaries between the Republic and "the Colony of British Honduras".[1]

* * * *

The earliest form of government in the Belize settlement was the Public Meeting. Though at first this had been open to all the settlers, in the beginning of the nineteenth century a property qualification had restricted its membership.[2] In 1853 it was replaced

---

p. 58. So uncertain were the settlers that in 1861 they renewed representations which they had previously made to become a colony. The Law Officers of the Crown in 1851 had hesitantly expressed the view that the settlement had become part of the Crown; but the British Government had refrained from changing "settlement" to "colony". In 1862, however, they expressed the view that the Belize settlement was *de jure* as well as *de facto* a part of Her Majesty's Dominions. As a result, British Honduras was by Letters of Patent declared a Colony in 1862. Humphreys, *op. cit.*, pp. 60 and 91.

[1] "The treaty was a clear recognition [by Mexico] of British sovereignty over British Honduras; it finally determined the boundaries between the colony and the republic; these boundaries have not since been questioned; and it is difficult to see on what valid ground the dispute could be reopened." *Ibid.*, p. 150.

[2] D. A. G. Waddell, *British Honduras* (Oxford University Press, 1961), p. 50.

by an elective Legislative Assembly.[1] Districts were created and magistrates appointed. Professor Waddell considers that by the end of the 1850s British Honduras had become a colony in all but name.[2]

The most important immediate result of the Anglo-Guatemalan Convention of 1859 was the change in British policy towards the settlement. For the first time Great Britain took firm control when in 1862 it acceded to the request of the Legislative Assembly and declared the settlement a colony.[3] The moment was opportune since the United States, which might have objected, and in fact did so twenty years later, was immersed in its Civil War. Spain made no comment.

The Colonial Office, which had been successful in replacing elected legislatures in most of the British West Indies colonies[4] in favour of direct administration through a Governor, took over direct control of British Honduras in 1871, when the Legislative Assembly abolished itself. Crown Colony Government was instituted.[5] The same pattern of placing good administration above the political training of a colony, which was the gospel of the nineteenth-century colonial office in the Caribbean, was being carefully followed.

After reserve powers had been conceded to the Governor following the 1932 hurricane which made the colony dependent on United Kingdom financial support, the Colonial Office agreed to the restoration in 1936 of elections for a portion of the legislature. The franchise, however, as in the case of other British colonies of the

[1] The property qualification of £400 for each of the 18 elected members was a high one, bearing in mind the low value of land in the settlement, which has continued to the present day. The Superintendent nominated three official members. The right of franchise required an income of £7 per year or a salary of £100 per year. *Ibid.*, p. 52.

[2] From 1860 to the introduction of the first Colonial stamps in 1866, letters in British Honduras were postally marked by handstamp or by manuscript writing. The first stamps of British Honduras, which were printed by De La Rue and Co. Ltd., bore the Queen's Head. The change was another manifestation of British sovereignty in British Honduras. From 1858 to 1860 British stamps had been used in British Honduras as in other Caribbean territories.

[3] Waddell, *op. cit.*, p. 53. Cf. Bianchi, p. 158, note 3.

[4] *Vide* Chapter III, p. 14, and Chapter XIV, pp. 141-142.

[5] ". . . In 1892, an unofficial majority on the Legislative Council was instituted. This, however, was not a very valuable concession as in the last analysis the unofficial nominated members owed their places to the Governor." Waddell, *op. cit.*, p. 54.

period, was severely restricted by a property or income qualification.[1]

Not until 1954 did Great Britain concede a constitution which could be termed in any way democratic. Probably the weak financial position of the colony, combined with the measure of Treasury control that traditionally accompanied financial subsidy, was the main reason for this slow advance. The scattered population, a substantial proportion of which spoke Spanish, undoubtedly had increased the difficulties of extending the franchise. However, the right to vote was now conferred on all literate adults. The new Constitution provided for nine elected members, three official members, and three nominated unofficial members with a nominated Speaker. In the Executive Council, the control of the Governor was absolute. In addition to his reserve powers, he could rely on the support of the three official Assembly members and two nominated members, which gave a majority over four elected members.

Unfortunately, outside events disorganized the well-meant British intentions of political advance for British Honduras. In September 1949, sterling was devalued.[2] British Honduras, which had maintained the parity of its dollar with the United States dollar after the first devaluation of sterling during World War II, continued to do so after this second devaluation. Though it was the only colonial territory to maintain this parity, there were important reasons for doing so. Half of its imports, of which food was an important part, came from the United States, against less than 12 per cent. from the United Kingdom. It was a period when agricultural implements and machinery and many other classes of manufactured goods were extremely difficult to secure from Great Britain, whose industry was only slowly recovering from the dislocation of the war. Infrequent shipping services to Great Britain, combined with manufacturers' delays, added to the difficulties.

With the sterling pool desperately short of dollars, however, Great Britain considered that the anomaly of one small colony's maintaining parity in its rate of exchange with the United States should cease. In support of this argument, it could point out that the export trade of British Honduras was changing with the rapid rise of a citrus industry

---

[1] In 1945, there were only 822 registered voters. By 1950 this had risen to 3695. *Ibid.*, p. 109.

[2] In 1939, sterling was devalued from $4.86 to £1 to $4.03 to £1. In 1949, it was further devalued to $2.80 to £1. In each case the British Honduras dollar had remained at parity with the U.S. dollar.

which was closely linked to British markets.[1] Great Britain considered that devaluation was likely to make the exports of British Honduras more competitive. Opinion, however, in the colony strongly opposed this course. Arguments continued until the end of 1949, when the Governor ultimately used his reserve powers to override the opposition of the legislature.[2]

On the credit side, the decision to devalue probably helped the citrus industry, though Great Britain was already committed by long-term agreement to taking a substantial part of its produce. Important in the long run was the granting to British Honduras of a 15,000-ton sugar export quota under the Commonwealth Sugar Agreement though a decade was to elapse before the colony could take full advantage of it.[3]

The effect of the Governor's action, however, on public opinion in the colony was dramatic.[4] That the wishes of the people had been

[1] At the end of World War II, the Ministry of Food made long-term arrangements for the supply of orange concentrate to Great Britain. In a period of continuing rationing, this was of considerable importance to children in the United Kingdom.

[2] The problem had been seriously mishandled by the British Government. Lord Listowel, Minister of State for Colonial Affairs, came to British Honduras and informed the Legislative Assembly on October 13 that the British Honduran dollar would not be devalued. This statement was well received. However, since the economic position was difficult, Mr. Ronald Garvey devalued the British Honduran dollar on December 31, in conformity with the recent sterling devaluation, using his Governor's reserve powers to override the unanimous opposition of the unofficial members.

The BH $ became worth 2·80 to £1 instead of 4·03. In terms of U.S. currency, it had fallen from par to about 70 cents. For an account favourable to devaluation, cf. Stephen L. Caiger, *British Honduras, Past and Present* (London, 1951), pp. 212-18.

Professor Waddell's assessment of the devaluation is more perceptive, since he stresses the opportunity given to an anti-colonial movement to base itself on the Colonial Office's action overriding the wishes of the territory. He considers, however, the long-term effects of devaluation to have been beneficial to the economy. Waddell, *op. cit.*, pp. 110-11.

[3] There was a provision to increase this up to 25,000 tons, which was finally confirmed at the Commonwealth Sugar Conference held in the latter part of 1959.

[4] An interesting comparison may be made with the introduction of the French franc at the end of 1947 in the Saar, which also shocked public opinion. Prices rose and protests were made. Even though economic conditions improved as a result of French policy, criticism was not assuaged. Jacques Freymond, *The Saar Conflict* (London, 1945-1955), pp. 45-8.

overruled by London could not be denied, and the British handling of the final negotiations had been clumsy. With a sharply rising cost of living, the way was prepared for a bitter political quarrel, with British Hondurans pitting what they considered were their interests against the policy of the Colonial Office. At a time when the federation of the British Caribbean colonies was being actively considered, this was most unfortunate for British policy. By 1950 the newly formed People's United Party had obtained control of the Belize City Council. Two of its leaders were imprisoned,[1] which, as in the case of other British territories, immediately enhanced the popularity of the party.[2] When in 1954 the General Election under adult franchise took place, the People's United Party won eight out of the nine seats, on a platform advocating independence combined with strong criticism of Great Britain. As in other British Caribbean territories, the party allied itself with labour through the medium of the General Workers Union.

The election had resulted in a new group of enthusiastic young men without experience obtaining a measure of power which was, however, still limited by the Constitution. Great Britain was following its policy of transferring authority gradually, as it had done in other Caribbean territories.

By 1956 George Price and Nicholas Pollard, who had been expelled from the secretaryship of the General Workers Union, had quarrelled with Leigh Richardson, who, however, retained control of the Union. At the 1957 General Election Price and Pollard led the People's United Party to victory over the Honduran Independence Party, which had been formed by Richardson. The decisive victory which gave every seat to the winners was a tribute to the electioneering ability of Price, whose attractive personality, combined with his ability to address audiences fluently in either English or Spanish, undoubtedly contributed to his success. The key issue in this contest had been Price's claim that Richardson, whose support was centred in the Negro population at Belize, favoured entering the West Indies Federation. The outcome was a blow to British colonial policy in the Caribbean.

As leader of the Legislative Assembly, Price brought a delegation to London in 1957 to discuss with the British Government

---

[1] Leigh Richardson and Philip Goldson, for seditious writing in the *Belize Billboard*. Waddell, *op. cit.*, p. 112.
[2] *Vide* Chapter XIV, p. 148.

constitutional development and the financial problems of British Honduras. During this visit, trouble flared when Price was accused by Alan Lennox-Boyd, Secretary of State for the Colonies, of entertaining overtures from Guatemala through the Guatemalan Minister in London. The discussions were immediately broken off by the British Government, and Price, on his return home, was dismissed from the Executive Council.[1]

Despite a break with Pollard, Price remained the leading political figure in the colony, with control of the People's United Party. Though Catholic, he managed by his political gifts and oratory to retain a substantial influence, not only in the Spanish-speaking country areas, which might have been attracted to a closer association with Central America, but more surprisingly with the Protestant Negro population in Belize.

The successful establishment of the West Indies Federation in 1958 had become the cornerstone of Great Britain's Caribbean policy. Dominated by the People's United Party, the British Honduras legislature continued its opposition to joining it. There can be no doubt that this reflected the views of the majority of British Hondurans, who remained rigidly opposed to any association with the West Indies colonies. The devaluation of the British Honduran dollar had not been forgotten. Moreover, there was fear of immigration from Jamaica, for whose people there was a traditional dislike, perhaps stemming back to the period when the remote Governor of Jamaica had a measure of authority over the territory, and fear too of an influx of the impoverished people of the Leeward and Windward Islands.[2] Wage rates were higher in British Honduras than in most of the other British Caribbean territories.

Price had often expressed the view that British Honduras should be more closely associated with Guatemala. This was probably a major

[1] He still, however, retained the confidence of the elected members of the Assembly.

[2] ". . . joining the West Indies Federation is not popular in the Colony—for the main reason that British Hondurans do not like Jamaicans". "A Colony in Dispute", *The Round Table*, London, March 1958.

"There were many Hondurans who at first sight saw in the proposed Federation, not progress towards the goal of independence, but merely a change of masters. They bitterly resented 'merging their identity' in a general West Indian amalgamation, where their comparatively small population would find British Honduras over-shadowed by such more fortunate rivals as Jamaica or Barbados." Caiger, *op. cit.*, p. 227.

factor in his split with Richardson,[1] causing the termination of what might otherwise have proved to be an effective partnership in a small community where inevitably the amount of political talent was very limited.[2]

After the overthrow of the Arbenz administration in 1954, Guatemalan pressure for incorporation of British Honduras within its territories increased, on the grounds that the 1859 Anglo-Guatemalan Convention had not been implemented by Great Britain. Governor Sir Colin Thornley attempted to force the issue by the introduction of a resolution in the Assembly pronouncing against association with Guatemala. Though carried with the help of nominated members, it was a Pyrrhic victory, since it implied that the Governor was not supported by the representatives of the majority of the electors. In response to a demand for increased political power and in pursuance of its policy of strictly preparing its territories for independence, the British Government amended the British Honduras Constitution in 1961, providing an elected majority in the Executive Council.

*　　*　　*　　*

If the British Government's action in devaluing the British Honduras dollar in 1949 had far-reaching political effects, it also produced changes in the economy of British Honduras. From obtaining half of its imports from the United States in the years before devaluation, a sharp diminution in the proportion took place which on an average for the years 1952-1954 fell to less than one-third. Imports from the United Kingdom which in the two years prior to devaluation had averaged under 12 per cent. of the total, had risen by 1952-1954 to over 35 per cent., surpassing the imports from the United States. With the relaxing of the restrictions on dollar imports, United Kingdom imports appeared to be stabilized at about 33 per cent. of the total for the average of the years 1958-1959. However, for the same period, United States imports had recovered to about 42 per cent., emphasizing the traditional orientation of commerce in the colony.

[1] Waddell, *op. cit.*, p. 129.
[2] It may be compared to the quarrel between Cheddi Jagan and Forbes Burnham, which was an important factor in the rise of racial antagonism in British Guiana. *Vide* Chapter XIV, p. 147. In British Honduras, however, Price seemed to hold the support of all sections of the population, while Richardson left the country to work in Trinidad.

165

Though the Colonial Development Corporation[1] devoted considerable attention to British Honduras, unfortunately some of its worst failures occurred in this territory. Wisely realizing that the lack of adequate hotel accommodation in the territory would be discouraging to prospective investors, it commenced the erection of the Fort George Hotel at Belize, which was opened in 1953.[2] Though its cost had been excessive and its operation was to prove difficult, it undoubtedly met a real need in British Honduras. Agriculture, naturally, was the principal interest of the Colonial Development Corporation in British Honduras. Here, too, success eluded it. An attempt was made to re-establish the banana industry in the Stann Creek valley which, as in other Caribbean countries, had been wiped out by Panama disease. This would have involved supplying the British market, since lacatan bananas, unacceptable in the United States but resistant to Panama disease, alone could be grown. Leaf-spot disease, however, brought about the failure of this project, although spraying had in some other countries proved to be an effective remedy. The banana project was abandoned in 1952.[3] Two thousand acres of land were purchased by the Corporation in 1950 in the El Cayo district to grow ramie. By 1953, Lord Reith, Chairman of the Colonial Development Corporation, declared that production was disappointing and yields poor, and the project was abandoned.[4] In the same district it had leased 70,000 acres for livestock, but the scheme came to nothing.

It would be unfair to judge the Colonial Development Corporation by its failure in British Honduras. As Lord Reith said, referring to its early operations as a whole, "The Colonial Development Corporation has paid heavily for inefficient management and supervision; it has also found that private enterprise has not always efficient

[1] *Vide* Chapter IX, pp. 79-80.
[2] The swampy nature of the ground on the Belize sea-front complicated the erection of the building. The capital was written down by £150,000. After providing depreciation on the reduced capital expenditure of £106,758, the hotel made a trading loss in 1953 of £4622. *Colonial Development Corporation Report 1953.*
[3] *Ibid.* Some plantings of oranges and cacao were made by the Colonial Development Corporation in the Stann Creek valley.
For the problem of disease and pest control in growing bananas, cf. Stacy May and Galo Plaza, *The United Fruit Company in Latin America* (New York, 1958), pp. 92-4.
[4] Expenditure of £169,236 had been incurred including losses for 1952 and 1953 of £45,163. *Colonial Development Corporation Report 1953*, p. 27.

166

management for hire."[1] Unfortunately, the Corporation's activities had a disastrous effect on the economic development of the country since it discouraged other potential investors.[2]

When reviewing these agricultural disasters, it seems strange that the Corporation overlooked what was to become one of the few successful industries in post-war British Honduras. Its 1950 report declared, "The production of sugar in British Honduras is considered to be commercially unattractive." Even when in 1953 an export quota of sugar was allocated to British Honduras with provision for an increase, the Corporation failed to realize the potentialities of this industry. Finally, private investors reorganized the small Corozal Sugar Factory, which increased its production from 2000 tons of sugar in 1955 to 27,500 tons in 1961.

The expansion of the citrus industry was also marked. The enterprise of the Citrus Company of British Honduras transformed the Stann Creek valley after the collapse of the first banana enterprise. Grapefruit and oranges were processed for export, mainly to the British market. It could be argued that if the political results of devaluation had been unfortunate, there had been a measure of compensation on the economic side. Undoubtedly British policy had contributed to the change in the economy of the colony from one based mainly on forest products and sold to the United States to one supported by an increasing agricultural production, much of which went to Europe.

Yet despite these efforts, British Honduras usually failed to pay its way and remained a grant-aided colony. It was a high-cost producer of commodities, because of poor communications, including the lack of a good deep-water port.[3] Roads had been constructed to connect Belize with the Mexican frontier in the north, and with the Guatemalan frontier in the east. The construction of the Hummingbird

[1] *Colonial Development Corporation Report 1954.*

[2] "A final factor affecting economic development must be mentioned. This is the pessimism about the prospects of British Honduras, which has been prevalent despite favourable pronouncements by experts on the country's potentialities. This scepticism is in part due to the failures of the Colonial Development Corporation, and to doubts about the attractiveness to investors of the country in its present condition, and in part also due to genuine uncertainty about the short-term outlook." Waddell, *op. cit.*, p. 108.

[3] For example, sugar from the Corozal factory was loaded into barges for a voyage of many hours through treacherous waters to Belize. There it was unloaded and stored in a warehouse to await shipment by lighter.

highway connecting the capital to the Stann Creek valley was made possible by the provision of funds in Great Britain.[1]

Though subject to hurricanes which devastated portions of the country in 1955 and 1961, British Honduras was able to extend its plantation economy. Yet it was unlikely for many years, if ever, to be a cheap exporter of sugar, citrus or cacao. Its cost of living was likely to remain high, with much of its foodstuffs imported, though this might be partly remedied by growing a wider variety for the home market.[2]

For any significant development, outside capital would be required. This small territory would have to stand in the queue with the other underdeveloped countries, hoping to attract investment. Thinly populated, it could at least consider an immigration scheme, provided a suitable one, financed from outside, were put forward. In an age when world agriculture was being rapidly mechanized, and when the application of scientific methods was steadily increasing production, a territory without the means of repairing heavy machinery, or the technical facilities necessary for agricultural research, was at an increasingly heavy disadvantage.

*　　*　　*　　*

The most remarkable feature of Great Britain's policy in regard to British Honduras has been its determination to hold this territory. While it may be true that in the seventeenth, eighteenth and nineteenth centuries the acquiring of overseas territory was highly regarded by the European powers for its own sake, yet British Honduras had no very obvious advantages to Great Britain. The climate was not suitable for European settlement, especially since malaria had not then been brought under control. There were no resources apart from the forests and no attempt was made to develop a plantation economy, which in any event was expressly prohibited by treaty. From a strategic point of view, it was too far from Veracruz or the Isthmus of Panama to be of practical use as a base against Spanish commerce. In fact, Great Britain left the British traders to their own devices. Compared to the value of the sugar-growing islands of the Caribbean, British Honduras was of small account.

[1] The cost of this road was £500,000.
[2] The whole subject of land use and farming in British Honduras which bristles with difficulties is examined in a recent report by A. C. S. Wright et al., *Land in British Honduras* (HMSO, London, 1959).

That the Belize settlement continued to exist is a tribute to the determination of its handful of colonists. Against the settlers' resolve to remain, the half-hearted efforts of Spain to eject them failed. No doubt the vast area of empty land in Spanish America was a major factor in the survival of the colony isolated as it also was from colonial Guatemala by the forests of Petén. Yet the difficulties which remained were formidable. A colony existed with a population less than that of a British parliamentary constituency. As seemed to be an almost universal practice, it sought independence. For reasons which it considered cogent, it had rejected entry into the West Indies Federation, thereby contributing to the failure of that attempt to unite the West Indies colonies. By following this course, it assumed for itself future responsibilities of representation overseas and of defence, both costly matters.[1]

Political and economic problems reacted on one another in British Honduras as everywhere else. The political future of the country was the responsibility of its inhabitants. It was unlikely that Great Britain would seek in any way to deflect it from the course which its population desired. There was no easy solution for British Honduras. Nor had the path of small states always been an easy one. The Baymen, however, had given proof enough in the past of their courage and determination, which would help to guide them through the difficulties which seemed to encompass them.

[1] Describing the political situation of British Honduras, Professor Preston E. James writes: "The result is an impasse, in which the Guatemalans are denied the access to the coast which might permit the economic development of the empty northern part of their country, and in which at the same time the British tax-payers must continue to carry the burden of a dependent colony. The people of British Honduras suffer from poverty and illiteracy, and from a rate of increase that has already outrun the local food supply." *Op. cit.*, p. 857.

CHAPTER XVI

CONCLUSION

Great Britain, France and the Netherlands put forth great efforts to establish themselves in the Caribbean during the seventeenth, and even more during the eighteenth, centuries. At the close of the Napoleonic Wars Britain was supreme at sea with a large and highly efficient navy. Yet, as sometimes happens, when a prize has been attained after great and prolonged effort, its worth turned out to be illusory. The very effectiveness of Great Britain's blockade of Europe had stimulated the beginnings of the continental sugar-beet industry, which, in the second half of the nineteenth century, played a major rôle in the decline of the prosperity of the sugar colonies. When the abolition of slavery created labour problems in most of the colonies, all three European powers resorted to the recruiting of Asian labour to replace the Negroes who, in many cases, were no longer prepared to work in the cane fields.

In the task of preparing for full citizenship the colonial populations, which consisted mainly of ex-slaves, indentured labourers and their descendants, the policies of the three European powers differed. Though it had finally freed its slaves fifteen years later than Great Britain, France was first to establish adult franchise. Both France and the Netherlands probably exceeded Great Britain in the quality of the primary education provided in their Caribbean territories. Great Britain, on the other hand, later established the University of the West Indies, a development which would not have been warranted in the much less populous French and Dutch territories, where students were enabled to pursue higher studies in Europe.

From the days of Colbert, France had favoured a close political and economic union with its colonies. Great Britain, on the other hand, had early conceded the substantial measure of self-government which flourished in the eighteenth century, far ahead of the systems adopted by Britain's rivals, even if the Netherlands had made a beginning with its College of Kiezers in its Guiana colonies.[1] In both the British and Dutch systems, however, there was a dichotomy between the

[1] *Vide* Chapter XIV, p. 139.

authority of the governor, who represented the metropolitan government, and the elected representatives of the colonists. In most of the British Caribbean colonies, the consequent constitutional difficulties were resolved by the institution of authoritarian Crown Colony government involving the abolition of the former elective Legislative Assemblies. The Colonial Office, which inspired this policy, acted from the highest of motives, convinced that it could govern the colonies in the general interest of the inhabitants more efficiently and fairly than the former Assemblies, which essentially represented a small group of planting and land-owning interests. A similar approach in a different context may be seen in the U.S. interventions in the Dominican Republic and in Haiti which while they lasted produced honest and more efficient administrations but politically provided no permanent solution since they were followed in each case by a prolonged period of undemocratic and corrupt government.[1] Though Great Britain, from the Reform Bill onwards, had expanded its own franchise, the widening of the electorate was not adopted as a solution in the colonies.

As the market for sugar worsened in the nineteenth century, the colonies became increasingly dependent on subsidy or other help from the metropolitan powers. The weakness of the island economies became increasingly apparent especially to the planters and merchants. Though trade was bad, there was a belief that a territory on its own would fare infinitely worse. The example of Haiti was not encouraging. Commercial depression may have contributed to the more ready acceptance of the Crown Colony system of government.

*   *   *   *

Both British and Dutch officials at home failed to appreciate how limited was the period that remained to prepare for self-government, despite the implied warning from the widespread unrest in the

---

[1] "Our intervention in Santo Domingo brought, while it lasted, the only period of safety, peace, and prosperity which the Dominican people had so far enjoyed—and some Dominicans doubt whether they have been better off since it ended. While the Dominican state, as such, temporarily lost much of its independence, the Dominican people temporarily gained more independence than they had before or were to have after. The state was worse off, but the human beings within the state were better off." Louis J. Halle, *American Foreign Policy* (London, 1958), pp. 165-6.

The United States administered the Dominican Republic from 1916 to 1924 and Haiti from 1915 to 1934.

171

Caribbean prior to World War II. As a result of this miscalculation, the period for the training of politicians was too short.[1] The establishment at an earlier date of an ever-increasing measure of self-government would have provided for island leaders and island electorates a longer preparation for the difficult tasks which faced them. These leaders, who in some cases sat as nominated members, would also have been in closer touch with the people. With the adoption of universal franchise after World War II, they were usually swept aside in the British territories. The system of a nominated Upper House, continued in the recent constitutions of Jamaica and Trinidad, inevitably meant that the senators would have a much weaker status than if they had been directly chosen by the electors.[2] This is tacitly admitted in the recent constitutions of Jamaica and Trinidad under which ministers drawn from the senate are limited to a maximum of three or a minimum of two.[3] The existence of a group of politicians, trained in the course of years of popular elections under a franchise restricted at first but ever expanding, might have saved British Guiana from the disasters of racial hatred: it would also have been of value in other territories. Unfortunately, the art of government cannot be acquired successfully from textbooks alone, since the holding of office is the best training for statesmanship. Too long a period of one party in power may even result in a weakening of the democratic machine.

*   *   *   *

The rise of nationalism in the Caribbean, especially since World War II, was comparable to that in many other parts of the world.

[1] "But a century and a half of the most carefully devised and unselfishly administered bureaucratic administration has conclusively proved that power without real responsibility is as much a failure in the East as in the West, and has demonstrated the truth of the statement of John Stuart Mill that self-government is ultimately far better than government by the most well-intentioned external authority." Sir Satyendra Sinha, the representative of India in the Imperial War Cabinet, *Address to private meeting of members of the Lords and Commons and members of Dominion Parliaments held at the Houses of Parliament, July 31, 1918.*

[2] An illustration of this principle may be seen in the much greater influence of the elected United States Senate in comparison with the nominated Canadian Senate.

[3] *Caribbean and North Atlantic Territories—The Jamaica (Constitution) Order in Council 1962*, No. 1550 (HMSO, 1962), Section 70, p. 54. Cf. *The Trinidad and Tobago (Constitution) Order in Council 1962*, No. 1875 (HMSO, 1962), Section 23, p. 21.

After the first great assault on colonialism had taken place in the New England colonies, closely followed by the successful revolt in St. Domingue, it was perhaps surprising that this movement did not immediately spread to the British, French and Dutch colonies. Many factors, however, contributed to restrain the pressure for independence. Political disturbances were usually limited to a single island. Since the metropolitan powers controlled sea communications, incipient revolts were quickly checked. Though Great Britain had been ready to encourage Simón Bolívar and other liberators, it had also unsuccessfully used armed intervention in an attempt to suppress the Haitian slave revolt, fearing its spread to Jamaica. Isolation from the mainland was a potent factor in the retention by Spain of Cuba and Puerto Rico long after the loss of the rest of its American empire.

The widespread riots in the years before World War II were the first indication of a decisive rise of nationalism. They led to the alliance of political parties with trade unions which in the British territories speeded political advance, even if later it was to cause problems of its own.'

In the early days, communication difficulties compelled the colonial powers to decentralize their administrations by the establishment of separate governments. This has been reflected in the post-World War II independence movements where the island remains the basic unit. Insularism played a major rôle in the failure of the West Indies Federation. Jamaica, with many citizens out of work and impoverished, was dismayed at the prospect of having to shoulder responsibility in regard to even poorer communities in the Leeward and Windward Islands. Fear of immigration from these islands made Trinidad insist on a delay in free movement of labour within the Federation. The individual units of the Leeward and Windward Islands struggled to maintain distinct governments which they could ill afford. So far these concepts seem largely to have prevailed, to the point that Jamaica and Trinidad have received independence. Great Britain appears to have now accepted the future establishment of a federation comprising Barbados, the Leeward and the Windward Islands; and of British Guiana, and British Honduras with its 90,000 inhabitants, as additional independent countries within the Commonwealth.

France has attempted to solve the whole problem by incorporating its Caribbean territories as French departments. The outcome of this experiment remains uncertain. Undoubtedly, France has much

173

to offer in culture, education and trade. If it were prepared to finance its Caribbean territories on a scale comparable to what the United States is attempting in Puerto Rico, it is conceivable that it might be successful, despite the fact that the standard of living in Puerto Rico is still below that of the poorest U.S. state. It is, however, extremely doubtful whether France, with its other overseas commitments, could possibly divert sufficient finance for this. As it is, the French officials in the overseas departments, higher paid and with other advantages, are a source of irritation to the impoverished colonists who overlook the vastly greater number of their own countrymen living in France.

* * * *

If the British islands failed to maintain their Federation, it may be wondered whether a wider federation of the whole Caribbean would be more successful. Here even greater problems of languages, laws, religions, customs and traditions exist. Perhaps the greatest weakness of any Caribbean federation would be the lack of commercial bonds to weld it together. A major difficulty is the production by the Caribbean territories of many of the same commodities which therefore must depend on outside markets. An extensive local trade might take long to develop. Usually an industrial complex, once established, expands and gains momentum as a result of demand from within. Industries attract further industries to supply their needs. Though theoretically transport should be cheap in an archipelago, it is less so in an area where seas may be turbulent, storms violent and, above all, harbour facilities antiquated.

Though separated by the Atlantic Ocean, the European Economic Community may prove to be of great value to the Caribbean countries by reason of its need for supplies of tropical produce and its high purchasing power, especially to those territories which may obtain entry through their direct association with a member nation, or by obtaining associate membership. Whether the amount of future aid will exceed what has been previously provided cannot be accurately forecast. It must be kept in mind that other and larger undeveloped countries will also look to the Common Market as an outlet for their products, and for development aid. Some of these countries may prove to be serious competitors.

Notwithstanding the immense influence of European culture in these territories, inevitably they will develop their own systems of

174

politics and culture. The influence of the racial backgrounds of Africa and of Asia may increase rapidly under independence. This will provide a study of great interest. It is unlikely that the development of Jamaica and of Barbados with a dominantly Negro population will follow precisely the same pattern as that of Trinidad and British Guiana with multi-racial backgrounds, despite past British influence upon all three. A comparison with the methods of handling multi-racial problems by African and Asian countries will be of particular interest. Influenced by Netherlands policy, the political development of Surinam with its diverse racial background will be of especial significance. The dream of philosophers such as Gilberto Freyre, and of José Vasconcelos who wrote that the future, particularly in the tropics, lay in a "cosmic" race, will be put to the test.[1]

Meanwhile, the sharply rising population in many of the Caribbean territories presents alarming features. Emigration at best will be a palliative, and immigration has already been restricted by Great Britain—a severe blow to the British Caribbean. Nor is it likely that the United States or Canada will in the future be ready to receive large numbers of Caribbean immigrants. There has been an unobtrusive but steady move of many persons from the French Antilles to France, but it has never been of a size to create the problems and antagonisms, which have arisen in London and certain other British urban areas.[2] With heavy unemployment in Martinique and Guadeloupe, however, the position might change rapidly. France would like to fill French Guiana with immigrants. It has wanted to do so for at least two centuries. Yet the population of the territory is less than it was a hundred years ago. The scheme of training army conscripts in engineering and agricultural work is the latest attempt to promote settlement in French Guiana.[3] However, it would not be surprising if the future pressure of emigration from the French Antilles was to Paris and not to Cayenne. In the Dutch territories, the success of the oil refineries in Curaçao and Aruba created a demand for immigrants. Recent reorganization has, however, reversed the position, making it necessary to repatriate some of the surplus non-Dutch labour, part of which had originated from the British islands. With its extensive area of land and successful small farms, Surinam has no surplus population. Free movement of citizens exists between the Netherlands and its partners and it would seem unlikely that difficulties will

[1] José Vasconcelos, La Raza Cósmica (Mexico, 1948), pp. 26-32.
[2] Vide Chapter IX, pp. 84-90. [3] Vide Chapter X, pp. 102-103.

175

arise in the immediate future. Yet the problems of increasing numbers, which the world of the future must face, is already becoming acute in some parts of the Caribbean. The Antilles afford a preview of some of the difficulties which other countries will one day be compelled to face.

*   *   *   *

Attacks on the colonial powers have been bitter and sustained. Certainly Great Britain, France and the Netherlands made mistakes in their policies towards their Caribbean territories. Admitting their imperfections, the colonial governments in the Caribbean will stand comparison with those of other countries in tropical America which have long enjoyed independence. Great Britain, France and the Netherlands have for centuries been leaders of Western democratic thought and have helped forward the civilization of the world, not least in the art of government. In the Caribbean territories which they have administered in our day, the standards of justice, including both the courts of law and the police services, have been high. Elections have been honest and there has been no evidence of widespread corruption in politics or commerce.

It may be that profit in the past has been well matched by expenditure in recent years. The Netherlands and Belgium have shown that the loss of colonies does not retard commercial prosperity at home: it may even promote it. Great Britain's desire to join the European Economic Community may have been influenced unconsciously by these examples, even if most British citizens also strongly desire the continuance of an effective Commonwealth. The Victorian concept of a tightly knit federal empire as an extension of Great Britain overseas was finally discarded when the Statute of Westminster, more suited to the nationalism of the twentieth century, was adopted in 1931.[1]

The territories of the three European powers have succeeded in maintaining a free press. To achieve this may be even more difficult in a small than in a large territory where newspapers are likely to be more numerous and therefore more varied in their comment. A single organ in a territory may be placed in an invidious position when it feels compelled to criticize a government or local institution. The effect of British press interests purchasing substantial stakes in organs of the press in Trinidad, Barbados and British Guiana is of too recent

[1] Sir J. R. Seeley, *The Expansion of England* (London, 1925), pp. 88-9.

176

origin to assess.[1] It would be reasonable to expect that the traditional freedom of the British press would blend with and strengthen that of the Caribbean territories. With the situation of censorship and of suppression which has existed in some of the neighbouring Caribbean republics, the maintenance of this is a matter of supreme importance.

Lying astride the principal routes of communications in the heart of the Americas, the strategic importance of the Caribbean is immense. The Cuban crisis of 1962 made this clear to the world. Though the interests of Great Britain, France and the Netherlands in this area are now small compared to those of the United States, their influence has not been eliminated. Their policies formed the pattern which much of the Caribbean has followed; the influence of centuries of administration continues. Should the free institutions, developed in these democratic European countries and extended to the Caribbean, meet with permanent acceptance, modified where necessary to suit local conditions, an extension of democracy will have been achieved in an area where it has often been lacking. Though weak and far from wealthy, these new countries have an opportunity of exerting beyond their boundaries a beneficial influence for humanity.

Great Britain, France and the Netherlands have implanted their concepts of democracy in these territories. If their administration has varied, their ideals have been similar. Educational systems on the whole have been effective, while freedom of speech, religious toleration, and honest administration have prevailed. To be fairly judged, their record must be viewed broadly in the context of what has been achieved elsewhere, for perfection in government has still eluded the human race.

[1] In April 1961, Thomson British Publications acquired control of the Trinidad Publishing Company, publishers of *The Guardian* and the *Sunday Guardian*. *Hispanic American Report*, Vol. XIV, p. 326.

This was followed in June 1961 by the announcement that Overseas Newspapers, part of the *Daily Mirror* group, and the *Liverpool Daily Post and Echo* had jointly purchased a majority interest in the *Barbados Advocate* and *Sunday Advocate*, with a substantial shareholding remaining in local hands. In the same month, the acquisition of the *Guiana Graphic* and the *Sunday Graphic* of British Guiana was announced by *Daily Mirror* Newspapers. *Hispanic American Report*, Vol. XIV, pp. 512, 513.

All these are leading newspapers in their territories.

BIBLIOGRAPHY

179

The Bibliography has been grouped into three main sections; Great Britain and British Territories; France and French Territories; the Netherlands and Netherlands Territories. In addition, a General section has been added, relating to more than one group of territories. Sources and studies mentioned have been included together with others of relevance.

Newspapers, periodicals and year books have been of considerable value, particularly in the research covering the post-World War II period. Those referred to in this book have been included, together with some others which have been of particular use.

ABBREVIATIONS

CDC	Colonial Development Corporation.
Cmd.	British White Paper.
Hansard	Parliamentary Reports.
HMSO	Her Majesty's Stationery Office, London.
n.d.	No date.
n.p.	No publisher.
U.C.W.I.	University College of the West Indies.
U.W.I.	University of the West Indies.

I. GREAT BRITAIN AND BRITISH TERRITORIES

SOURCES

A. *Official Documents*

ACWORTH, ANGUS W., *Colonial Research Studies No. 2*, HMSO, London, 1951.
Annual Report on British Guiana, 1959, British Guiana Government, Georgetown.
British Caribbean Standing Closer Association Committee: *Report 1948-1949* (Rance Report), Advocate Co., Bridgetown, Barbados, 1949.
British Dependencies in the Caribbean and North Atlantic, 1939-1952, Cmd. 8575, Colonial Office, London, 1952.
British Guiana: land of opportunity, 1958, Government of British Guiana.
British Honduras, Peace Handbooks, Historical Section of the Foreign Office, Vol. XXI, HMSO, London, 1920.
British Honduras, 1957, HMSO, London, 1959.
British Honduras: new sugar factory, an investment opportunity, Government of British Honduras, n.d.
British Virgin Islands, 1959 and 1960, HMSO, London, 1962.
Caribbean and North Atlantic Territories 1959, The Jamaica (Constitution) (Amendment) Order in Council, 1959, No. 2202, HMSO, London, 1959.
Caribbean and North Atlantic Territories, The Jamaica (Constitution) (Amendment) Order in Council, 1961, No. 571, HMSO, London, 1961.
Caribbean and North Atlantic Territories, The Jamaica Constitution Order in Council, 1959, No. 862, HMSO, London, 1959.
Caribbean and North Atlantic Territories, The Jamaica (Constitution) Order in Council, 1962, No. 1550, HMSO, London, 1962.
Caribbean and North Atlantic Territories, The Trinidad and Tobago (Constitution) Order in Council, 1961, No. 1192, HMSO, London, 1961.
Caribbean Commission, *Caribbean Timbers, their Utilisation and Trade within the Area*, Report of the timber conference held at Kent House, Trinidad, on April 15-22, 1958, Kent House, Port-of-Spain, 1955.
Caribbean Market Survey: Rice, Caribbean Commission Central Secretariat, Port-of-Spain, Trinidad, 1955.
Colonial Development and Welfare 1946-1955, Lewis, Roy, Central Office of Information, 1956.
Colonial Development Corporation Report and Accounts, 1948, 1950-1953, 1958, 1960, 1961, HMSO, London.
Commonwealth Immigrants Act, 1962, 10 & 11 Eliz. II. Ch. 21, HMSO, London, 1962.
Commonwealth Prime Ministers' Meeting 1962: Final Communiqué, Cmd. 1836, London, 1962.
Comptroller's Reports on Development and Welfare in the West Indies, 1952, Sir George Seel, Colonial No. 291, London, 1953.
Conference on the Closer Association of the British West Indian Colonies, Montego Bay, Jamaica, 11-19 Sept. 1947, *Pt. 1, Report . . . 1948; Pt. 2, Proceedings . . . 1948*, HMSO, London, 1948.

Development and Welfare in the West Indies, 1957, Luke, Sir Stephen, K.C.M.G., Comptroller, Colonial No. 337, London, 1958.

The Economic Development of British Guiana: Report of a Mission organized by the International Bank for Reconstruction and Development at the request of the Government of British Guiana, Johns Hopkins Press, Baltimore, 1953.

The Economic Development of Jamaica, Report by a Mission of the International Bank for Reconstruction and Development, Johns Hopkins Press, Baltimore, 1952.

The Economics of Nationhood, Government Printing Office, Trinidad, September 11, 1959.

Economic Survey of Jamaica 1959, Government Printer, Kingston, Government of Jamaica, Central Planning Unit, 1960.

An Economic Survey of the Colonial Territories, 1951: Vol. IV, *The West Indian and American Territories*, Colonial No. 281, London, 1953.

European Integration and West Indian Trade, Office of the Premier and Ministry of Finance, Trinidad and Tobago, 1960.

Extracts from Papers Relative to the West Indies, printed by order of the House of Commons, 1839, Clowes and Sons, London, 1840.

A Fiscal Survey of the British Caribbean, PREST, A. R., HMSO, London, 1957.

Industrial Development in Jamaica, Trinidad, Barbados and British Guiana: Report of a Mission of U.K. Industrialists, Oct.-Nov. 1952, Colonial No. 294, London, 1953.

Industrial Development in the United Kingdom Dependencies, Central Office of Information, London, 1960.

Jamaica: The Making of a Nation, Central Office of Information Reference Pamphlet, HMSO, London, 1962.

Land in British Honduras, Report of the British Honduras Land Use Survey Team, D. H. Romney, ed., Colonial Research Publications No. 24, HMSO, London, 1959.

The Modern Commonwealth, Sandys, Duncan, HMSO, London, 1962.

Report by the Conference on British Caribbean Federation held in London in February, 1956, Cmd. 9733, London, 1956.

Report by the Honourable E. F. L. Wood on his Visit to the West Indies and British Guiana, Dec. 1921-Feb. 1922, Cmd. 1679, Colonial Office, London, 1922.

Report by the joint committee of the House of Lords and the House of Commons appointed to consider the Petition of the State of Western Australia, HMSO, London, 1935.

Report by the Leeward Islands and Windward Islands Constitutional Conference, Cmd. 1434, London, 1961.

Report of the Board of Inquiry into a Trade Dispute in the Sugar Industry of Trinidad, Government Printing Office, Trinidad, 1960.

Report of the British Caribbean Federal Capital Commission, Colonial No. 328, London, 1956.

Report of the British Guiana Commission, April 1927, Cmd. 2841, London, 1927.

Report of the Commission of Enquiry into the Banana Industry of Jamaica, 1959, Vol. I, Government Printer, Kingston, Jamaica, 1959.

182

Report of the Commission of Enquiry on the Sugar Industry of Jamaica, January 1960, Goldenberg, H. Carl, O.B.E., Q.C., Chairman; Kingston, Jamaica, 1960.

Report of a Commission of Inquiry into Disturbances in British Guiana in February 1962, Colonial No. 354, 1962.

Report of the Conference on Movement of Persons within a British Caribbean Federation, Port-of-Spain, Trinidad, 1955.

Report of Royal Commission appointed 1938 (Moyne Report), Cmd. 6607, London, 1945.

Report of the Royal Commission appointed to inquire into the public revenues, expenditures, debts, and liabilities of the Islands of Jamaica, Grenada, St. Vincent, Tobago and St. Lucia, and of the Leeward Islands, 1884, C. 3840.

Report of the West Indies Constitutional Conference, 1961, Cmd. 1417, London, 1961.

Report on Closer Association of the British West Indian Colonies, Cmd. 7120, Colonial Office, London, 1947.

Report presented to the Comptroller for Development and Welfare in the West Indies by the Regional Economic Committee of the British West Indies, British Guiana and British Honduras for the period July 1954-December 1955, Port-of-Spain, Trinidad.

Statement of Action Taken on the Recommendations of the West India Royal Commission, Cmd. 6656, London, 1945.

Technical Assistance from the United Kingdom for Overseas Development, Cmd. 1308, London, 1961.

This is the Rupununi, Melville, Edwina, Government Information Services, British Guiana, 1956.

Trinidad and Tobago: The Making of a Nation, Central Office of Information Reference Pamphlet, HMSO, London, 1962.

The U.K. Colonial Development and Welfare Acts, Central Office of Information, London, 1960.

The West Indies: a Nation in the Making, Central Office of Information Reference Pamphlet No. 30, HMSO, London, 1958.

The West Indies: Report of the Trade and Tariffs Commission, Parts I and II, Government of the West Indies, 1958.

West India Royal Commission, 1938-1939: Recommendations, Cmd. 6174, London, 1940.

West India Royal Commission, 1938-1939: Statement of action taken on the Recommendations, Cmd. 659, London, 1945.

Yallahs Valley Land Authority, 1951-1961, Ten Years of Progress, Kingston, Jamaica, n.p., n.d.

B. Unofficial Documents and Pamphlets

The Booker Group of Companies, Booker Bros., British Guiana, n.d.

Cambridge Expedition to British Honduras, 1959-1960, General Report, Cambridge, 1960.

Central Banking Arrangements for the West Indian Federation, Bloomfield, A. I., U.C.W.I., Jamaica, 1962.

183

An Economic Study of Small Farming in Jamaica, Edwards, David, Institute of Social and Economic Research, U.C.W.I., Jamaica, 1961.
Into Peace, Mitchell, Harold, Hutchinson and Co., London, 1945.
Jamaica Supplement, *The Times*, London, August 3, 1962.
Kaiser Bauxite—The Story of the World's Largest Open Pit Bauxite Mining Operation, Kaiser, Jamaica, 1960.
Migration and Development in the West Indies, Reubens, E. P., U.C.W.I., Jamaica, 1962.
Nationalism and Industrial Development in the British Caribbean, Rawle, Farley, *Daily Chronicle*, Georgetown, British Guiana, 1957.
The Ras Tafari Movement in Kingston, Jamaica: a Report, Smith, Augier and Nettleford, Institute of Social and Economic Research, U.C.W.I., Jamaica, 1960.
A Report on Jamaican Migration to Great Britain, Senior, Clarence and Douglas Manley, Government Printer, Kingston, Jamaica, 1955.
SINHA, Sir SATYENDRA, *Address to private meeting of members of the Lords and Commons and members of Dominion Parliaments held at the Houses of Parliament, 31 July, 1918*, Empire Parliamentary Association, London, 1918.
Survey of Industry in the West Indies, Voelker, Alter D., U.C.W.I., Jamaica, 1961.
Trinidad and Tobago, Independence Supplement, Sunday Guardian, Port-of-Spain, August 26, 1962.
The Voice of the Dominions, Addresses by Sir Robert Borden, Prime Minister of Canada, and Lt.-Gen. J. C. Smuts, Minister of Defence, South Africa, The Empire Parliamentary Association, London, 1917.
What Independence Means to you, Government Printing Office, Trinidad, 1962.

C. *Newspapers, Periodicals and Year Books*

BARBADOS
Barbados Advocate

BRITISH GUIANA
Daily Argosy
Daily Chronicle
Guiana Graphic
Sunday Chronicle
Sunday Graphic
The Sunday Argosy
Thunder

BRITISH HONDURAS
The Belize Billboard
The Belize Times

JAMAICA
The Daily Gleaner
Handbook of Jamaica

Jamaica Times
Public Opinion
Social and Economic Studies, U.W.I.
Spotlight
Sunday Gleaner
The West Indian Economist
West Indian Review
Who's Who in Jamaica

TRINIDAD AND TOBAGO
Caribbean Quarterly, U.W.I.
Federal Information Service Press Releases
Sunday Guardian
The Nation
Trinidad Guardian
Trinidad and Tobago Year Book
West Indies Federal Review

A. *Books*

ABRAHAMS, PETER, *Jamaica: an Island Mosaic*, HMSO, London, 1957.
AMERY, L. S., *A Balanced Economy*, Hutchinson, London, 1954.
AMERY, L. S., *The Empire in the New Era*, Edward Arnold, London, 1928.
ASPINALL, Sir ALGERNON, *A Wayfarer in the West Indies*, Methuen, London, 1928.
ASPINALL, Sir ALGERNON, *The Pocket Guide to the West Indies*, Methuen, London, 1960.
ATTLEE, C. R., *Purpose and Policy*, Hutchinson, London, 1946.
AYEARST, MORLEY, *The British West Indies*, Allen & Unwin, London, 1960.
BECKFORD, WILLIAM, *A Descriptive Account of the Island of Jamaica*, Vol. I, Egerton, London, 1790.
BIANCHI, W. J., *Belize*, Las Americas Publishing Co., New York, 1959.
BLACK, CLINTON V., *History of Jamaica*, Collins, Glasgow, 1958.
BOYD, CHARLES W., ed., *Mr. Chamberlain's Speeches*, Constable, London, 1914.
BRYCE, WYATT et al., *Historic Port Royal*, Tourist Trade Development Board, Kingston, Jamaica, 1952.
BURDON, J. A., *Archives of British Honduras*, 3 Vols., Sifton Praed, London, 1931-1935.
BURNS, Sir ALAN, *History of the British West Indies*, Allen & Unwin, London, 1954.
CAIGER, STEPHEN L., *British Honduras, Past and Present*, Allen & Unwin, London, 1951.
Canada and the West Indies Federation, Mount Allison University Publication No. 2, Sackville, New Brunswick, Canada, 1957.
CHURCHILL, Sir WINSTON S., *A History of the English-Speaking Peoples*, Cassell, London, 1957.
COUDRIER DE CHASSAIGNE, J., *Les Trois Chamberlain*, Flammarion, Paris, 1939.
CUMPER, G. E., ed., *The Economy of the West Indies*, U.C.W.I., Kingston, 1960.
CUNDALL, FRANK, ed., *Lady Nugent's Journal*, Adam and Charles Black, London, 1907.
CURTIN, PHILIP D., *Two Jamaicans*, Harvard University Press, Cambridge, Massachusetts, 1955.
EISNER, GISELA, *Jamaica, 1830-1930: a Study in Economic Growth*, Manchester University Press, Manchester, 1961.
GARVIN, JAMES L., *The Life of Joseph Chamberlain*, Macmillan, London, 1932.
GLASS, RUTH, *Newcomers: the West Indians in London*, Centre for Urban Studies, Report No. 1, Allen & Unwin, London, 1960.
GRIFFITH, J. A. G., JUDITH HENDERSON, MARGARET USBORNE, and DONALD WOOD, *Coloured Immigrants in Britain*, Oxford University Press, London, 1960.
HARLOW, V. T., *History of Barbados, 1625-85*, Oxford, 1926.

HUMPHREYS, R. A., *The Diplomatic History of British Honduras: 1638-1901*, Oxford University Press, 1961.
JONES, A. CREECH, *New Fabian Colonial Essays*, Hogarth Press, London, 1959.
KINGSLEY, CHARLES, *At Last: a Christmas in the West Indies*, Macmillan, New York, 1871.
KLASS, MORTON, *East Indians in Trinidad*, Columbia University Press, 1961.
LE PAGE, R. B. and DAVID DE CAMP, *Jamaican Creole*, Macmillan, London, 1960.
LEWIS, MATTHEW, G., *Journal of a West India Proprietor*, Murray, London, 1834.
LOWENTHAL, DAVID, ed., *The West Indies Federation*, Columbia University Press, 1961.
MACLEOD, IAIN, *Neville Chamberlain*, Frederick Muller, London, 1961.
MAUNDER, W. F., *Employment in an Underdeveloped Area—a sample survey of Kingston, Jamaica*, Yale University Press, 1960.
MITCHELL, Sir HAROLD, *In My Stride*, Chambers, London, 1951.
NAMIER, L. B., *The Structure of Politics at the Accession of George III*, Macmillan, London, 1929.
OLIVIER, LORD, *Jamaica, the Blessed Island*, Faber & Faber, London, 1936.
PARES, RICHARD, *A West India Fortune*, Longmans, London, 1950.
PROUDFOOT, MARY, *Britain and the United States in the Caribbean*, Praeger, New York, 1953.
RAGATZ, LOWELL J., *The Fall of the Planter Class in the British Caribbean*, New York, 1928.
ROBERTSON, E. ARNOT, *The Spanish Town Papers*, The Cresset Press, London, 1959.
RUCK, S. K., ed., *The West Indian Comes to England*, Family Welfare Association, Routledge & Kegan Paul, London, 1960.
SEELEY, Sir J. R., *The Expansion of England*, Macmillan, London, 1925.
SCOTT, MICHAEL, ed., *Tom Cringle's Log*, Gibbings, London, 1894.
SHERLOCK, PHILIP M., *Caribbean Citizen*, Longmans, London, 1957.
SMITH, R. T., *British Guiana*, Oxford University Press, London, 1962.
TREVELYAN, G. M., *Illustrated History of England*, Longmans, London, 1956.
WADDELL, D. A. G., *British Honduras*, Oxford University Press, London, 1961.
WHEARE, K. C., *The Constitutional Structure of the Commonwealth*, Oxford University Press, London, 1960.
WILLIAMS, ERIC, *History of the People of Trinidad and Tobago*, PNM Publishing Co., Port-of-Spain, Trinidad, 1962.
WISEMAN, H. V., *A Short History of the British West Indies*, University of London Press, 1950.

B. *Articles*

ARCHIBALD, CHARLES H., "The Failure of the West Indies Federation", *The World Today*, London, June 1962.
BETHEL, JEANETTE, "A National Accounts Study of the Economy of Barbados", *Social and Economic Studies*, Vol. 9, No. 2, Institute of Social and Economic Research, U.C.W.I., Jamaica, June 1960.

"Canada—West Indies Economic and Political Relations", *The West Indian Economist*, Kingston, Jamaica, December 1958.

"A Colony in Dispute", *The Round Table*, London, March 1958.

"Coloured Immigrants: Still Open Door?", *The Economist*, London, February 25, 1961

CROCKER, JOHN, "West Indies Bases Talks Leave Both Sides Content", *New York Herald Tribune*, January 8, 1961.

DE GRAFF, EDWARD, "Cheddi Jagan y el futuro de la Guayana Británica", *Cuadernos*, Paris, February 1952.

"The Economics of Federation", *The West Indian Economist*, Kingston, Jamaica, July 1958.

"The Economy of Trinidad", *The West Indian Economist*, Kingston, Jamaica, March 1960.

FARLEY, RAWLE, *Trade Unions and Politics in the British Caribbean, Daily Chronicle*, British Guiana, 1957.

FAUCHILLE, PAUL, "Le conflit de limites entre le Brésil et la Grande-Bretagne et la sentence arbitrale du Roi d'Italie", *Revue Générale de Droit International Public*, Vol. XII, Paris, 1905.

FOX, DAVID J., "Recent Work on British Honduras", *Geographical Review*, New York, January 1962.

GLASS, RUTH, "West Indian Search for Exits", *The Times*, London, November 23, 1961.

GREENRIDGE, C. W. W., "The British West Indies", *International Affairs*, Vol. XXV, No. 1., London, January 1949.

"Guiana Elections", *Manchester Guardian Weekly*, August 24, 1961.

"Is British Honduras a Reality?", *The West Indian Economist*, Kingston, Jamaica, December 1961.

JAGAN, CHEDDI, "Socialism and Democracy", *Monthly Review*, New York, February 1962.

JEPHCOTT, PEARL and TONY LYNES, "Jobless Young West Indians", *Manchester Guardian Weekly*, January 18, 1962.

KNIGHT, RUDOLPH H., "La Planificación y la Política en el Caribe Británico", *Revista de Ciencias Sociales*, Vol. IV, No. 1, Universidad de Puerto Rico, March 1960.

LEWIS, W. ARTHUR, "The Industrialisation of the British West Indies", *Caribbean Economic Review*, Vol. II, No. 1, Port-of-Spain, Trinidad, May 1950.

MITCHELL, Sir HAROLD, "Finance and Federation", *The West Indian Review*, Kingston, Jamaica, October 1957.

"Multi-Racial Britain?", *The Economist*, London, December 30, 1960.

"Political Perils", *The West Indian Economist*, Kingston, Jamaica, March 1961.

PROCTOR, JESSE HARRIS, Jr., "Britain's Pro-Federation Policy in the Caribbean: an Inquiry into Motivation", *The Canadian Journal of Economics and Political Science*, Vol. 22, No. 3, University of Toronto Press, August 1956.

RABINOWITZ, VICTOR, "Guiana Rightist Riots no Surprise to Jagan", *National Guardian*, New York, February 1962.

187

RAGATZ, LOWELL J., "L'absentéisme chez les grands propriétaires des Antilles anglaises, 1750-1830", *Revue d'Histoire des Colonies*, Paris, 1937.

ROBERTS, G. W. and D. O. MILLS, "Study of External Migration affecting Jamaica: 1953-1955", *Social and Economic Studies*, (Supplement to Vol. 7, No. 2), Institute of Social and Economic Research, U.C.W.I., Jamaica, June 1958.

SHERIDAN, RICHARD B., "The West India Sugar Crisis and British Slave Emancipation", *Journal of Economic History*, New York, December 1961.

STOCKDALE, Sir F., "The Work of the Caribbean Commission", *International Affairs*, Vol. XXIII, No. 2, London, April 1947.

SWAYNE, Brigadier-General Sir E., "British Honduras", *Geographical Journal*, London, September 1917.

THORNE, ALFRED P., "Size, Structure and Growth of the Economy of Jamaica", Supplement to *Social and Economic Studies*, Vol. 4, No. 4, U.C.W.I., Jamaica, 1955.

"To Aid or Not to Aid: Will the United States aid Premier Cheddi Jagan of British Guiana in Democratic Socialism?", *Monthly Review*, New York, December 1961.

II. FRANCE AND FRENCH TERRITORIES

SOURCES

A. *Official Documents*

Commission de modernisation et d'équipement des départements d'outre-mer, Rapport général, Paris, 1959.

France, institut national de la statistique et des études économiques. Annuaire statisque de la Guadeloupe 1949-53, Paris, 1954.

France, institut national de la statistique et des études économiques. Situation démographique dans les départements de la Martinique, de la Guadeloupe et de la Réunion, Paris, 1961.

French Guiana, Handbooks No. 137, Foreign Office, Historical Section, HMSO, London, 1920.

Journal Officiel de la Martinique.

La Guadeloupe, Ministère de la France d'Outre-Mer, Agence des Colonies, Paris, 1946.

La Martinique, Département français d'outre-mer, Secrétariat Générale du Gouvernement, Direction de la Documentation, Paris, 1961.

La Martinique, Ministère de la France d'outre-mer, Paris, 1941.

Rapport Général de la Commission de Modernisation et d'Equipement des Départements d'Outre-Mer, Guadeloupe et dépendances, Guyane française, Martinique, Réunion, Commissariat Général au plan de l'équipement et de la productivité, 1959.

Rapports au Conseil Général, Préfecture de la Guadeloupe.

Résultats statistiques du recensement général de la population des départements d'outre-mer effectué le 1er juillet 1954, Antilles françaises: Martinique, Guadeloupe, Guyane, Paris, 1956.

Revue Agricole du Service de l'Agriculture de la Guadeloupe et dépendances, Pointe-à-Pitre.

Sentence du Conseil fédéral suisse dans la question des frontières de la Guyane française et du Brésil, du 1er décembre 1900, Imprimerie Staempfli, Berne, 1900.

B. *Unofficial Documents and Pamphlets*

A French Pattern for Technical Assistance, Service de Presse et d'Information, Ambassade de France, New York, 1959.

Annuaire Noria: Martinique et Guadeloupe 1960-1961, Larose, Paris.

French Guiana, Service de Presse et d'Information, Ambassade de France, New York, 1959.

Guadeloupe, Service de Presse et d'Information, Ambassade de France, New York, 1956.

Martinique, Service de Presse et d'Information, Ambassade de France, New York, 1956.

Progress Report on the New French Community, Service de Presse et d'Information, Ambassade de France, New York, 1959.

The Community, Service de Presse et d'Information, Ambassade de France, New York, December 1959.

C. *Newspapers, Periodicals and Year Books*

FRENCH GUIANA	MARTINIQUE	GUADELOUPE
Radio Presse	*Le Courrier*	*Match*

STUDIES

A. *Books*

ABBONENC, E., J. HURAULT and R. SAHAN, *Bibliographie de la Guyane française concernant la Guyane et les territoires avoisinants*, Larose, Paris, 1957.

ALDUY, PAUL, *Principles and Methods of Colonial Administration*, "La naissance du nationalisme outre-mer", Colston Research Society and University of Bristol, Butterworths Scientific Publications, London, 1960.

BOUCHE, PIERRE, *La côte des esclaves*, E. Plon, Nourrit et Cie, Paris, 1885.

BROGAN, D. W., *The Development of Modern France*, Hamish Hamilton, London, 1940.

CHAILLEY-BERT, J., *Les compagnies de colonisation sous l'ancien régime*, Armand Colin, Paris, 1898.

CLÉMENT, PIERRE, *Histoire de la vie de l'administration de Colbert*, Guillaumin, Paris, 1846.

CORBIÈRE, EDWARD, *Le négrier*, Editions Jean Cres, Paris, 1936.

DE GAULLE, CHARLES, *Discours de guerre*, Egloff, Fribourg, 1944.

189

DE GAULLE, CHARLES, *Mémoires de guerre*, Plon, Paris, 1954.
DU TERTRE, PÈRE J.-B., *Histoire générale des Antilles*, 3 Vols., Paris, 1667-1671.
DUCHÊNE, ALBERT, *Histoire des finances coloniales de la France*, Payot, Paris, 1938.
DUCHÊNE, ALBERT, *La politique coloniale de la France*, Payot, Paris, 1928.
FAUVEL, LUC, *Developments Towards Self-Government in the Caribbean*, "Les conséquences économiques et sociales de l'assimilation administrative des Antilles françaises", Van Hoeve, The Hague, 1955.
FIDEL, CAMILLE, *La Paix Coloniale*, Sirey, Paris, 1918.
GUIEYSSE, MARCEL, *La Martinique, les colonies françaises d'Amérique*, Notre Domaine Coloniale, Paris, 1923.
HEARN, LAFCADIO, *Two Years in the French West Indies*, Harper Bros., New York, 1890.
JACOB, LÉON, *Les colonies françaises d'Amérique*, Notre Domaine Coloniale, Paris, n.d.
LASSERRE, GUY, *La Guadeloupe*, 2 Vols., Union Française d'Impression, Bordeaux, 1961.
LORIN, HENRI, *La France, puissance coloniale*, Augustin Challamel, Paris, 1906.
MÉRIMÉE, PROSPER, *The Slave Ship* (Tamango), trans. by Eliot Fay, Northwestern University Library, Evanston, Illinois, 1934.
PARKER, FRANKLIN D., *The Caribbean: British, French, Dutch, United States*, "Political Development in the French Caribbean", University of Florida Press, Gainesville, 1950.
PRIESTLEY, HERBERT INGRAM, *France Overseas: a Study of Modern Imperialism*, Appleton-Century, New York, 1938.
REVERT, EUGÈNE, *Les Antilles*, Armand Colin, Paris, 1954.
REVERT, EUGÈNE, *La France d'Amérique*, Société d'Editions Géographiques, Maritimes et Coloniales, Paris, 1949.
REVERT, EUGÈNE, *La Martinique*, Nouvelles Editions Latines, Paris, 1949.
REVERT, EUGÈNE, *Le Monde Caraïbe*, Editions Françaises, Paris, 1958.
REVERT, EUGÈNE, *Principles and Methods of Colonial Administration*, "La politique coloniale de la France: étude retrospective", Colston Research Society and University of Bristol, London, 1950.
ROBERT, Amiral GEORGES, *La France aux Antilles de 1939 à 1943*, Plon, Paris, 1950.
ROBERTS, W. ADOLPHE, *The French in the West Indies*, Bobbs Merrill, New York, 1942.
SABLÉ, VICTOR, *La transformation des îles d'Amérique en départements français*, Larose, Paris, 1955.
SCHOELCHER, VICTOR, *Esclavage et colonisation*, Presses Universitaires de France, Paris, 1948.
SPITZ, GEORGES, *Developments towards Self-Government in the Caribbean*, "La Martinique et ses institutions depuis 1948", A Symposium held under the Auspices of the Netherlands Universities Foundation for International Cooperation at The Hague, September, 1954, Van Hoeve, The Hague, 1955.
TRAMOND, JOANNÈS and ANDRÉ REUSSNER, *Eléments d'histoire maritime et coloniale*, Challamel, Paris, 1924.

WEYGAND, MAXIME, *En lisant les mémoires du Général de Gaulle*, Flammarion, Paris, 1955.

B. *Articles*

"Au chevet de la Guyane", *Le Monde*, Paris, March 21, 22, 23, 1950.

CÉSAIRE, AIMÉ, "Crise dans les départements d'outre-mer ou crise de la départementalisation?", *Le Monde*, Paris, March 29, 1961.

CHENEVIÈRE, GUILLAUME, "Un genevois et un français dans la jungle guyanaise", *La Tribune de Genève*, Geneva, July 4-5, 7, 17, 1959.

CLOS, MAX, "Que se passe-t-il à la Martinique?", *Le Figaro*, Paris, February 24, 25, 1960.

CRABOT, CHRISTIAN, "Chômage, racisme et centralisation excessive sont à l'origine du malaise à la Martinique", *Le Monde*, Paris, December 29, 1959.

DECRAENE, PHILIPPE, "Dans l'intention de prévenir des revendications politiques: le gouvernement prend diverses mesures économiques et sociales en faveur des départements d'outre-mer", *Le Monde*, Paris, October 4, 1961.

DECRAENE, PHILIPPE, "La Guyane à l'abandon", *Le Monde*, Paris, August 17, 18, 19, 1962.

DECRAENE, PHILIPPE, "Terres françaises des Antilles", *Le Monde*, Paris, September 11, 12, 13, 14, 1962.

DE GRANDMAISON, DANIEL, "La vérité sur le tourisme", *Le Courrier*, Martinique, November 11, 18, 26, 1961.

DE GRANDMAISON, DANIEL, "Quelques problèmes", *Le Courrier*, Martinique, March 12, 1960.

GLISSANT, EDOUARD, "Culture et colonisation: l'équilibre antillais", *Esprit*, Paris, April 1962.

HOY, DON. R., "The Banana Industry of Guadeloupe", *Social and Economic Studies*, Vol. 11, No. 3, U.W.I., September 1962.

JULIAN, CLAUDE, "Un paradis plein de problèmes", *Le Monde*, Paris, May 2, 1960.

MARIE-JOSEPH, E., "Réalités économiques", *Esprit*, Paris, April 1962.

NIGER, PAUL, "L'assimilation, forme suprême du colonialisme", *Esprit*, Paris, April 1962.

PETIT, CAMILLE, "La Martinique, département français des Antilles", *Le Monde*, Paris, May 11, 1961.

VAUSSARD, MAURICE, "La Guyane peut-elle renaître?", *L' Aube*, Paris, May 9, 10, 11, 1950.

III. THE NETHERLANDS AND NETHERLANDS TERRITORIES

SOURCES

A. *Official Documents*

Charter of the United Kingdom of the Netherlands, The Hague, 1954.

Explanatory Memorandum of the relationship between the three parts of the Kingdom of the Netherlands, Netherlands Government, The Hague, n.d.

Facts and Figures about Surinam, Government Information Service, Paramaribo, 1959.
Five Years of Economic Reconstruction in the Netherlands, Ministry of Economic Affairs, Netherlands Government Printing Office, 1950.
Holland Carries On (The Netherlands West Indies), Netherlands Information Bureau, New York, 1943.
Investment and Taxation in Suriname, Ministry of Finance, Paramaribo, 1961.
The Netherlands (1945-1955): A Decade of Decision, Netherlands Ministry of Economic Affairs, Netherlands Information Service, San Francisco, n.d.
The Netherlands Antilles: A Short Survey, Government of the Netherlands Antilles, Curaçao, 1955.
The Netherlands Antilles: their geography, history, and political, economic and social development, Government Information Service, Curaçao, 1961.
The Netherlands Commonwealth and the Future: Important Statements of H.M. Queen Wilhelmina on Post-War Aims, Netherlands Information Bureau, 1945.
Netherlands "Regeringsvoorlichtingsdienst", Netherlands Government Information Service, The Hague, 1948. Series of four historical articles on the occasion of the inauguration ceremony of Queen Juliana in September 1948.
NYSTROM, J. WARREN, *Surinam, A Geographic Study*, Netherlands Information Bureau, New York, 1940.
Surinam—A Land of Many Resources, Surinam Planning Office, under the supervision of the Minister of Finance, Paramaribo, n.d.
Surinam in the Making, Government of Surinam, Paramaribo, 1955.
Surinam: Recommendations for a Ten Year Development Plan. Report of a Mission organized by the International Bank for Reconstruction and Development at the request of the Governments of the Netherlands and of Surinam, Johns Hopkins Press, Baltimore, Maryland, 1952.
VAN HELSDINGEN, W. H., *La charte du royaume des Pays-Bas*, reprinted by Librairie Générale de Droit et de Jurisprudence, Paris, 1956.
VAN RAALTE, E., *The Parliament of the Netherlands*, Netherlands Government Printing Office, The Hague, 1959.
WILHELMINA, Queen of the Netherlands: *From Curaçao to New Guinea, the Netherlands Empire Stands Fast.* Radio speech on May 10, 1941, from London, printed as pamphlet by the Netherlands Government.

B. *Unofficial Documents and Pamphlets*

The Brokopondo Development, A Hydroelectric Project, Suralco (Surinam Aluminium Company), n.p., July 1961.
Gids van Suriname, To mark the visit of H.M. Queen Juliana and H.R.H. Prince Bernhard to Surinam in October-November, 1955, n.p.
Hollandsche Bank-Unie Annual Report 1959-1960, Holdert, Amsterdam, 1960.
Landen Documentatie, Koninklijk Instituut voor de Tropen, Amsterdam, 1960.

LOUDEN, ALEXANDER, *Holland (A History of Freedom)*, Address delivered at Harvard University, July 10, 1940.
Netherlands Overseas Territories, The Royal Institute of International Affairs, London, 1941.
The Netherlands Windward Islands, The Netherlands West Indies Tourist Bureau, New York, n.d.
Surinam and the Netherlands Antilles: From Dependency to Partnership, n.p., n.d.
Wosuna 1954-1959, Netherlands Foundation for the Advancement of Research in Surinam and the Netherlands Antilles (Wosuna), Amsterdam, 1960.

C. Newspapers, Periodicals and Year Books

CURAÇAO

Antillean Nieuwsbrief
Amigoe di Curaçao
Beurs en Nieuwsberichten
La Cruz
La Prensa

ARUBA

Arubaansche Courant
Echo of Aruba

ST. MAARTEN

Windward Islands' Opinion

SURINAM

De Nieuwe Tijd
De West
Suriname Nieuwsbrief
Voor Elkaar

STUDIES

A. *Books*

ALTING, J. H. CARPENTIER and W. E. COOK BUNING, *The Netherlands and the World War*, Vol. III, "The Effects of the War Upon the Colonies", Yale University Press, New Haven, Connecticut, 1928.
ASHTON, H. S., *The Netherlands at War*, Routledge & Kegan Paul, London, 1941.
BARNOUW, A. J., *The Making of Modern Holland*, Allen & Unwin, London, 1948.
BLOK, PETRUS JOHANNES, *History of the People of the Netherlands*, G. P. Putnam's Sons, New York, 1912.
BORDEWYK, Prof. H. W. C., *The Netherlands and the World War*, Vol. IV, "War Finances 1918-1922 in the Netherlands", Yale University Press, New Haven, Connecticut, 1928.
BOUSQUET, G. H., *La Politique Musulmane et Coloniale des Pays-Bas*, Centre d'Etudes de Politique Etrangère, Paris, 1938.
BRUIJNING, C. F. A. and LOU LICHTVELD, *Suriname: Geboorte van een Nieuw Volk*, Wetenschappelijke Uitgeverij, Amsterdam, 1957.
BRUIJNING, C. F. A. and LOU LICHTVELD, *Suriname, a New Nation in South America*, Radhakishun, Paramaribo, 1959.

193

DE JONG, L. and JOSEPH W. F. STOPPELMAN, *The Lion Rampant*, Querido, New York, 1943.
DE KAT ANGELINO, A. D. A., *Colonial Policy*, Martinus Nijhoff, The Hague, 1931.
DE KLERCK, E. S., *History of the Netherlands East Indies*, W. L. and J. Brusse, Rotterdam, 1938.
DE KOCK, VICTOR, *Those in Bondage*, Allen & Unwin, London, 1950.
DE LEEUW, HENDRIK, *Crossroads of the Zuider Zee*, J. B. Lippincott, Philadelphia and New York, 1938.
DE WIT, T. P. M., *The Wageningen Rice Project in Surinam*, Mouton, The Hague, 1960.
DONNER, W. R. W., *The Financial Mechanism of the Netherlands Antilles*, Drukkerij en Uitgeverij Werto, Amsterdam, 1961.
HERMANS, HANS G., *The Caribbean: British, Dutch, French, United States*, "Constitutional Development of the Netherlands Antilles and Suri-nam", University of Florida Press, Gainesville, Florida, 1958.
HOETINK, H., *Het Patroon van de Oude Curaçaose Samenleving*, Van Gorcum, Assen, 1958.
KLEINTJES, Ph., *Institutions Politiques et Administratives des Pays d'Outre-Mer Néerlandais*, Etablissements Généraux d'Imprimerie, Brussels, 1935.
KRAAL, JOANNA FELHOEN, *Colonial Administration*, "Principles of Adminis-tration in the Netherlands West Indies", Symposium presented by the Colston Research Society and the University of Bristol, Butterworths, London, 1950.
LANDHEER, BARTHOLOMEW, ed., *The Netherlands*, University of California Press, Berkeley, California, 1943.
LOGEMANN, J. H. A., *Developments Towards Self-Government in the Caribbean*, "The Constitutional Status of the Netherlands Caribbean Territories", Van Hoeve, The Hague, 1955.
MOTLEY, JOHN L., *History of the United Netherlands*, John Murray, London, 1875.
PANDAY, R. M. N., *Agriculture in Surinam, 1650-1950*, H. J. Paris, Amsterdam, 1959.
PREGER, W., *Dutch Administration in the Netherlands Indies*, Cheshire, Melbourne, 1944.
RIEMENS, HENDRIK, *The Netherlands*, Eagle Books, New York, 1944.
VAN EYSINGA, W. J. M., *Lectures on Holland for American Students*, A Symposium of lectures delivered at the University of Leiden during the first Netherlands week for American students, July 7-12, 1924, A. W. Sijthoff's Publishing Co., Leiden, 1924.
VAN DE POLL, WILLEM, *Suriname*, Van Hoeve, The Hague, 1959.
VAN LIER, R. A. J., *Developments Towards Self-Government in the Caribbean*, "Social and Political Conditions in Suriname and the Netherlands Antilles: Introduction", Van Hoeve, The Hague, 1955.
VISSERING, G. and J. WESTERMAN HOLSTIJN, *The Netherlands and the World War*, Vol. IV, "War Finances in the Netherlands", Yale University Press, New Haven, Connecticut, 1928.

VLEKKE, BERNARD H. M., *Evolution of the Dutch Nation*, Roy, New York, 1945.

B. *Articles*

HALLET, ROBERT M., "Queen Juliana's Visit Cements Caribbean Ties", *The Christian Science Monitor*, Boston, November 2, 1955.

KENNEDY, PAUL P., "Automation Cuts Payrolls in Curaçao and Threatens the Economy", *The New York Times*, New York, October 8, 1962.

SCHNORR, DANIEL L., "Dutch Union Government Takes Shape", *The Christian Science Monitor*, Boston, April 21, 1952.

SHELLABY, ROBERT K., "Dutch Speed Twin Goals in West Indies", *The Christian Science Monitor*, Boston, May 20, 1947.

VAN KLEFFENS, E. N., "The Democratic Future of the Netherlands Indies", *Foreign Affairs*, New York, October 1942.

WRIGHT, JOHN K., *The Netherlands West Indies*, Reprint from the *European Possessions in the Caribbean Area*, American Geographical Society, New York, 1941.

IV. GENERAL

SOURCES

Newspapers, Periodicals and Year Books

Bank of London and South America Fortnightly Review, London.

The Canadian Journal of Economics and Political Science, Toronto.

The Caribbean, University of Florida Press, Gainesville, Florida.

Caribbean Studies, Institute of Caribbean Studies, University of Puerto Rico.

The Christian Science Monitor, Boston, Massachusetts.

The Chronicle of the West India Committee, London.

Combat, Paris.

Combate, San José, Costa Rica.

Cuadernos, Paris.

The Daily Telegraph, London.

The Economist, London.

Esprit, Paris.

Foreign Affairs, New York.

The Geographical Journal, London.

Geographical Review, New York.

The Guardian, Manchester.

Handbook of Latin American Studies, University of Florida.

Hispanic American Report, Stanford University, California.

International Affairs, London.

Journal of Economic History, New York.

Journal of Inter-American Studies, University of Florida.

La Tribune de Genève, Geneva.

L'Aube, Paris.

Le Figaro, Paris.
Le Journal de Genève, Geneva.
Le Monde, Paris.
L'Humanité, Paris.
The Listener, London.
Manchester Guardian Weekly, Manchester.
Monthly Review, New York.
National Guardian, New York.
Nederlandse Regeringsvoorlichtingsdienst, The Hague.
Netherlands News, Netherlands Embassy, London.
The New Statesman, London.
The New York Herald Tribune, New York.
The New York Times, New York.
Revista de Ciencias Sociales, University of Puerto Rico, Rio Piedras.
Revue générale de droit international public, Paris.
The Round Table, London.
San Juan Star, Puerto Rico.
The South American Handbook, London.
The Sunday Times, London.
Time, Latin American edition, New York.
Time and Tide, London.
The Times, London.
The West Indies and Caribbean Year Book, London.
The World Today, London.
Washington Post, Washington.
Washington Star, Washington.

STUDIES

A. *Books*

ANGELL, NORMAN, *The Great Illusion*, William Heinemann, London, 1912.
ARCINIEGAS, GERMÁN, *Caribbean, Sea of the New World*, Knopf, New York, 1946.
AUGIER, F. R. and S. C. GORDON, *Sources of West Indian History*, Longmans, London, 1962.
AUGIER, F. R., S. C. GORDON and M. RECKORD, *The Making of the West Indies*, Longmans, London, 1960.
BAILEY, THOMAS A., *A Diplomatic History of the American People*, Appleton-Century-Crofts, New York, 1958.
BAUER, P. T. and B. S. YAMEY, *The Economics of Under-developed Countries*, Nisbet & Cambridge University Press, Cambridge, 1957.
BEMIS, SAMUEL FLAGG, *A Diplomatic History of the United States*, Henry Holt, New York, 1955.
BLANSHARD, PAUL, *Democracy and Empire in the Caribbean*, Macmillan, New York, 1947.
BOULDING, K. E., *The Organizational Revolution*, Harper, New York, 1953.
BUTLAND, GILBERT, J., *Latin America: a Regional Geography*, Longmans, London, 1960.

CAMPOS MENÉNDEZ, ENRIQUE, *Se Llamaba Bolívar*, Empresa Editora Zig-Zag, Santiago, Chile, 1956.

CARLSON, F. A., *Geography of Latin America*, Prentice-Hall, Englewood Cliffs, New Jersey, 1952.

CASEY, LORD, *Personal Experience, 1939-1946*, Constable, London, 1962.

CASTRO, AMÉRICO, *Iberoamérica*, Dryden Press, New York, 1954.

CHANDOS, LORD, *The Memoirs of Lord Chandos*, The Bodley Head, London, 1962.

CLARK, GROVER, *A Place in the Sun*, Macmillan, New York, 1937.

COCHRAN, THOMAS C., *The Puerto Rican Businessman: a Study in Cultural Change*, University of Pennsylvania Press, Philadelphia, 1959.

DE MADARIAGA, SALVADOR, *Cristóbal Colón*, Editorial Sudamericana, Buenos Aires, 1940.

DE MADARIAGA, SALVADOR, *The Fall of the Spanish American Empire*, Hollis & Carter, London, 1947.

Developments Towards Self-Government in the Caribbean, A Symposium held under the auspices of the Netherlands Universities Foundation for International Cooperation, at The Hague, September 1954, Van Hoeve, The Hague, 1955.

EASTON, STEWART C., *The Twilight of European Colonialism*, Holt, Rinehart & Winston, New York, 1960.

EDMUNDSON, GEORGE, *Anglo-Dutch Rivalry*, Clarendon Press, Oxford, 1910.

EDWARDS, BRYAN, *The History of the British Colonies in the West Indies*, Stockdale, London, 1801.

FREYMOND, JACQUES, *The Saar Conflict, 1945-1955* (Published under the auspices of the Carnegie Endowment for International Peace), Stevens, London, 1960.

GUÉRIN, DANIEL, *The West Indies and their Future*, Dobson, London, 1961.

HALLE, LOUIS J., *American Foreign Policy*, Allen & Unwin, London, 1960.

HANCOCK, RALPH, *Puerto Rico: a success story*, D. Van Nostrand, Princeton, New Jersey, 1960.

HANSON, EARL P., *Transformation: the Story of Modern Puerto Rico*, Simon & Schuster, New York, 1955.

HARING, C. H., *The Spanish Empire in America*, Oxford University Press, New York, 1947.

HAYEK, FRIEDRICH A., *The Constitution of Liberty*, Routledge & Kegan Paul, London, 1960.

HEILPERIN, MICHAEL A., *Studies in Economic Nationalism*, Librairie E. Droz, Geneva, 1960.

HERRING, HUBERT, *A History of Latin America*, Jonathan Cape, London, 1954.

IRELAND, GORDON, *Boundaries and Conflicts in South America*, Harvard University Press, Cambridge, Massachusetts, 1938.

JAMES, PRESTON E., *Latin America*, Odyssey Press, New York, 1959.

JONES, CHESTER LLOYD, *Caribbean Backgrounds and Prospects*, Appleton, New York and London, 1931.

JONES, CHESTER LLOYD, *The United States and the Caribbean*, University of Chicago Press, 1929.

197

LEWIS, W. ARTHUR, *The Theory of Economic Growth*, London, 1955.

LEYBURN, J. G., *The Haitian People*, Yale University Press, 1941.

MAY, STACY and GALO PLAZA, *The United Fruit Company in Latin America*, National Planning Association, Washington, D.C., 1958.

MORISON, SAMUEL E., *Admiral of the Ocean Sea*, Little, Brown & Co., Boston, 1942.

NABUCO, CAROLINA, *Life of Joaquim Nabuco*, ed. Ronald Hilton, Stanford University Press, Stanford, California, 1950.

NAIPAUL, V. S., *The Middle Passage*, Deutsch, London, 1962.

The New Cambridge Modern History, Potter, G. R., ed., Cambridge University Press, 1957-1960.

NEWTON, A. P., *The European Nations in the West Indies*, London, 1933.

O'CALLAGHAN, SEAN, *The Slave Trade*, Anthony Blond, London, 1961.

PARES, RICHARD, *War and Trade in the West Indies, 1739-63*, Oxford, 1936.

PARRY, J. H. and P. M. SHERLOCK, *A Short History of the West Indies*, Macmillan, London, 1960.

PERLOFF, HARVEY S., *Puerto Rico's Economic Future*, University of Chicago Press, Chicago, Illinois, 1949.

PETRIE, C. and L. BERTRAND, *The History of Spain*, Eyre & Spottiswoode, London, 1952.

POTTER, E. B. and CHESTER W. NIMITZ, *Sea Power*, Prentice-Hall, Englewood Cliffs, New Jersey, 1960.

PRATT, JULIUS W., *A History of United States Foreign Policy*, Prentice-Hall, Englewood Cliffs, New Jersey, 1955.

Principles and Methods of Colonial Administration, Colston papers based on a Symposium promoted by the Colston Research Society and the University of Bristol, April, 1950, Butterworths, London, 1950.

RAYNAL, ABBÉ G. T., *History of the Indies*, trans. by J. Justamond, London, 1783.

RECORD, SAMUEL J. and ROBERT W. HESS, *Timbers of the New World*. Yale University Press, New Haven, Connecticut, 1943.

RIPPY, J. FRED, *Latin America*, University of Michigan Press, Ann Arbor, Michigan, 1958.

RODWAY, JAMES, *Guiana: British, Dutch and French*, T. Fisher Unwin, London, 1912.

RUBIN, VERA, ed., *Caribbean Studies: a Symposium*, Institute of Social and Economic Research, Jamaica, 1957.

SALISBURY-JONES, Sir GUY, *So Full a Glory*, Weidenfeld and Nicolson, London, 1954.

SENIOR, CLARENCE, *Land Reform and Democracy*, University of Florida Press, 1958.

SHERRARD, O. A., *Freedom from Fear: the Slave and his Emancipation*, The Bodley Head, London, 1959.

SNOW, ALPHEUS H., *The Administration of Dependencies*, G. P. Putnam's Sons, New York, 1902.

Symposium Intercolonial, juin/juillet, 1952, Organisé par la Faculté des Lettres de Bordeaux et l'Institut de la France d'Outre-Mer, Imprimeries Delmas, Bordeaux, 1954.

STEAD, W. H., *Fomento—The Economic Development of Puerto Rico*, National Planning Association, Washington, D.C., 1958.

STRAUSZ-HUPÉ, R. and H. W. HAZARD, *The Idea of Colonialism*, Praeger, New York, 1958.

THOMAS, A. B., *Latin America: a History*, Macmillan, New York, 1956.

TILLYARD, E. M. W., *The Athenian Empire and the Great Illusion*, Bowes & Bowes, Cambridge, 1914.

TIMOSHENKO, VLADIMIR P. and BORIS C. SWERLING, *The World's Sugar*, Stanford University Press, Stanford, California, 1957.

TREND, J. B., *Bolívar and the Independence of Spanish America*, Hodder and Stoughton, London, 1946.

VAN HOOK, ANDREW, *Sugar: its Production, Technology and Uses*, Ronald Press, New York, 1949.

VASCONCELOS, JOSÉ, *La Raza Cósmica*, Collección Austral, Mexico, 1948.

WILGUS, A. CURTIS, ed., *The Caribbean*, University of Florida Press, Gainesville, Florida, 1950-1958.

WORCESTER, D. E. and W. G. SCHAEFFER, *Growth and Culture of Latin America*, Oxford University Press, New York, 1956.

B. *Articles*

ARCHIBALD, CHARLES H., "Question-Mark over the Caribbean", *The New Commonwealth*, Vol. 39, No. 8, London, August 1961.

FLECKER, H. L. O., "West Indian Education", *The Times Review of the British Colonies*, London, Spring 1952.

MITCHELL, SIR HAROLD, "The West Indies", *The World Today*, London, November 1962.

SEALY, THEODORE, "Why the West Indies Need Help", *The Listener*, Vol. XLVII, No. 1199, London, February 21, 1952.

"West Indies' Need for British Market", *The Times Review of Industry*, Vol. 9, No. 104 (New Series), London, September 1955.

INDEX

Acworth, Angus W., 19n
Adams, Sir Grantley:
  deputy leader of the Federal Labour
    Party, 50
  Prime Minister of the West Indies
    Federation, 51
  taxation controversy, 52-3, 74
  conference on constitutional reform,
    53-4, 56
  question of dominion status, 58
  deportation of Trinidad immigrants,
    59
  the Chaguaramas base question, 59,
    64-5
  support of the Federation, 63n, 70, 72
  views on West Indian immigration,
    86-7, 89
Adams, John, 6n
Agriculture:
  British policy, 79, 81, 91-3, 151, 166-8
  Dutch policy, 129-30, 133, 135-6, 175
  French policy, 8, 112-3
Akers, Aretas, 5n
Alduy, Paul, 34
Alejandinho, 20
Aluminum Company of America, 132
Aluminium industry, 132
American Civil War, 27
American War of Independence, 6, 173
Amery, Julian, 54
Amery, L. S., 142
Amsterdam, influence of merchants on
  Netherlands policy, 2, 7, 26, 27
Angell, Norman, 20
Anglo-American Caribbean Commis-
  sion, 41
Annabay, 3, 30, 128
Antigua, 8, 12, 14n, 52, 80n, 109
Antilles, 1, 2
Arbenz, 165
Archambaud, Pedro, 57n
Archibald, Charles H., 51n
Architecture, 19
Arévalo, Juan José, 158
Arnett, Vernon, 55n, 57, 58
Art, 19
Aruba:
  economic conditions and policy: oil
    industry, 29-30, 110, 118, 128-9,
    134, 135, 137, 175
  widening of economy, 133-5
  industrialization, 134-5
  political parties, 117-8
  population, 117, 118
  representation, 125n

Asquith Commission for Higher Educa-
  tion in the Colonies, 82n
Asquith, Herbert, 18
Atlantic Charter, 38, 40, 41
Attlee, Clement, 47
Attorney, 7
Aublet, Christian, 23
Australia, federal constitution of, 74n,
  75

Bahamas, 14
Baldwin, Stanley, 18, 142
Balfour Declaration, 18
Banana industry:
  in British colonies, 35, 81, 84, 110n, 166
  in French colonies, 106, 110, 112
Barbados:
  colonization of, 2
  constitution, 14, 18, 46, 72
  proposed federation with Windward
    Islands, 45-6
  West Indies Federation and, 50, 51
Barrère, Pierre, 23
Batista, Fulgencio, 145
Battle of the Saints, 5n, 6
Bauxite industry:
  in British colonies, 82, 84, 90, 92,
    110, 130n, 133, 150, 152
  in Netherlands colonies, 39, 110, 130,
    132, 133, 137
Bayard, Thomas, 17n
Belize, 155, 156
Bemis, Professor S. F., 143n
Berbice, 6n, 13, 138, 139
Bermuda, 12n, 45, 141
Bermuda Conference (1940), 37
Betancourt, President Rómulo, 144n
Bevan, Aneurin, 19n
Bianchi, William J., 158n
Blackburne, Sir Kenneth, 71
Bolívar, Simón, 21n, 173
Bonaire, 117, 118, 125n
Bordeaux, influence of merchants on
  French policy, 2
Borden, Sir Robert, 20
Boulanger, Ernest-Théophile, 24n
Bousquet, Professor G. H., 31
Bradshaw, Robert, 63-4
Brazil:
  sugar cane industry, 4
  slave trade, 4
  site of capital, 49
  emancipation of slaves, 140
  independence, 142
  boundary disputes with Britain, 142-3

Commonwealth ideal, 33, 40-1
political parties committed to self-
  government, 18, 45
West Indies Federation, *q.v.*, 44-75
independence of Jamaica, 70-2,
  124, 173
independence of Trinidad, 70, 72
  124, 173
changes in British Guiana, 140-1
British Guiana Commission, 141
the 1928 constitution of British
  Guiana, 141-2
amendments of 1943 and 1953, 144
suspension of the British Guiana
  constitution, 97, 146-7
the 1961 constitution, 147, 150, 153
demands for independence in
  British Guiana, 148, 152, 153
constitution of British Honduras,
  97, 159-61, 165, 169
survey of policy, 170, 171-4, 176-7
training in self-government, 170-2
economic: slave trade, 4, 9n, 10, 140
emancipation of slaves, 7, 10, 13,
  14, 22, 140, 150, 155n, 170
sugar industry, 6-7, 10, 12, 13, 14,
  16, 17, 35, 80-1, 83-4, 92-3, 109,
  140, 141, 150, 151, 152, 162, 167,
  168, 170, 171
management of estates, 7-8
preferences, 14, 17-18, 80-1, 162
economic policy from 1815 to 1939,
  15-18
protective tariffs, 16, 17, 18, 91,
  92-3, 151
free trade, 16, 17
Ottawa Agreements, 18, 33, 77, 84
policy in World War II, 34, 35-6, 42
Colonial Welfare and Development
  Fund, 35-6, 47, 73, 81-2, 90
Caribbean Commission, 41-2
Colonial Development Corporation, 47, 78-80, 90, 133, 150, 166-7
post-war economic policy, 76-94,
  150-3
weaknesses of Caribbean economies, 76, 92-3, 151-3, 171
industrialization, 76, 77-80, 82, 90,
  91, 150-1, 152-3, 174
problem of markets, 78, 83-4, 90-1,
  93, 152, 161-3, 174
tax concessions to new industries,
  78, 91
productivity index, 78-9
agriculture, 79, 81, 91-3, 151, 166-8
banana industry, 35, 81, 84, 110n,
  166
citrus industry, 81, 93, 161-2, 167
high-cost production, 80, 90-1, 93,
  151, 152, 167, 168

bauxite industry, 82, 84, 90, 92, 110,
  130n, 133, 150, 152
increase in population, 84, 90, 175-6
emigration, 84-91, 175-6
immigration into Great Britain,
  84-90
Commonwealth Immigrants Act,
  33n, 87-90,
foreign capital, 90, 168
oil industry, 81, 82, 90, 92, 110
tourist industry, 90, 92, 111, 134,
  166
unemployment, 92-3
policy in British Guiana, 140, 150-3
importation of indentured labour,
  140, 150, 170
gold-mining, 130, 150
hydro-electric power, 150-1, 152
rice, 151, 152
policy in British Honduras, 154-5,
  157, 161-3, 165-8.
devaluation of the dollar, 161-3,
  164, 165
economic aid programme, 82, 165-7
transport, 167-8
survey of policy, 170, 173-7
education, 82-3, 170
finance, 56, 73, 76, 77-8, 149, 161,
  167-8, 171
social: Moyne Report, 18-19, 35-6
Colonial Welfare and Development
  Fund, 35-6, 47
Caribbean Commission, 41-2
in Barbados, 46n
health, 144-5
Great houses, 7, 19
Grenada, 13, 16, 14n, 52
Guadaloupe:
colonization, 2, 9-10
constitution: representation in French
  National Assembly, 95
reorganized as a department, 96
cultural influence, 19
economic: slave labour, 21
production of rum, 23n
unemployment, 99, 175
sugar industry, 109
political: dissatisfaction with administration, 97-8, 104
political parties, 97, 104
Guatemala:
boundary disputes, 16-17
Anglo-Guatemalan Treaty, 156-8, 160
relations with Great Britain, 158-9,
  165
projected association with British
  Honduras, 164-5
Mexico and, 158, 159
U.S.A. and, 156
Guisan, Samuel, 23n